STUDIES IN CLASSICS

edited by
Dirk Obbink
Oxford University

Andrew Dyck
The University of California, Los Angeles

A ROUTLEDGE SERIES

RHETORIC IN CICERO'S
PRO BALBO

Kimberly Anne Barber

LONDON AND NEW YORK

First published 2004 by
Routledge

2 Park Square, Milton Park, Abingdon, Oxon OX14 4RN
711 Third Avenue, New York, NY 10017, USA

Routledge is an imprint of the Taylor & Francis Group, an informa business

First issued in paperback 2016

Library of Congress Cataloging-in-Publication Data

Barber, Kimberly Anne, 1956-
   Rhetoric in Cicero's Pro Balbo / Kimberly Anne Barber.
      p. cm. -- (Studies in classics ; v. 6)
   Includes bibliographical reference (p.   ) and index.
      ISBN 0-415-96995-6 (alk. paper)
    1. Cicero, Marcus Tullius. Pro Balbo. 2. Speeches, addresses, etc.,
Latin--History and criticism. 3. Balbus, Lucius Cornelius. 4.
Rhetoric, Ancient. I. title. II. Series: Studies in classics (Routledge
(Firm)) ; v. 6.
   PA6279.B33B37 2004
   875'.01--dc22   2003021586

ISBN 978-0-415-96995-6 (hbk)
ISBN 978-1-138-99736-3 (pbk)

Series Editors' Foreword

Studies in Classics aims to bring high-quality work by emerging scholars to the attention of a wider audience. Emphasizing the study of classical literature and history, these volumes contribute to the theoretical understanding of human culture and society over time. This series will offer an array of approaches to the study of Greek and Latin (including medieval and Neolatin), authors and their reception, canons, transmissions of texts, ideas, religion, history of scholarship, narrative, and the nature of evidence.

While the focus is on Mediterranean cultures of the Greco-Roman era, perspectives from other areas, cultural backgrounds, and eras are to be included as important means to the reconstruction of fragmentary evidence and the exploration of models. The series will reflect upon the role classical studies has played in humanistic endeavors from antiquity to the present, and explore select ways in which the discipline can bring both traditional scholarly tools and the experience of modernity to bear on questions and texts of enduring importance.

Dirk Obbink, Oxford University
Andrew Dyck, The University of California, Los Angeles

To the memory of my mother and father,
optimis parentibus,
and to Sylvanus.

Contents

Acknowledgments

I WOULD LIKE TO THANK THE UNIVERSITY OF TEXAS AND THE DEPARTMENT of Classics for financial support during my doctoral studies. I am also grateful to my readers, Professors David Armstrong, Michael Gagarin, James May, and Gwyn Morgan, all of whom contributed to this dissertation with their keen eye for detail and excellent suggestions. In particular, I would like to thank my co-supervisors, Professors Karl Galinsky and Andrew Riggsby, who in addition to offering a careful reading and invaluable advice, also encouraged me and shepherded this dissertation through to completion. I would also like to thank my editors, Dr. Andrew Dyck, for his careful reading and helpful suggestions, Mr. Paul Foster Johnson, for his patience and good humor, and Ms. Nathalie Martinez.

Introduction

AS CICERO'S FIRST EXTANT FORENSIC SPEECH AFTER LUCA, THE *PRO BALBO* was delivered during a momentous historical period in Rome.[1] The defendant was a highly influential political adviser of Caesar, who during the civil war was to become one of his right-hand men, and eventually the first non-Italian consul.[2] The rhetorical issues raised by the particular legal context of the *Pro Balbo* are significant, as it is one of only two extant speeches in which Cicero defends a person charged under the *lex Papia* for an illegal grant of citizenship. The *Pro Archia*, dealing with similar legal issues, has received more attention from scholars largely because of its encomium of the arts. The *Pro Balbo* also invites study because it is from a period noted for Cicero's richness and maturity of style.[3]

Despite these factors scant scholarly attention has been directed towards the speech. In the last quarter of the 19th century and the early 20th century, only four important works were devoted to the *Pro Balbo*. Jullien's dissertation (1886) focuses on the life of Balbus and examines the circumstances surrounding the speech, although it does not tackle the speech itself. Gasquy (1886) addresses the historical and biographical circumstances surrounding the speech, and certain issues regarding citizenship and treaties. But his historical discussion of the speech itself is descriptive rather than analytical.

Kaden (1912) deals primarily with the life of Cornelius Balbus and the question of citizenship, saving a rhetorical and stylistic discussion of the speech for the last twelve pages. Here he breaks up the speech into its divisions according to traditional rules, justifies his divisions, since in some cases they differ from those of his predecessors, and outlines the contents of each part. He then adds a brief stylistic discussion of some tropes and figures contained in the speech. There is no attempt to examine each part for what it contributes to the whole or to analyze how the individual sections fit together, or in the stylistic portion, how style functions in relation to the rhetoric. Hoche's (1882) work deals mostly with Balbus' life, but also divides the speech into its rhetorical parts, giving a synopsis of each. This study, like Kaden's, does not provide much rhetorical analysis. There are also two commentaries, but these are only slightly more helpful: one by J. S. Reid (1890), the other by Cousin (1962). Both provide useful biographical and historical background to the speech, and grammatical notes. Cousin's also has a thorough discussion of the term *populus fundus*. But again stylistics is short-changed.

Historians tend to use the speech as a treasure trove of information on the citizenship issue while ignoring other aspects. For example, E. G. Hardy (1917) employs one particular section to prove that Italian communities, when franchised, became *fundi* to Roman law. Some scholars have turned to the speech to discuss specific laws mentioned by Cicero.[4] Others have searched for information on Rome's relations with and power over her colonies.[5] Brunt (1982) presents a more thorough examination of the legal issues as a whole in the speech. Both Goodfellow (1935) and Sherwin-White (1973) rely heavily upon the *Pro Balbo* for information regarding Roman colonial relationships and the granting of citizenship. The scope of scholarship directed towards this speech, therefore, has been very narrow, with focus on legal and historical issues. The lack of any substantial rhetorical or stylistic study is evident, yet surprising, since the *Pro Balbo* is certainly worthy of such study.

In the interval since the last studies of the *Pro Balbo* appeared, several useful approaches have developed in Ciceronian scholarship. The first is largely due to the work of Kennedy and May, who concentrate on the role of ethos in persuasion.[6] May examines the orator's artistic manipulation of ethos in a study of individual speeches from four periods of Cicero's life. By analyzing the different techniques Cicero employs in portraying ethos, and demonstrating how these techniques affect the overall argumentation of the speeches, May documents the important role of ethos as a persuasive tool. He also follows the development and changes in the portrayal of ethos, particularly in Cicero's portrayal of his own ethos, in response to changes in the circumstances of his own life.[7]

Another approach is that of Craig (1979). He examines the use of enthymemes in five Ciceronian speeches. His methodology is to analyze four aspects of rational argumentation: the premises which the hearer is meant to accept, the logical development of the argument, the effects of thematic resonance, and the arrangement of the arguments on the hearer's readiness to accept any given premise. On this basis, Craig analyzes each *argumentatio* on three levels: on the first, he examines the general structure of the *argumentatio* as a whole; on the second, the interrelation and arrangement of arguments for a given contention; and on the third, the premises, supporting points, and conclusions.

The third approach is that of Neumeister, Stroh, Classen, and Gotoff.[8] Their method of interpretation is prompted by a reaction to 19th-century Ciceronian scholarship, which they view as simplistic and unanalytical in its approach to rhetoric. The above scholars examine the compositional strategies of the orator in the light of persuasion, which they see as the prime function of forensic oratory.[9] Everything else in a forensic speech is subordinated to persuasion, including aesthetics. For example, an orator can use intentionally unbalanced proportioning of the speech parts or inelegant, rough diction, if it is useful to his goal of persuasion. Although they recognize the importance of ancient rhetorical theory in interpreting speeches, they rightly stress that theory is meant as a guide to the beginner, that is, as a sort of pedagogical convenience, not as a set of rigid rules for the accomplished orator.[10]

According to Neumeister, the orator proceeds from a few general principles, and these the interpreter must also adopt.[11] First, the orator must accommodate his speech to the audience (*inventio*),[12] then he must persuade his listeners step-by-step (*dispositio*).[13] Each part of the speech is built upon the preceding one, providing logical and psychological preparation for the following (*dispositio*).[14] The third principle is the deliberate concealment of this structure from the audience, since the orator does not want the audience to know that, let alone how, it is being manipulated (again *dispositio*).[15] The fourth principle is style, which greatly assists persuasion (*elocutio*).[16] It is used to explain thoughts clearly and also has suggestive forcefulness. The interpreter must examine the speech in the light of these four principles, and in particular discover the hidden structure, the techniques used gradually to persuade the audience.

In analyzing Ciceronian speeches, these scholars seek to clarify whether the arguments selected actually belong to the circumstances of the individual case or whether they are brought in for their particular effect and without regard for the actual legal aspects of the case. They analyze the order of arguments and discuss how the style, the structure of the sentences, and the diction support the attempt to persuade the audience.

Whereas Neumeister is interested in how the orator adapts his speech to the audience, Nisbet explores the other side of the issue: the response of the audience to the speech. This is particularly relevant to judicial speeches, where the correct audience response is vital. Nisbet combines a reader response approach with an emphasis on detailed reading and analysis of the text, regarding which, he rightly states: "Talk of literature too often loses sight of the words on the page."[17]

Although each of these methods focuses on one particular area of interpretation, they all offer a valuable means of analysis. In this study of the *Pro Balbo*, a speech which none of the above scholars discusses, I combine these modes of interpretation for a more integrated approach. In addition, I will emphasize the function of pathos more than they do. By pathos I mean the type of argument whose purpose is to arouse an emotional reaction in the audience. Aristotle had already shown the importance of pathos as one of the three types of *pisteis*, and both Cicero and Quintilian believed that pathos was the most important of the three types of *inventio*.[18] Hence it deserves special scrutiny. In synthesizing the different but complementary methods of Kennedy/May, Craig, Neumeister/Stroh/Classen/Gotoff, and Nisbet, and focusing them on one speech, I aim to achieve a broader and more thorough understanding of the *Pro Balbo*.

I will examine the speech in respect to the kinds of arguments employed (*inventio*: ethos, pathos, and logos), the arrangement of the arguments (*dispositio*), and the style (*elocutio*). This follows the ancient divisions of rhetoric and provides the best methodology for tackling the rhetoric. Neumeister (1964), Classen (1985), and Kirby (1990) have employed this approach to interpretation: Neumeister subdividing these divisions into his four principles, Classen using different speeches to illustrate *inventio, dispositio,* and *elocutio,* and Kirby analyzing one speech.

In the chapter on ethos I examine the tactics Cicero employs in character portrayal and how they function to make character persuasive. The interrelation of the characters is also discussed, especially in terms of association and polarization. One of the major challenges facing Cicero in the *Pro Balbo* is to present Balbus' ethos in such a way that the *invidia* directed at him is diminished. One of the ways in which the orator achieves his goal is to focus the speech on Pompey by substituting him as defendant. Balbus is then associated as closely as possible with the general, while the prosecutor is presented as the antithesis to Pompey. Cicero dwells on Pompey's *auctoritas* and great military and (alleged) legal experience, which he contrasts with the ignorance and inexperience of the prosecutor. Cicero also avoids regenerating ill will against the defendant by universalizing and generalizing his praise of brave men who help Rome, rather than specifically praising Balbus too often. The Gaditans are also lauded as longstanding loyal allies of Rome, and again Balbus is closely associated with them. To rebut arguments that he is caving in to the "triumvirate," Cicero employs his own ethos to present an example of how the wise Roman, who wants to place the state before his own personal interests, should behave towards Caesar and Pompey. The remaining characters are minor ones: Crassus disappears after a brief laudation in the *exordium* since he is a peripheral player, the Gaditans are *exempla* of loyal allies, and Caesar is used to add prestige to Balbus through their friendship, and to arouse pity in the audience in the *peroratio*. The interrelation between ethos and pathos in this speech provides a greater understanding of the function of each. Often pathos is aroused through the use of character, as in the *digressiones* on Pompey and Marius.[19] Here intense feelings of admiration, and in the Marius' case, longing, are stirred in the audience and mingled with strong feelings of patriotism. The mention of Caesar in the *peroratio* is meant to stir strong feelings of pity. In other instances Cicero works on emotions that are not related to ethos, as when he plays on the audience's fears of Rome's inability to find allies in times of grave national danger. The chapter on logos examines the structure of the syllogisms presented in the speech, with particular attention to premises and conclusions, especially unstated ones. Types of arguments are examined, as are techniques, such as universalization and association, both of which Cicero also employs in his "ethical" argumentation. Of special interest is the extent to which Cicero manipulates syllogisms to give the appearance of rational arguments.

The chapter on *dispositio* studies the placement of arguments and the manner in which the interrelations among ethos, pathos, and logos affect persuasion in the speech. Attention is directed towards the effect the position of arguments has upon the audience's acceptance of the premises and how the arrangement induces the audience to accept weak arguments.

The chapter on *elocutio* investigates the relation between style and rhetoric. Particularly important here is how the diction, sentence structure, and transitions help focus (and sometimes purposely to misfocus) and strengthen the arguments. The linkage between "ethical," "pathetic," and rational argumentation and style is examined, and also the use of style in the different parts of the speech. The final chapter contains my conclusions.

Since understanding of the rhetoric of the *Pro Balbo* will be enhanced by understanding of the background to the speech, I shall provide a brief explication of the situation, including the relationship between Pompey and Cicero, and Balbus' background. The trial took place in late summer or early fall of 56 B.C. Because Cicero refers to the *De Provinciis Consularibus* in the *Pro Balbo* (61), Balbus' trial obviously took place after that speech. No mention, however, is made of Pompey's and Crassus' consulships of 55 B.C., and Cicero doubtless would have mentioned such a fact as this, which would enhance Pompey's *auctoritas* with the audience.

Cicero's relationship with Pompey was long-standing, but not without its vicissitudes. It is likely that they first met each other in the early 90s B.C. in Rome, where their families lived in the same neighborhood,[20] and they likely served together in the *consilium* of Cn. Pompeius Strabo, Pompey's father, in 89 B.C.[21] There is evidence that they had personal contact with each other through mutual friends among the Terentii, the Pompeii, and Q. Mucius Scaevola, the Pontifex, and the Metelli.[22] It is also likely that Pompey and Cicero co-operated in 73 B.C. during the trial of Verres, in which several of Pompey's clients provided evidence for the prosecution.[23] Cicero and Pompey also possibly worked together in favor of the praetor L. Aurelius Cotta's bill of 70 B.C. to divide the juries equally among the Senate, the Equites, and the Tribuni Aerarii.[24]

Cicero continued to support Pompey throughout the 60s. As praetor in 66 B.C., Cicero spoke in favor of the *lex Manilia*.[25] After Cicero's consulship in 64 B.C., during which he put down the Catilinarian conspiracy and took credit for saving the Republic, there was a cooling of the relationship between them on the part of Pompey, who was probably resentful and jealous.[26] The formation of the coalition, the so-called "First Triumvirate," in 60 B.C. among Pompey, Caesar, and Crassus further alienated Cicero from Pompey.[27] Caesar attempted to draw Cicero into the coalition, but Cicero remained cool to the idea. Then, in 59 B.C., while defending Antonius at trial, Cicero criticized the violence used by the coalition.[28] Immediately afterwards, with Pompey acting as augur and Caesar as *pontifex maximus*, Cicero's enemy Clodius was adopted into a plebian family.[29] This allowed him to run for the tribunate, which he did successfully in 58 B.C.. He alienated Pompey from Cicero by various machinations, and used his tribunate to exact vengeance on Cicero, by introducing a law that exiled anyone who put to death a Roman citizen without trial. The target of this legislation was Cicero, who had put to death the Catilinarian conspirators. Pompey abandoned Cicero, and Cicero went into exile. His exile lasted only one year; he returned with the assistance of Pompey.[30] In gratitude to Pompey, Cicero spoke in favor of a special command for Pompey over the grain supply.[31] By 56 B.C., it appeared that the coalition was breaking apart. Cicero tried to draw Pompey back into the arms of the Optimates, and proposed in the Senate on 6 April the repeal of the *lex Campana*, legislation which Caesar had introduced.[32] Cicero's plan was unsuccessful: the coalition did not fall apart. Pompey, Caesar, and Crassus renewed their agreement to work together at Luca. As a result of the meeting at Luca, Cicero was restrained by Pompey from further attacks on Caesar's legislation.[33]

Balbus had quite an illustrious career: after being enfranchised by Pompey, Caesar had appointed him *praefectus fabrum*, and later Balbus became Caesar's political adviser. Balbus, working for Caesar, attempted unsuccessfully to bring Cicero into a coalition with Caesar and Pompey in 59 B.C. (*Ad Att.* 2.33). While Caesar was in Gaul, Balbus mostly remained with him, but also made trips to Rome to look after Caesar's affairs there.[34] We know from the amount of time Cicero spends in the *Pro Balbo* on defusing *invidia*, that jealousy ran high against this foreigner, who had risen to the position of political adviser to one of Rome's most powerful political figures. It is possible that the charges against Balbus were preferred before Luca, when it seemed the coalition between Caesar, Pompey, and Crassus was disintegrating. With the collapse of the "first triumvirate," and Caesar far away in Gaul, perhaps enemies of Caesar and Balbus thought the latter would be an easy target. This scenario is tempting, but since there is no solid evidence that this is in fact what happened, Cousin's suggestion that optimates, angered at Balbus for his suspected role in helping Caesar to draw Pompey away from them, were behind the charges is equally plausible.[35]

Pompey granted Balbus citizenship uder the *lex Cornelia* of 72 B.C., a law which allowed Pompey to confer individual grants of citizenship upon foreigners.[36] The charges were brought forward under the *lex Papia* of 65 B.C., by a Gaditan, who, as we know from a remark Cicero makes in the *Pro Balbo* (32), had lost his Roman citizenship. Under the *lex Papia*, procedures were established to determine the legality of citizenship grants, and foreigners could be expelled from Rome.[37] If the prosecutor won this case against Balbus, he would regain his Roman citizenship.

The legal issues of the case are whether Pompey had authority under the *lex Cornelia* to grant Balbus citizenship, since the *lex Cornelia* did not allow a grantor of citizenship to violate anything sacrosanct.[38] If the treaty between Gades and Rome was sancrosanct, and if the treaty did not allow a grantor to grant citizenship to a Gaditan without the consent of the Gades, then Pompey would have violated a sacrosanct treaty with Gades by conferring citizenship upon Balbus without Gades' sanction.[39] Cicero deals with this issue by arguing that Rome's treaty with Gades was not sacrosanct, since it had not been ratified by the Roman people.[40] Cicero also argues that even if the treaty were sacrosanct, there is nothing in the treaty that stipulates that Gades had to sanction a grant of Roman citizenship upon a Gaditan.[41] Moreover, the treaty did contain a clause which indicates that the treaty was not between equals, but between a superior (Rome) and inferior (Gades) state.[42] A second issue is whether Gades, as a state with a treaty with Rome, had to adopt (*fundus*) the *lex Cornelia* before a Gaditan citizen could obtain citizenship under that law.[43] Cicero handles this issue by arguing that *fundus* had nothing to do with whether a state had a treaty with Rome, since since some states without treaties with Rome had adopted Roman laws.[44] Cicero also argues that a foreigner who became a Roman citizen was no longer subject to the laws of his previous state, and in any case, by making Balbus *hospes*, Gades gave implicit acceptance of Balbus' Roman citizenship.[45]

It is hypothetical to speculate what the prosecutor's speech contained. As Quintilian and Alexander point out,[46] it is impossible to reconstruct a prosecutor's entire speech from a defense speech. However, a defense speech can contain useful information about the case for the prosecution, as Alexander also recognizes.[47] Given this caveat, it is possible that the prosecution's arguments focused on the Gaditans' alleged right to give consent and on Balbus' character.

The ill will against Balbus would have provided the prosecutor with plenty of ammunition, and it would have been foolish for a prosecutor not to take advantage of this opportunity. Since Cicero rebuts at great length the consent argument, it is possible that this was one of the prosecutor's main arguments. Rebuttals of other arguments are almost non-existent, and if the prosecutor had made other arguments, Cicero probably would have acknowledged them, even if he did not elaborate on them.

It is unlikely that the prosecutor directed most of his speech against Pompey, as Cicero says he does, for several reasons. First, it would be foolish for the prosecutor to ignore Balbus who was a highly unpopular figure, and attack Pompey, who was generally liked. In addition, Pompey was a powerful figure, and as such more dangerous for the prosecutor to attack directly than Balbus. And finally, Cicero tells us (*Pro Balbo* 59) that in his speech, Pompey begged the prosecutor to attack him instead of his friend Balbus. Histrionics aside, if the prosecutor had actually spent his speech attacking Pompey, Pompey's plea for *miseratio* would have been rather ridiculous.

Cicero's speech is a fine example of forensic argumentation. The dominant form of argumentation in the *Pro Balbo* is "ethical" and consists of a defense of Pompey's character. The second major argument is legal and consists of a rebuttal of the proposition that the Gaditans had to give consent for the enfranchisement to be legitimate. These two main arguments are bolstered by other "ethical," "pathetic," and legal arguments, in particular the use of precedents and *exempla*. Cicero won his case and Balbus rose to even greater heights, backing Caesar and then Octavian in the civil wars, and eventually becoming Rome's first non-Italian consul.

Rhetoric in Cicero's *Pro Balbo*

Chapter One
Inventio: Ethos

ARISTOTLE CONSIDERS ETHOS THE MOST IMPORTANT OF HIS THREE *entechnoi pisteis*.[1] Although primarily interested in the moral character of the speaker, he also discusses the characterization of a third party, and the character of the jury.[2] In order to persuade through character, Aristotle names wisdom, virtue, and goodwill as qualities necessary to make a speaker credible.[3]

In his *De Oratore*, Cicero more or less abandons the schema of analyzing speeches through their rhetorical parts, which he employed in *De Inventione*. Instead he adapts Aristotle's tripartite division of arguments, but replaces the Greek with Latin terms. In so doing he changes the emphasis of the terminology. Ethos becomes *conciliare*, stressing the goal of character portrayal rather than the content of this type of argument.[4] This is not to say, however, that Ciceronian ethos is solely limited to focus on the audience. Wisse convincingly argues that Ciceronian ethos can also focus on the speaker or client, and less frequently, on the material of the speech.[5] Cicero's conception of character as expressed in *De Oratore* is somewhat different from Aristotle's.[6] Whereas Aristotle wanted the speaker to present his character in such a way as to render it credible, Cicero is more interested in using character to sway the audience.[7] Thus in *De Oratore* character depiction appears as a form of (mild) "sympathetic" emotional appeal, calculated to win the goodwill of the audience (2.178; 2.212).[8]

Since character already played such a large role in Roman politics and oratory, Cicero's adoption of the Aristotelian approach to ethos as one of three major argument types found throughout a speech fit in naturally with traditional Roman forensic practice.[9] In a society that so highly respected tradition, important ancestors, and authority, character portrayal was a potent force for persuasion.[10] As May phrases it: "The Roman respect for an individual's rank, reputation, dignity, and authority thus became a special weapon for advocates and clients who were in possession of such *desiderata* and a considerable liability for those who lacked them."[11]

The exigencies of Roman judicial oratory also presented rich opportunity for character depiction. As both Kennedy and May have noted, the use of a patron,[12] or several patrons, to deliver speeches on behalf of a client enabled the speaker to present his own persona as well as that of his client, the opponent, and the opponent's patron, if any.[13]

The *Pro Balbo* relies heavily upon ethos for its major arguments. In discussing ethos, the most important character in the speech is Pompey, but Cicero also deals with the prosecutor, Balbus, himself, and to a lesser extent, Caesar, the jury, and Crassus, who is dropped after brief mention in the *exordium* as Cicero focuses more and more on Pompey. The most important "ethical" strategy in the entire speech is the substitution of Pompey for Balbus as "defendant." This strategy enables Cicero to defend a more popular and important person than Balbus, which raises the stature of the case and takes pressure off Balbus. Another prevalent strategy is the identification of Balbus with Pompey, Cicero, Caesar, and the association of these latter three with the good of the Republic. These associations imply indirectly that Balbus' good should be identified with the good of the Republic.

Pompey and Crassus, who had delivered speeches the previous day, are introduced at the outset of the *exordium*. Cicero has a threefold purpose in the presentation of their characters. First, he is striving to win the goodwill of the audience by emphasizing the prestige and importance of Pompey and Crassus.[14] *Auctoritas*, the second word of the speech, becomes the defining characteristic of Pompey and Crassus. The concept of *auctoritas* is fundamental to the Roman social, political, and legal system.[15]

In all aspects of life a Roman would seek advice from and rely upon one who had *auctoritas*; for example, the consul (in theory) upon the senate; the citizen upon eminent jurists. As to the last, as Frier indicates, the jurists' *responsa* influenced the jurors (who were laymen) decisions.[16] The greater the *auctoritas* of the orator, the greater his influence upon the jurors.[17] Pompey and Crassus are described as having the greatest *auctoritas* possible. *Amplissimis*, which modifies *viris* (1), is a term applied to those who hold or have held the highest offices, such as the consulship or censorship.[18]

In section 1 the two men are described in terms of their experience (*usus*); they are most skilled (*peritissimus*); their natural ability (*ingenia*), demonstrates they are most eloquent (*eloquentissimi*), and their strong attachments (*studia*)[19] indicate they are very close friends (*amicissimi*) with Balbus. In *Topica*, Cicero links these qualities with *auctoritas*.[20] They are all qualities, which are prerequisites to having authority, and which demonstrate the worth of Pompey and

Crassus and stress their status in the eyes of the jurors. *Peritissimi* refers to practical experience, which was highly valued in Roman society, and was an essential prerequisite for *autoritas*. The *ingenium*, or natural talent of the two is expressed in terms of their ability as orators, as is appropriate, since this is a trial. This quality, *eloquentia*, is referred to in the *Pro Quinctio* (1) as one of the most powerful qualities in the Roman state. Its presence can result in one acquiring *gravitas* (seriousness of purpose).[21] The use of the superlative adjective suggests that Pompey and Crassus have tremendous expertise in the law-courts. This is not true of Pompey,[22] and in regard to Crassus, Cicero gives a different picture of his talents elsewhere (*Brutus* 233). One should note, however, that Cicero used superlatives more freely than we do. All the above terms carry a great deal of association, but their relative weight depends on the listener. As a result the audience becomes more involved in the speech.

After a short reference to himself, Cicero returns to Pompey, this time focusing on him alone. Cicero praises his speech, in which Pompey showed *gravitas*, a word which indicates weight of words, but also carries connotations of intellectual and moral influence;[23] *gravitas* indicates that what he said was said seriously and should be taken seriously; *facultas*, which translates both as fluency and the ability to do anything easily; and *copia*, an important rhetorical concept, which translates as abundance and sometimes signifies *eloquentia* in general.[24] To make the audience receptive to his own speech, Cicero reminds them of their reaction to Pompey's.[25] Their obvious approval of Pompey's speech becomes a subtle kind of proof of the accuracy of Cicero's praise and encourages them to accept other arguments Cicero will make. The reminder of their reaction also forges a tie between Cicero, Pompey, and the audience, by placing the three in the same psychological camp.[26]

McClintock makes the following statement about Ciceronian judicial speeches:

> Thus from the outset of the speech, when Cicero appeals in the exordium to the sympathy and sense of honor of the judges and jury and has won their ear, he uses three methods to steer the audience's reactions as he wishes them to go. He establishes a bond of familiarity with the audience, which places Cicero and them on the same side of a joke, a secret, or an emotional judgment; a climate of approbation direct and indirect, about his client; and an atmosphere of disapprobation or irreverence about the opponents or their accusations.[27]

In this case Cicero uses the first method, that of creating a bond with an emotional judgment. Because of the ill feeling towards his client[28] he cannot openly create a climate of approbation towards Balbus. But Cicero does create such an atmosphere indirectly through his portrayal of Pompey, who is linked to Balbus as his patron and the man who gave him citizenship.[29] Thus ethos is employed here to create a feeling of approbation—*conciliare* as opposed to *movere* (pathos).

Cicero's second goal was touched upon in the preceding paragraph: to associate Balbus as closely as possible with Pompey and Crassus (*amicissimi*). By identifying the defendant with these two, the former acquires prestige and respect through his close friendship with them. In his consular and post-reditum speeches Cicero commonly uses this technique of patron-client association by associating his client with himself.[30] Here he alters the tactic somewhat, by substituting other powerful patrons for himself.[31]

The third purpose of the characterization of Pompey in the *exordium* is to set the scene for the explanation of events in later sections. Everything that Pompey has done in respect to Balbus' enfranchisement will be seen in the light of these characteristics. A vital part of Cicero's defense strategy is the assertion that Pompey made a legitimate decision in giving Balbus citizenship. By praising Pompey for his experience at the outset of the exordium, Cicero is preparing the premise to an argument he will make later that Pompey is too experienced a person to make an inadvertently illegal decision about citizenship.[32] Thus the promotion and commendation of Pompey is important not only for securing the goodwill of the jury, but also serves as strategic preparation for the *argumentatio*.

Cicero then shifts in his portrayal from praise of the manner in which Pompey spoke, to praise of the content of his speech.[33] In a series of seven phrases, Cicero elaborates upon Pompey's practical experience. He lauds Pompey's explanation of the law, his knowledge of precedents, treaties, warfare and state affairs, his eloquence, and his modesty (2).

Cicero caps this praise with two references: one to a Stoic paradox,[34] which states that for a man who has a firm grasp of all the virtues, everything turns out well (3). The implications of this are that Pompey has a firm grasp on all the virtues, and that everything (including both the original citizenship grant and the present court case) will turn out well for him.[35] The second reference provides a comparison of Pompey to the famous orator Lucius Crassus,[36] stating that Pompey spoke so well that even Crassus could not have surpassed him, even though Pompey had only been able to devote a small portion of time to the study of oratory, between his continuous wars and victories. Again the emphasis is that Pompey is successful in whatever he undertakes, even if it is something to which he has not devoted his entire life.

In the conclusion to the *exordium* Cicero presents an *apologia* for his focus on Pompey, by stating that the latter had mentioned that "qui sui facti, sui iudici, sui benefici voluit me esse . . . praedicatorem et actorem" (4) (". . . he [Pompey] wanted me to be both the herald and defender of his action, of his judgment, of his patronage . . .").[37] Pompey's request that Cicero defend him also suggests that Cicero will have more to say about Pompey and introduces the notion that Pompey is somehow on trial.

First, however, Cicero must demonstrate that a defense of Pompey is both necessary and relevant to the case. Cicero states the *status* of his case as follows:[38] "quod fecisse Cn. Pompeius constet, id omnes ei licuisse concedant" (5). ("What it is established that Pompey has done, everyone should concede he was permitted to do"). Since everybody agreed Pompey had done the act, Cicero states the *status* in positive form, but what Cicero wants is for everyone to concede that Pompey acted within his rights: hence the orator phrases the issue as qualitative: whether Pompey's bestowal of citizenship was legitimate or not.[39]

Cicero further defends his focus of the *causa* on Pompey in the *narratio* by stating that the prosecutor has attacked Pompey: ". . . in Pompeio causa laedatur, poena sit nulla nisi famae" (6) (". . . with reference to Pompey, the defense is wronged but there is no penalty except for [Pompey's] reputation"); "praestantissimi imperatoris factum condemnari volunt. Ergo in iudicium caput Corneli, factum Pompei vocatur." (6) ("[The prosecution] want an act of the most pre-eminent general to be condemned. Therefore Balbus' citizenship rights and an act of Pompey are summoned before the court."); and "Ubi igitur est crimen? Quod eum Pompeius civitate donavit. Huius crimen? Minime, nisi honos ignominia putanda est. Cuius igitur? Re vera nullius, actione accusatoris eius unius, qui donavit." (7) ("Therefore where is the charge? That Pompey bestowed citizenship upon him. A charge with which my client has anything to do? Not in the least, unless honor is to be thought ignominy. A charge against whom, then? In truth against no one, but so far as the prosecutor's contention is concerned, against the one man who enfranchised him.") By presenting his defense of Pompey as a response to the prosecutor, who according to Cicero pled his case as if he were prosecuting Pompey, Cicero makes the attention to Pompey seem relevant, and he also gains the sympathy of the jury.[40] More importantly, by making Pompey the target Cicero is taking the pressure off Balbus. The jurors might not like Balbus, but they would be less likely to object to Pompey. Thus Cicero substitutes Pompey for Balbus as defendant.

Cicero shapes the argument by asking what Pompey's character defect was in whose absence the jury would hold that the privilege of citizenship was given legitimately. By narrowing the scope of the argument in this way, Cicero disregards any other possible cause for an illegal grant. Cicero is assuming that the grant of citizenship could only have been bestowed illegally if Pompey can be proved to be "ethically" deficient. Such an assumption may not be accurate, but Cicero has prepared the audience for the acceptance of this assumption with his discussion of Pompey in the *exordium*.

Thus, rather than arguing the issue on strict legal grounds, Cicero argues from ethos:[41] whether Pompey was the sort of commander who would bestow citizenship illegally. The molding of the argument in this way enables Cicero to elaborate on Pompey's virtues: namely his experience, including his military career, triumphs, and victories; his ability, including his courage and good fortune; and his honor, integrity, piety, and application. His *religio*, a quality not mentioned earlier in the speech, is used later (13) to refute the argument that Pompey would have intentionally violated a treaty. Cicero continues to list Pompey's excellent qualities, including his uprightness, his self-control, his righteousness, his *auctoritas*. The description of these characteristics, particularly *auctoritas*, is calculated to inspire confidence in Pompey. Pompey's *auctoritas* becomes the major defense of the citizenship grant. Here Cicero is playing upon the Roman tendency to rely upon and trust a man of political influence. This tendency is clearly seen in political life, especially in the role of the senate, which functioned through its exercise of *auctoritas senatus*, that is through the prestige and influence of its members.[42]

Cicero has skillfully shifted the focus of the case from Balbus to Pompey,[43] thereby raising the stakes in regard to the outcome. Since Pompey was a more important figure in Rome than Balbus, this makes the trial a more significant one to the jury[44] in addition to making the defense easier. Pompey also had far more *auctoritas* than Balbus, and reaped the benefits from this, such as far more respect in the eyes of the jury. In addition the power Pompey possessed made "convicting" him a more serious matter than convicting Balbus. By putting Pompey at the center of the charges Cicero is also able to defuse some of the envy and jealousy directed at Balbus, since Balbus becomes almost a peripheral object.

After he has built up Pompey into a paradigm of all the virtues, Cicero suggests that it is disgraceful that the point at issue is whether it was lawful or contrary to the treaty and against the sacred obligation of the Roman people for Pompey to have given Balbus citizenship.[45] The suggestion Cicero makes here is that this case ought never have come to trial. The case *has* come to trial, however, so Cicero presents two *exempla* which serve as analogies for this case and offers suggestions as to how the jury should act. The first *exemplum* concerns Quintus Metellus Numidicus (11). When this man was on trial the jury refused to look at his account books, lest anyone think they doubted his honesty.[46] The second example is a Greek man, who lived "sancte graviterque" (a venerable life with seriousness of purpose"), and when on trial the jury protested that he did not need to take an oath, since they "spectati viri noluerunt religione videri potius quam veritate fidem esse constrictam" (12) ("would not allow it to be thought that the credibility of a respected man was better secured by religious observance than by truthfulness of character"). This second example allows Cicero to provide a positive example of a foreigner for the jurors.[47]

By comparing Pompey to these men, Cicero is imbuing Pompey with their qualities: "ille vir, cui patriae salus dulcior quam conspectus fuit, qui de civitate decedere quam de sententia maluit" (11) ("that man, to whom the safety of his country was sweeter than the sight of it, who preferred to give up his state rather than his beliefs")[48] and "sancte graviterque vixisset" (12) ("he had lived a venerable life with seriousness of purpose"). These examples, by reference to *ius* and *mos maiorum* also suggest to the jury that they ought to behave as did these earlier juries by granting authority of character precedence over excessively strict observance of the law.[49] This message is softened by section 12: ". . . nos etiam in ipsa religione et legum et foederum conservanda qualis fuerit Cn. Pompeius dubitamus?" ("shall we, moreover, doubt the kind of man Gnaeus Pompeius was in maintaining respect for both laws and treaties?"), where Cicero suggests that because his client is good, it is therefore implausible that he violated the law.

The author of the *Rhetorica ad Alexandrum* (8) states that an orator should use *exempla* when he wants to say something unconvincing or something that cannot be proved by an argument from probability. (It is also reasonable to infer that an orator might use *exempla* for an argument that is not immediately and obviously convincing.) Credibility for such a statement can be gained if the orator shows that a similar action occurred in the past. In this case the use of *exempla* also enables Cicero to state in a subtle and oblique manner a point which would be insulting to the jurors if expressed openly.[50] Rather than declaring outright that the jurors ought not to observe the law too closely, a statement which might offend the jury, he simply draws an analogy and poses a question.

The second *exemplum* also provides a transition to the rebuttal of the prosecutor, when Cicero, immediately after presenting it, asks the prosecutor if he thinks Pompey violated the treaty knowingly. Since Cicero has already commented extensively on Pompey's *religio*, and asserted that he is *castior* and *sanctior*, the audience should say no. Even the prosecutor gestured a "no," according to Cicero (14).

Cicero has narrowed his interpretation of the prosecution's argument to this: Pompey must have knowingly bestowed the citizenship illegally.[51] But according to the ethos Cicero has presented of Pompey from the very outset of the *exordium*, such an argument would be invalid. His portrait is of a man who is master of everything he undertakes, from giving speeches (as the audience has already agreed) to winning wars and making treaties. According to Cicero, Pompey's specialty is treaties. Therefore it is impossible that Pompey could have made a mistake in giving Balbus citizenship. Cicero concludes his defense of Pompey with a repetition of the latter's knowledge of Spain and Gades and their treaties and laws, and a caution about envy.

An important technique Cicero uses in presenting ethos consists of the repetition of Pompey's qualities, with increasing elaboration.[52] Also, by depicting character traits in the *exordium* and *narratio* which will be germane to the *argumentatio*, the audience becomes so familiar with them in these first divisions of the speech that the *argumentatio* serves only to confirm what the audience has already been persuaded of. This is a far more powerful manner of persuasion than to list the charge and then rebut it by mentioning the character traits for the first time.[53]

The portrayal of the prosecutor provides an antithesis to both Pompey and Balbus. Pompey has tremendous *auctoritas*, a brilliant military career, a thorough knowledge of treaties. The Gaditan prosecutor, on the other hand, is not even graced with a name by Cicero, an omission which emphasizes his insignificance.[54] Little information is given about the background of the prosecutor. He is first mentioned in the *narratio* as wanting an innocent man and a brilliant commander condemned (6), and is accused of directing the prosecution against Pompey (7). Although these statements are designed to depict the opposition in a negative light,[55] they are only preparatory to the main attack on the prosecution. As is customary with Cicero, he does not begin an outright attack upon the opposition until the *argumentatio*. The earlier remarks about the prosecutor, however, are designed to sow seeds of doubt about his ability as an advocate. He is characterized as an *obtrectator* (16) before Cicero focuses on his incompetence as a lawyer. Cicero's main method is to address the opposition with biting sarcasm, as if exasperated by his stupidity.[56] By ironically presenting a depiction that is clearly the opposite of the picture Cicero wants the jury to have of the prosecutor, Cicero raises a laugh from the audience. His wit diffused a potentially difficult situation, for if Cicero had criticized the prosecutor outright, in a serious manner, the criticism might have aroused sympathy for the Spaniard, since the contest between the two was so clearly unequal. More importantly, his wit also solves a problem for Cicero: he cannot use ethnic stereotypes in a negative manner because his client is also a Spaniard. If he maligns the prosecutor as an ignorant foreigner, he might unwittingly encourage the jurors to view Balbus in this light. By making the jury laugh, however, Cicero brings them over to his side. His language makes the prosecutor appear pretentious and ridiculous:[57]

O praeclarum interpretem iuris, auctorem antiquitatis, correctorem atque emendatorem nostrae civitatis, qui hanc poenam foederibus adscribat, ut omnium praemiorum beneficiorumque nostrorum expertis faciat foederatos! Quid enim potuit dici imperitius quam foederatos populos fieri fundos oportere? (20)

Here is a magnificent interpreter of the law, promoter of antiquity, improver and amender of our community, since he attaches a punishment to treaties in order that he may deprive our allies of all our rewards and benefits. For what could be more inexperienced to say than that allied people must give consent?

Clarus is a term applied to men who were illustrious or well known either because of their noble family or their own actions.[58] Romans did not use it for just any noble, but only for the most important ones. Cicero employs *clarissimus* elsewhere in the *Pro Balbo* to describe: a victory of Pompey's: "cuius res gestae omnis gentis cum clarissima victoria terra marique peragrassent . . ." (16) ("whose acts, ever attended by glorious victory on land and sea, had spread to every race . . ."); several illustrious Romans, such as Q. Maximus, a consul, C. Laenas, a legatus, Q. Philippus, the son of a consul, C. Cato, a consul, Q. Caepio, a consul, and P. Rutilius Rufus, another consul (28); Marius (49); Pompey (64); and all the generals who ever enfranchised foreigners (65). *Praeclarus*, as an intensification of *clarus*, would only be used for the most illustrious Romans. Cicero employs the term only once again in the speech, when describing in emotive language the Roman laws: "O iura praeclara!" (31) ("O magnificent laws!"). Cicero could employ *praeclarus* seriously to describe Pompey. When used to describe the unnamed prosecutor, however, the word is incongruously and bitingly funny.

The use of *auctor* to characterize the prosecutor is also amusing. Hellegouarc'h defines the word as follows: "L'*auctor*, c'est avant tout la personnalité qui par ses hautes qualités possède assez de *fides* pour exercer une influence sur les actions d'autrui."[59] *Auctor* is etymologically related to the term *auctoritas*.[60] (The term is elsewhere in the *Pro Balbo* used to describe Pompeius Strabo (51).) The word is used here with a dependent genitive which gives it the meaning of "supporter" or "sponsor" in a broad sense.[61] It is impossible to believe that the prosecutor could have influence on any Roman. In fact, the idea that an obscure foreigner (with no ancestors) might support and promote *Roman* antique usages is a contradiction in logic.

The description of the prosecutor as a "correctorem atque emendatorem nostrae civitatis" (20) ("improver and amender of our community") is hyperbolic, and presents the prosecutor as a would-be censor of morals. That he is censoring the morals (according to Cicero) of a city to which he does not even hold citizenship suggests a tremendous (and ridiculous) impudence and impertinence on his part. Although the phrase is employed sarcastically in reference to the prosecutor, it could be used seriously to describe Pompey.[62] The term *imperitius*, applied implicitly to the prosecutor, follows logically from the preceding characterization of him, and the word recalls the contrasting *peritissimus* that characterized Pompey in the *exordium*.[63] The implicit comparison with Pompey is operative throughout the speech.

Later Cicero resumes his attack: "Hanc tu igitur, patrone foederum ac foederatorum, condicionem statuis Gaditanis, tuis civibus . . ." (25) ("Therefore do you, O patron of treaties and allies, assign this condition to the Gaditans, your fellow citizens . . ."). The term *patronus* was generally applied to men of a certain importance, who were able to protect their clients.[64] In the courts, the prosecutor under the *lex repetundarum*, who represented the foreigners accusing the defendant, was called a *patronus*.[65] By styling the prosecutor in the *Pro Balbo* as *patronus*, Cicero is portraying him as the protector of treaties and Roman allies. This title is ridiculous, given the man's lack of status, and indeed, the appellation emphasizes that point. Added to the sarcasm is the assertion that the prosecutor is actually attempting to deny his fellow citizens rights they ought to enjoy; and therefore even as a mock patron, he is not acting in his clients' best interests (since they would self-evidently prefer to have Roman citizenship).

After repeatedly asserting that the prosecutor is ignorant and inexperienced, Cicero elaborates the characterization by specifying that the man knows little about Roman or Gaditan laws: "Sed cum est illud imperitissime dictum de populis fundis . . . tum vero ius omne noster iste magister mutandae civitatis ignorat . . ." (27) ("But as he spoke most unknowingly about peoples giving consent . . . so in particular is that instructor of ours ignorant of every law of changing citizenship . . .") and: "Ignosco tibi, si neque Poenoruum iura calles (reliqueras enim civitatem tuam) neque nostras potuisti leges inspicere; ipsae enim te a cognitione sua iudicio publico reppulerunt."[66] (32) ("I forgive you, if you neither understand Carthaginian laws (for you had left your community) nor were able to become acquainted with our laws; for these laws themselves, by means of a public trial, held you back from acquiring knowledge of them"). The criticism of the prosecutor's lack of knowledge about Roman and Gaditan law prepares the jurors for the arguments Cicero makes in sections 28–37. The reminder of his loss of Roman citizenship after a trial provides an insinuation of illegal activity on the part of the prosecutor and suggests an unsavory character.

After delivering this damning and contemptuous portrayal of the prosecutor, Cicero asks a cunning question: "Quos igitur prudentissimos interpretes foederum, quos peritissimos bellici iuris, quos diligentissimos in exquirendis condicionibus civitatum atque causis esse arbitramur? eos profecto, qui iam imperia ac bella gesserunt" (45) ("Whom, therefore, do we think are the most skilled interpreters of treaties, whom the most experienced in military law, whom the most careful in seeking out the status and legal position of states? By all means those who have already held command and waged wars").

Implicit in the question is the assumption that the most credible man, the person the jury ought to vote for, is the one who fulfills the criteria Cicero offers. The criteria contain characteristics which have been associated with Pompey throughout the speech. The words *peritissimus* and *diligentia* have both been used to describe the general earlier: ". . . ab amplissimis viris L. Corneli causa defensa est, si usus, a *peritissimis* . . ." (1) (". . . the case of Lucius Cornelius has been defended by the most distinguished men, if experience [holds weight], by the most skilled men . . .") and: "An pudor, an integritas, an religio in eo, an *diligentia* umquam requisita est?" (9) ("Have decency, or integrity, or religious scruples, or diligence ever been found lacking in him?") The prosecutor, on the other hand, has been depicted as possessing none of these qualities. In fact throughout the speech he is characterized as the opposite of Pompey, with a lack of any practical experience (*imperitissimus*), ignorant of all law, both Roman and Gaditan, and hardly scrupulous in his inaccuracies. Cicero has created two completely antithetical characters. By juxtaposing two black and white characters, Cicero makes the choice easy for the jury. Since Pompey has the greater *auctoritas*, and has fulfilled the qualifications to be the best interpreter of citizenship laws, the jury must side with him.

To drive home this point, Cicero introduces the *exemplum* of Titus Matrinius of Spoletium, who had been given citizenship by Marius, and was prosecuted by Lucius Antistius: ". . . Quem cum disertus homo L. Antistius accusaret, non dixit fundum Spoletinum populum non esse factum—videbat enim populos de suo iure, non de nostro fundos fieri solere") (48) ("When the well-spoken man, Lucius Antistius accused him, he did not say that the people of Spoletium had not given their consent [for he was aware that people were accustomed to give consent about their own law, not about ours]").

L. Antistius, although he had a better grasp of law than the present prosecutor, still lost the case to Marius: "sed tamen tanta auctoritas in C. Mario fuit ut non per L. Crassum, adfinem suum, hominem incredibili eloquentia, sed paucis ipse verbis causam illam gravitate sua defenderit et probarit." (49) ("But nevertheless Gaius Marius had such authority that he defended and proved that case not with the aid of Lucius Crassus, his relative by marriage and a man of incredible eloquence, but he himself, with a few words and his own dignity.")

The message in the analogy is clear: Pompey's prestige is similar to Marius' and the present prosecutor has a worse understanding of the law than Antistius. Therefore the jurors ought *a fortiori* to do in this case the same as the earlier ones did. Pompey ought to be vindicated on the strength of his *auctoritas*. (But it should be noted at the same time that Cicero never concedes the legal point. He does not have to: it is disputed, and therefore there are already people who think it legal.)

The prosecutor is also presented, as mentioned earlier, as an antithesis to Balbus. The prosecutor does not have the prestige among his fellow-citizens that Balbus has, since the Gaditans support the latter. Their support is demonstrated by their appointing Balbus as their guest-friend at Rome, and the deputation they have sent to Rome on Balbus' behalf.[67] The prosecutor is also depicted as desiring to harm the Gaditans' interests, since he wants to remove their right of becoming Roman citizens if as individuals they wish to (25). Balbus, on the other hand, has used his influence to do the utmost to help his fellow-citizens: ". . . et magno opere iis esse laetandum huius L. Corneli benevolentiam erga suos remanere Gadibus, gratiam et facultatem commendandi in hac civitate versari? Quis est enim nostrum cui non illa civitas sit huius studio, cura, diligentia commendatior?" (43) (". . . and consequently it must be a matter of great rejoicing for them that Gades retains the goodwill of this man, Lucius Cornelius, towards his fellow citizens, and that he employs his influence and his capability of recommending favors in this community? For who is there among us by whom that community is not more favorably viewed because of the zeal, the concern, and the diligence of this man?") According to Cicero, Balbus, then has shown a lack of self-interest,[68] whereas the prosecutor is consumed by bettering his own position to the detriment of his fellow-citizens.

Perhaps the most difficult character for Cicero to portray is Balbus himself, because of the jealousy which the jury feels towards the Spaniard (18–19), a jealousy which the prosecutor has attempted to intensify (56–57).[69] In *De Oratore*, Cicero states that *invidia* is the strongest emotion: ". . . sed haud sciam an acerrimus longe sit omnium motus invidiae nec minus virium opus sit in ea comprimenda quam in excitanda." (2.209) (". . . but I might say that the emotion of jealousy is by far the fiercest of all, nor is there less work in curbing it than there is in arousing it.")[70] Cicero goes on to describe those of whom one might be jealous: "Invident autem homines maxime paribus aut inferioribus, cum se relictos sentiunt, illos autem dolent evolasse . . ." (2.209) ("Moreover men are especially jealous of those who are their equals or inferiors, when they perceive themselves left behind, moreover they feel pain at the others flying upward . . .").

The envy directed at Balbus was undoubtedly quite fierce, especially since he was a non-Italian and held the position of powerful adviser to Caesar.[71] Cicero, who had suffered from the attacks of jealous men, and was never fully accepted by all elements of the senatorial class,[72] mentions his own jealousy of Balbus in a letter.[73]

Since Cicero is attempting to disarm *invidia* rather than arouse it (*conciliare* rather than *movere*), and since the prime method of diminishment is through the projection of Balbus' character, I will discuss *invidia*, insofar as it pertains to Balbus' character portrayal, in this section.

Cicero does not begin to discuss Balbus until he has softened up the audience with his praise of Pompey and references to himself. To create sympathy for Balbus, Cicero declares the Spaniard is fighting for his very existence (5). This kind of depiction is employed in other speeches, such as the *Pro Sex. Roscio* (13)[74] and *Pro Rabirio Postumo* (48). This hyperbolic (but also standard) interpretation of the penalty flatters the jury and also increases the importance of the trial in the eyes of the jurors. In the *Pro Balbo* Cicero makes the bid for favor even stronger by adding that Balbus has not been charged with any offense.

When summarizing Balbus' military career under Pompey, the fierceness of the wars is stressed by the frequent use of superlatives: "in Hispania durissimo bello . . ." and ". . . acerrimis illis proeliis et maximis . . . interfuisse" (5) (". . . when there was a most harsh war in Spain . . ." and "he took part in those fiercest and most important battles . . ."). Balbus' experience appears as extensive, with service both on land and at sea, in several important battles: the siege of New Carthage, at Sucro, and Turia. Descriptions of Balbus' loyalty are interwoven into the description of the harsh battles, which makes the Spaniard's loyalty seem all the more admirable: "numquam a Memmio discessisse . . . cum Pompeio ad extremum belli tempus fuisse." (5) ("He never left Memmius . . . he was with Pompey until the end of the war.") Balbus' military record reads like that of a young Roman noble, and indeed is one any Roman would be proud of, and his military experience also links him with Pompey.

Balbus' qualities of character are briefly enumerated: "Haec sunt propria Corneli, pietas in rem publicam nostram, labor, adsiduitas, dimicatio, virtus digna summo imperatore, spes pro periculis praemiorum . . ." (6) ("These qualities are Cornelius' own: a sense of duty towards our state, toil, unremitting application, furious fighting, courage worthy of the expectations of a great general, hope of rewards in proportion to dangers . . ."). Such a character depiction is the type advocated by rhetorical handbooks to disarm jealousy: "ad sedandum autem, magno illa labore, magnis periculis esse parta nec ad suum commodum, sed ad aliorum esse conlata. . . ." ("but to assuage [jealousy], it must be said that they were acquired by great labor, at great risk not directed for his own advantage, but for that of others . . .")[75]

The qualities Cicero attributes to Balbus are highly charged. In political terms, *pietas* signifies a sense of duty; a *pius* man is one who has fulfilled his *officia* and the debt that he owes to the state.[76] The concept of *virtus* traditionally expressed the ideal of the Roman nobility: personal achievements in service of the state.[77] Cicero appropriated the term to describe the *novus homo* as a man worthy of his new rank and status because of his own individual merit rather than an illustrious lineage.[78] Although technically Balbus is not a *novus homo* at the time of Cicero's speech,[79] he has risen beyond his original status through military service under Pompey,[80] and then by becoming a Roman citizen and adviser to Caesar. Therefore the rhetoric of the *novus homo* applies to him. The above-mentioned qualities are also important traditional Roman character values.[81] The fact that Balbus is shown to possess the kinds of qualities which Romans value and like to see in themselves, is a good argument that Balbus is the type of man that would make a good Roman.

After a brief return to Pompey, Cicero resumes Balbus' biography, which repeats and elaborates what the orator said earlier:

Hunc enim in ea civitate in qua sit natus honestissimo loco natum esse concedis,
et ab ineunte aetate relictis rebus suis omnibus in nostris bellis nostris cum imperatoribus esse versatum, nullius laboris, nullius obsessionis, nullius proeli expertem
fuisse. Haec sunt omnia cum plena laudis tum propria Corneli, nec in iis rebus
crimen est ullum.[82] (6)

For you agree that my client was born to a very distinguished family in his native
city, and from the earliest age, after abandoning all his own interests, he occupied
himself in our wars with our generals, and there was no toil, no blockade, no battle in which he did not take part. As all these praiseworthy qualities are Cornelius'
own, so there is no ground for a charge in them.

Important in the attempt to quench envy is the reference to Balbus' honorable birth, his courage, and the statement that Balbus has renounced all personal interests.[83] *Rebus suis*, although perhaps intentionally vague, probably refers to
political interests that Balbus had in Gades, as well as property and possessions.[84]
Clearly hyperbolic, this statement is meant to contrast Balbus' own personal
interests, which according to Cicero he completely renounced, with the interests
of the Roman state, which Balbus fostered by participating in every battle possible. The picture which emerges is that of a self-sacrificing individual completely devoted to Rome.

It is not until section 18 that Cicero openly pleads with the jury to set aside
the envy and prejudice directed towards his client. He attempts to reduce the ill
will first by speaking in general terms about rise in fortune:

. . . quiddam de communi condicione omnium nostrum deprecandae malivolentiae causa breviter commemorandum videtur. Si quo quisque loco nostrum est,
iudices, natus, aut si, in qua fortuna est nascendi initio constitutus, hunc vitae statum usque ad senectutem obtinere debet . . . (18)

. . . it seems to me that, in order to ward off a cause of spitefulness, something
must be mentioned briefly about a circumstance which affects one and all of us.
If each one of us, judges, is bound to keep right up to old age that position in life,
in which he was born, or whatever position fortune established for him at birth .
. .

Cicero's introduction to the subject is clever, since he draws in the jury by
addressing each individual juror's ambition for himself. The prejudice against
social mobility is therefore something which potentially could be directed
against them personally.[85] Words such as *omnium nostrum* emphasize this.
Although Cicero does not employ the term *novus homo* here, the *novus homo*
would be an instance of the phenomenon being discussed. The term could
describe a senator whose ancestors had not been of senatorial rank, or it could
mean a consul who was the first in his family to become one.[86]

Because Sulla had doubled the number of senators it is conceivable that there would be several men on the jury in Balbus' case who were either *novi homines* or whose fathers had been *novi homines* in the first sense of the term.[87] As Wiseman points out, prejudice against new men was not restricted only to senators, but was directed also against *equites* who were the first of their family to attain that rank: "Like *nobilitas* among the senators, *vetustas equestris nominis* gave a man high social status among his peers in the order, though constitutionally his position was the same as theirs."[88] The *equites* of lengthy pedigree employed these stratified systems of status to protect their position against the new men in their ranks.[89] Thus any new men among the *equites* in the jury, no doubt, would also have experienced the prejudice Cicero describes in 18 and 19.

Cicero's statement also serves to remind the jury that he himself is a man who has risen to a station higher than that to which he was born, thereby associating himself with Balbus. The statement also implicitly associates both Cicero and Balbus and Lucius Cossinius, one of the jurors, whose father (as Cicero tells us in the *Pro Balbo* 53) won Roman citizenship, and to any other of the jurors who were *novi homines*.[90]

The argument that *fortuna*, *labor*, *industria*, *virtus*, *ingenium*, and *humanitas* should not be begrudged, especially if accompanied by modesty, as in Balbus' case, is a rhetorical trope designed to mitigate jealousy.[91] The terms carry powerful connotations. *Labor* and *industria* express the approved concept of hard work (on behalf of Rome). *Fortuna* suggests the gods are on one's side, and is linked with the concept of *virtus*.[92] *Virtus* is courage and is often applied to brave actions in the service of the state.[93] *Virtus* and *ingenium* go together, since *virtus* is the functioning of *ingenium*. As is typical of a *novus homo*, Balbus enhanced his status by means of his *virtus* as well as through *labor* and *industria*.

Later in the speech Cicero describes the bravery and risks that certain allies have undertaken on Rome's behalf. Although Balbus is not mentioned by name, it is clear he is meant as such a man:

> . . . si quis ex his [Gaditanis, Massiliis, Saguntinis] populis sit exortus qui nostros duces auxilio laboris, commeatus periculo suo iuverit, qui cum hoste nostro comminus in acie saepe pugnarit, qui se saepe telis hostium, qui dimicationi capitis, qui morti obiecerit, nulla condicione huius civitatis praemiis adfici possit? (23)

> . . . if anyone has come forward from these peoples [the Gaditans, Massilians, Saguntines] who has assisted our military leaders with his hard work, or helped our supply convoys at his own private risk, who often fought against our enemy in hand to hand combat, who often opposed the spears of the enemy, who battled for his life, who threw himself in the path of death, can he under no circumstances obtain the reward of Roman citizenship?

and:

> . . . grave est non posse uti sociis excellenti virtute praeditis, qui velint cum periculis nostris sua communicare; in socios vero ipsos, et in eos de quibus agimus foederatos, iniuriosum et contumeliosum est iis praemiis et iis honoribus exclusos esse fidelissimos et coniunctissimos socios quae pateant stipendiariis, pateant hostibus, pateant saepe servis . . . (24)

> . . . it is burdensome not to be able to employ allies endowed with surpassing courage, who wish to associate their own danger with ours; certainly in regard to those allies and those with whom we have treaties, whom we are dealing with now, it is unjust and insulting that the most loyal and friendly allies should be absolutely shut out from those rewards and those honors which are accessible to members of tributary states, to our enemies, and often to slaves.

By talking about the genus (courageous foreigners) of which Balbus is a species, Cicero is able to elaborate on the risks the Spaniard took and bravery he showed for Rome's advantage. Balbus comes off to advantage by association with the best of the allies. It is safer for Cicero to talk about excellent allies in general, rather than to elaborate specifically about Balbus as he did about Pompey. By praising Balbus too much he could create more jealousy rather than dissipate it: "Videndumque hoc loco est ne, quos ob benefacta diligi volemus, eorum laudem atque gloriam, cui maxime invideri solet, nimis efferre videamur;" ("And here we must take care least we appear to proclaim excessively the laudable actions and glory (of which people are especially jealous) of those whom we want to be loved on account of their good deeds.")[94] The praise of stalwart allies also heightens the importance of the case through universalization, because Cicero is not just talking about one ally, but about all good allies.[95]

Cicero also employs the technique of association to put Balbus in a good light when he describes how Balbus aided his family during his exile: "Non modo non exsultavit in ruinis nostris vestrisque sordibus Cornelius, sed omni officio,—lacrimis, opera, consolatione,—omnes me absente meos sublevavit . . ." (58) ("Not only did Cornelius Balbus not exult in my downfall and your mourning, but in my absence he supported my whole family with every service: with his tears, with his actions, and with his consolation"). Balbus did not show *invidia*, he showed *miseratio*, even *magnitudo animi*.

The exile is depicted not only as a catastrophe for Cicero, but also for the Roman Republic.[96] By extending help and sympathy to Cicero's family during this difficult time, Balbus also helped the Republic because it was distressed by Cicero's exile. By associating Balbus' efforts so closely with Cicero and the Republic, Balbus acquires luster and prestige from Cicero's persona. This identification of client with Cicero and Cicero with the Republic (and thereby client with Republic) in common in the post-reditum speeches.[97]

Cicero openly tackles the envy directed at his client once more in the *refutatio* (56). The passage is interesting for its rebuttal of luxury, extravagance, and greed. It is likely the prosecutor attacked Balbus in much the same way Cicero attacked the freedman Chrysogonus in the *Pro Roscio Amerino*. In the *Pro Roscio*, however, Cicero had managed to separate Chrysogonus from Sulla in the minds of the jurors, so that they were able to take exception to Chrysogonus' behavior without feeling they were insulting Sulla.[98] In this trial it appears the prosecutor was unable to separate the two, and Cicero binds Pompey so closely to Balbus and his case that the jury feels a condemnation of Balbus would also be a condemnation of his patron.

Cicero's tactics of rebuttal in the *refutatio* are straightforward. He denigrates the prosecutor by stating that those who are hostile to Balbus are malevolent, unjust, and envious (56). Then he rebuts the character defects with which the opposition had tarred Balbus. Balbus' wealth was acquired by careful management, not ill acquired; his extravagance was a general slander (56). Balbus' purchase of the villa at Tusculum was not an example of him overreaching himself because it had been formerly owned by a freedman (56).[99] The membership in the prestigeous *tribus Clustumina* was the result of Balbus' success in a court-case (hard work and talent) (57), and his much-criticized adoption by Theophanes was to enable him to inherit his own relatives' property (57). In each instance, Cicero strives to neutralize the charges by giving a reasonable explanation which demonstrates positive character traits or by simply dismissing the accusation.[100]

After refuting the charges, Cicero employs a strategy inverse to that of the prosecutor. He portrays Balbus as a man who is suffering injustices at the hands of those who hate his client's friends (58). Such a depiction creates sympathy for Balbus and also hostility towards the prosecution for cowardly behavior, since it suggests the opposition did not have the courage to attack the men they actually opposed.

Cicero's portrayal of his own ethos requires skilful management. After showing an independent streak when he thought the coalition among Caesar, Pompey, and Crassus was breaking apart, in particular by attempting to have the Senate repeal some of Caesar's legislation, Cicero was sharply reined in by Pompey after the Conference at Luca, where Caesar, Crassus, and Pompey renewed their alliance.[101] May states:[102]

> The *post reditum* speeches span some of the most difficult years of Cicero's life and career. His return from humiliating exile, his struggle to repair his private fortune and his personal *dignitas*, the horrible year of Luca, and the *De Provinciis Consularibus*, all exerted a profound effect upon him, his oratory, and his use of ethos in that oratory.

The results of Luca, then, put him in a very awkward situation.[103] If the jury interpreted Cicero's defense of Caesar's henchman as kowtowing to Caesar and Pompey, it would severely damage his *dignitas* and *auctoritas*, and therefore his credibility as Balbus' advocate. It is vital for Cicero to turn this potentially disadvantageous situation into an advantageous one.

Cicero begins his self-portrait with a projection of modesty.[104] He describes his qualifications, repeating three of the four qualities with which he had earlier credited Pompey and Crassus: "*auctoritatis* tantae quantam vos in me esse voluistis, *usus* mediocris, *ingeni* minime voluntati paris" (1) ("As much influence as you desire me to have, moderate experience, a natural ability in no way equal to my goodwill").[105] In the latters' case he coupled these qualities with superlatives, however when describing himself he uses litotes. This *deprecatio* is geared to win over the goodwill of the jury; especially the phrase "auctoritas tantae, *quantam vos in me esse voluistis*" consists of a flattering (but also more or less true) suggestion to the jury that they are responsible for Cicero's *auctoritas*, and have the power to grant or deny it. He sets up an implied comparison with Pompey and Crassus, depicting himself as their inferior in regard to *auctoritas*, *usus*, and *ingenium*. But since it would not be appropriate for him to have too much less *studium* than they in regard to the case, he twists the last to say his *ingenium* is not equal to his *voluntas*. The comparison to Pompey also serves to highlight Pompey's ability.

Also implied is a comparison of Pompey, Crassus, and Cicero with the prosecutor. If Cicero, an ex-consul and a member of the Senate, describes himself as having less *auctoritas* than Pompey and Crassus, and *usus mediocris* despite his illustrious career in the courts, then the prosecutor in turn, who has lost his Roman citizenship and undoubtedly never held office, and has nowhere near Cicero's experience in the courts, must have no *auctoritas* and very little *usus*.

Immediately afterwards, Cicero explains his motivation for defending Balbus. It is crucial that Cicero establish that he is defending his client out of duty. This is necessary in ordinary circumstances and doubly so in the present case.[106] Cicero mentions a debt he owes Balbus, and creates anticipation by elaborating only briefly: "principio orationis hoc pono, me omnibus qui amici fuerint saluti et dignitati meae, si minus referenda gratia satis facere potuerim, praedicanda and habenda certe satis esse facturum." (2) ("Here at the beginning of my speech I assert this: to all those who were friends to my welfare and dignity, if I will not have been able to repay their favors sufficiently, I will certainly satisfy them by proclaiming and acknowledging it"). The phrase "amici fuerint saluti et dignitati mei" is an oblique reference to those who helped bring about an end to Cicero's exile. The use of the plural *amici* suggests that Cicero is referring to more than one person, not only to Balbus but also to Pompey, who was largely responsible for Cicero's recall and who had asked Cicero to speak on behalf of the Spaniard.[107] The debt to Balbus is explained in the *refutatio*, when Cicero equates his ill fortune with that of the Republic: "Sive meum sive rei publicae fatum" (58) ("either my ill-fortune or that of the state").[108]

Pompey's assistance was well known and did not require elaboration. Allusions to *amici* who aided Cicero provide justification for his undertaking of Balbus' defense, since friendship entailed reciprocal obligations.[109]

After stressing that the jury should approve Balbus as they cherish all who helped himself, Cicero tackles the issue of his own about-face in supporting Pompey and Caesar. Here he masterfully interprets his own behavior in the best light possible.[110] He depicts himself as a prudent, patriotic elder statesman, who offers advice to the jurors and uses his own situation as a model for them to follow. His capitulation to Pompey and Caesar, which could be viewed as cowardice, is instead presented as an act of political foresight and shrewdness. As in the case of his exile, this action is portrayed as being in the best interests of the state. Using the well-worn ship of state metaphor, Cicero declares it is not inconsistent to steer a ship according to the weather.[111] The important issue is the welfare of the Republic. Political controversy in defending a cause one believes in is only prudent as long as it does not injure the Republic. Cicero has moved to adapt to the present circumstances and rise above personal enmity, he states, because he does not want the Republic to suffer harm.

The argumentation here is the same as that Cicero used in the *De Provinciis Consularibus*, where he is somewhat blunter in admitting his enmity to Caesar:

> Ergo ego senator— inimicus, si ita vultis, homini— amicus esse, sicut semper fui, rei publicae debeo. Quid? si ipsas inimicitias depono rei publicae causa, quis me tandem iure reprehendet? praesertim cum ego omnium meorum consiliorum atque factorum exempla semper ex summorum hominum factis mihi censuerim petenda.[112] (19–20)

> Therefore I, a senator—a personal enemy of that man, if you wish to put it thus— am under an obligation to be a friend to the republic, as I always have been. What If I lay aside those hostilities for the sake of the republic, who at length will justly blame me? Especially when in all my deliberations and actions I have been of the opinion that I must always seek precedents in the actions of the greatest men.

In the *Pro Balbo*, Cicero adds that anyone who has the Republic's best interests at heart must do as Cicero and accommodate Pompey and Caesar. This implies that anyone who convicts Balbus is going against Pompey and Caesar and thereby harming the interests of the state. This heightens the antithesis set up earlier (58) between Cicero and his defendant, who are working for the Republic's best interests and his opponents, who are attempting to injure the state (60–62).

The *Pro Balbo* offers only a sketchy portrayal of Caesar. Like Balbus, he is interesting for his absence throughout most of the speech.[113] Caesar is first introduced with a description of the benefits he proferred as governor to Gades: he settled disputes, established codes of law, stamped out a certain barbarity, and in

general showed interest in and favor to the Gaditans. "Omitto quantis orna-
mentis populum istum C. Caesar, cum esset in Hispania praetor, adfecerit, con-
troversias sedarit, iura ipsorum permissu statuerit, inveteratam quandam bar-
bariam ex Gaditanorum moribus disciplinaque delerit, summa in eam civitatem
huius rogatu studia et beneficia contulerit" (43). ("I pass over the great honor
that G. Caesar, when he was praetor in Spain, bestowed upon that people; how
he settled disputes, established laws with their consent, expunged a certain long-
standing barbaric practice from Gaditan customs and institutions, and conferred the greatest goodwill and benefits upon that state, at the request of
Balbus.") The characterization is that of a magnanimous and skilled adminis-
trator. Cicero next mentions him with a reminder to the audience of the honors
recently bestowed upon the general by the senate, at Cicero's request: "C.
Caesarem senatus et genere supplicationum amplissimo ornavit et numero
dierum novo: idem in angustiis aerari victorem exercitum stipendio adfecit,
imperatori decem legatos decrevit, lege Sempronia succedendum non censuit.
Harum ego sententiarum et princeps et auctor fui . . ." (61) ("The senate hon-
ored Gaius Caesar with the most distinguished kind of thanksgiving which lasted an unprecedented number of days: it bestowed a stipend upon his victorious
army notwithstanding the indigence of the public treasury, it decided upon ten
legates for the general, and it moved that he should not be succeeded under the
Sempronian law. I was the sponsor and initiator of these measures . . .").

Caesar is characterized in such a way as to bring credit upon Balbus for associating with him. He is most discerning (*prudentissimus*), has a large circle of
friends, and values positive qualities such as judgment, loyalty, services rendered,
and respect. If he enjoys advantages now, he (like Balbus) earned them through
hard work (63). Cicero completes his characterization of Caesar with brief but
pointed mention of the general's military achievements:[114] Caesar is now at the
boundaries of the world, where he is enlarging Roman dominion (64). Here
Cicero suggests that Caesar is the real target of the prosecution: ". . . nolite . . .
hunc illi acerbum nuntium velle perferri, ut suum praefectum fabrum . . . non
ob ipsius aliquod delictum, sed ob suam familiaritatem vestris oppressum sen-
tentiis audiat" (64) (". . . do not desire that this harsh news be brought to him
[Caesar], that he may hear that his chief engineer has been crushed by your verdict not because of some transgression of his own, but because of his friendship
with him."). The stress on Caesar's military record and the downplaying of his
political activity should be noted. In fact the emphasis on Pompey and on
Balbus is the same. Perhaps the object here is to find some uncontroversial common ground. Then any disagreement can be devalued as *invidia*.

Cicero portrays the jury differently from the other players. In the case of the
jurors, Cicero often assumes them to have characteristics that he would like
them to possess: ". . . aequitas vestra . . ."[115] (18) ("your sense of justice") and

"iudices . . . vestros quidem animos certe confidimus non oratione nostra, sed humanitate vestra esse placatos."[116] (62) ("judges . . . I certainly trust that your minds have been appeased not by my speech, but by your own humanity.") *Humanitas* incorporates the concepts of *iustitia* (justice) and *clementia* (mercy).[117] Such an appeal to *humanitas* is made in other Ciceronian speeches: in the *Pro Archia* (31), the other speech regarding citizenship, and in a few speeches in which there was ill feeling towards the defendant: the *Pro Caelio* (75) and *Pro Sulla* (92). These qualities are attributed to the jury both to win their favor and to suggest to them how they should act in judging this case.

Cicero reminds the jury of the emotions roused by Pompey's speech in order to reactivate those favorable feelings for his own speech (2, 4). He tells them what their duty is, in a charge in 5: ". . . hoc proprium esse vestri offici . . . ut, quod fecisse Cn. Pompeium constet, id omnes ei licuisse concedant." (". . . this is your own duty . . . what it is established that Pompey has done, everyone should concede he was permitted to do.")

Exempla are offered to suggest indirectly the behavior the jurors should emulate (11, 12, 13).[118] The jurors in the Metellus case refused even to examine evidence against Metellus, and those in the venerable Greek's case preferred to consider the character of the defendant rather than ritual observances.[119] Such paradigms are useful since they allow Cicero to get across a message that he would not want to state directly. *Exempla* are also provided for other grants of citizenship:

> Quod ius si Cn. Pompeius ignoravit, si M. Crassus, si Q. Metellus, si Cn. Pompeius pater, si L. Sulla, si P. Crassus, si C. Marius, si senatus, si populus Romanus, si qui de re simili iudicarunt, si foederati populi, si socii, si illi antiqui Latini, videte ne utilius vobis est honestius sit illis ducibus errare quam hoc magistro erudiri.[120]

> If Gnaeus Pompeius, if Marcus Crassus, if Quintus Metellus, if Gnaeus Pompeius' father, if Lucius Sulla, if Publius Crassus, if Gaius Marius, if the senate, if the Roman people, if those who have given decisions on similar lawsuits, if people bound to us by treaties, if our allies, if the ancient Latins, were ignorant about this law, consider that it may be more useful and honorable for you to err with those men as leaders rather than to be schooled with this man for a teacher.

In these *exempla*, Cicero lines up the authority of the whole Roman world on one side, and that of the prosecutor, whom he ironically refers to as *magister*, on the other. Clearly the *auctoritas* of famous Roman generals, the senate, the Roman people, other judges, and ancient Latins outweigh the prosecutor as a model for the jury to follow. The *auctoritas* of the generals mentioned has already been discussed, and that of the Roman senate and people is obvious. The concept of *antiqui Latini* also held potent connotations, and is related to the idea of *mos maiorum*. In *De Republica*, Cicero, quoting Ennius, states that: "moribus antiquis res stat Romana virisque" ("The Roman state stands firm on ancient customs and on men") (5.1). The early republic was seen, in an idealized manner, as a time when men and morals were better, and individual actions of those early times were cited as worthy of emulation.[121] As Earl notes, the actions of the ancients became a criterion by which actions of later generations were judged.[122] The behavior of earlier generations had an *auctoritas maiorum* which formed for later Romans a quasi-judicial import.[123] Therefore precedents such as those cited by Cicero would have a strong impact on the jurors, such a strong impact, in fact, that Cicero could suggest that it would be better to make a mistake in company with the *antiqui* than to be correct by following the prosecutor.

Sometimes desirable qualities of character are suggested to the jury in the form of a request: "Est autem petendum ne oderitis ingenium, ne inimici sitis industriae, ne humanitatem opprimendam, ne virtutem puniendam putetis." (19) ("I must, however, ask you not to hate natural ability, not to be hostile to diligence, and that you should not think that human feelings should be crushed and courage punished.") This request has several purposes. Cicero could just as easily have asked the jury not to hate Balbus. But by naming the qualities, Cicero provides himself with an opportunity to repeat Balbus' excellent characteristics. Also by focusing on the characteristics rather than the man, Cicero avoids stirring up further animosity against Balbus. Thirdly, the qualities he attributes to Balbus, *ingenium, industria, humanitas*, and *virtus*, are all qualities Cicero knows the jury already approve of. Therefore Cicero is asking a question to which he knows the jury must answer positively.

Cicero also requests the jurors to show certain attitudes: "speroque, iudices, ut eos, qui principes fuerunt conservandae salutis aut dignitatis meae diligitis et caros habetis, sic, quae ab hoc pro facultate hominis, pro loco facta sunt, et grata esse vobis et probata." (59) ("and I hope, judges, that as you esteem and hold dear those men who were the leaders in preserving my welfare and dignity, so what was done by this man, considering his opportunities and the position he was in, will be pleasing to and approved by you.") This is the culmination of this theme, developed and expanded throughout the speech. This request emphasizes the bond between Balbus and Cicero, but also between Cicero and the jurors. Just as Cicero himself stated at the outset of the speech that he owed a debt to those who helped him (and Balbus was one of them), after developing the bonds between himself and Balbus and himself and the Republic, he is now able to ask the jury to look favorably upon Balbus because of this.

At another time Cicero gives a strong hint at a request he would like to make, but does not. Instead he declares that he is afraid to make the request: "non intellego cur potius invidia violatura virtutem L. Corneli quam aequitas vestra pudorem eius adiutura videatur. Itaque quod maxime petendum est a vobis idcirco non peto, iudices, ne de vestra sapientia atque de vestra humanitate dubitare videar" (18–19) ("I do not understand why it appears that ill-will will injure Lucius Cornelius' merit rather than that your sense of fairness will help a man of his modesty. Therefore a request which it is most important to make, I do not make on this account, judges, lest I appear to doubt your wisdom and human feelings."). The unstated request is to acquit Balbus. The *praeteritio* is clever, in effect equating an acquittal with the *aequitas* and *humanitas* of the jurors. The pretended delicacy and fear of doubting the jury brings Cicero their sympathy and a willingness to listen to him.

It is evident that ethical argumentation is central to the *Pro Balbo*. The major tactics Cicero employs in presenting ethos are the shifting of focus from Balbus to Pompey, and the subsequent narrowing of the scope of the entire case to Pompey's character, and in particular, his *auctoritas*. By making Pompey the "defendant" Cicero creates a more powerful antithesis between defense and prosecution than with the focus on Balbus as defendant. An important tactic in the presentation of Pompey's character is the repetition of Pompey's characteristics with increasing elaboration. The negative portrayal of the unnamed prosecutor, in particular his ignorance and inexperience, provides opposition to Pompey and highlights the latter's virtues. The prosecutor is also an antithesis to Balbus and to Cicero. Cicero's major tactic in presenting the prosecutor is a withering irony, as for example when he calls him *praeclarus*, *auctor*, and *patronus*. In the portrayal of Balbus, *invidia* presented difficulties, and the Spaniard's ethos is meant to dissipate the jealousy. Here Balbus' loyalty to Rome, his hard work, self-sacrifice, and compassion to Cicero's family during the exile are stressed. In his own portrayal, in order to circumvent accusations of cravenness, Cicero depicts himself as a prudent, elder statesman, willing to set aside personal enmities for the good of the state. This tactic of turning his own disadvantageous position into a strong one through his self-portrait as a strong, wise statesman providing an example of correct behavior towards the "triumvirate," is one of the most important tactics. Another pervasive technique is patron-client association. Balbus is strongly associated with Pompey, Cicero, and Caesar. Cicero, Pompey, and Caesar are strongly associated with the Roman state, and therefore Balbus, through identification with these men becomes associated with the good of the Republic.

Chapter Two

Inventio: Pathos

IN ARISTOTELIAN RHETORIC, PATHOS IS DISTINGUISHED FROM ETHOS BY ITS POINT of origin: pathos originates from the audience, and ethos from the speaker.[1] The corresponding Latin terms, *commovere* and *conciliare* are generally both understood in terms of the audience.[2] Eventually both are combined under the term *adfectus* (*auditoris*), with *commovere* referring to the more vehement emotions and *conciliare* to the milder.[3]

Some modern commentators have encountered difficulties in defining pathos.[4] Lussky, in following Cicero's definition of pathos, is unable to distinguish the intense emotion of pathos from the milder ethos[5] and since he believes Cicero is unclear about the distinctions, he concludes there is no difference between ethos and pathos.[6] Kennedy, May, Vasaly, and Kirby, on the other hand, all follow Quintilian in differentiating ethos from pathos in terms of intensity.[7] Wisse qualifies this idea, and distinguishes ethos as character portrayal which has sympathy as its goal and pathos as the rousing of violent emotions.[8]

Cicero does in fact differentiate the two types adequately by characterizing pathos as *atrox, vehemens*, and having *vis* and *contentio*, and ethos as *lene* and having *lenitas*.[9] The key to making the distinction is that pathos is concerned with rousing intense emotion in the audience, and ethos with the portrayal of character, which involves milder emotional expression: "In utroque autem genere dicendi et illo, in quo vis atque contentio quaeritur, et hoc, quod ad vitam et mores accommodatur . . ." (*De Or.* 2.213) ("Moreover in each kind of speaking, both the former, in which force and strife are sought, and the latter, which is adapted to the presentation of the life and character . . ."). The above describes the general distinction between ethos and pathos. But there are also nuances in the characterization of pathos: the appeal to pathos begins gradually (*De Or.* 2.213); it does not appear like a sudden blast and remain on one intense level, but rises and falls according to the orator's strategy. As to the distinction between ethos and pathos, Cicero admits that there may be grey areas and some overlap between the two (*De Or.* 2.212), but in my view that is no reason to jettison his classifications. Instead it indicates that the two different argument types are complementary and often function together in a given passage to achieve the orator's rhetorical goals.[10] I will present first a brief overview of Cicero's characterization of pathos in *De Oratore,*[11] and then explain how I shall approach pathos in this chapter.

Cicero believes pathos is the most important of the three types of arguments.[12] He defines it as a *ratio orationis* that arouses the emotions of the jury.[13] In *De Oratore* Cicero has Antonius present his defense of Norbanus as a paradigm for emotional appeal, and sum up the case as follows:

> Quod ubi sensi me in possessionem iudici ac defensionis meae constitisse, quod et populi benevolentiam mihi conciliaram, cuius ius etiam cum seditionis coniunctione defenderam, et iudicum animos totos vel calamitate civitatis vel luctu ac desiderio propinquorum vel odio proprio in Caepionem ad causam nostram converteram, tum admiscere huic generi orationis vehementi atque atroci genus illud alterum [ethos], de quo ante disputavi, lenitatis et mansuetudinis coepi. . . . (2.200)

> But when I perceived that I stood in firm possession of the court and my defense, and that I had procured the goodwill of the people, whose rights moreover I had defended even when associated with sedition, and had turned all the minds of the jurors to our case either by means of the calamity suffered by the state, or by grief or longing for relatives, or personal hatred of Caepio, then I began to mix with this vehement and harsh kind of speaking that other kind, the mild and gentle one, which I discussed previously. . . .

Here Antonius characterizes pathos as being *vehemens* and *atrox,* terms which respectively, indicate force or vehemence, and bitterness or violence. The emotions aroused are powerful ones: grief (*luctus*), longing (*desiderium*), and hatred (*odium*). The above-quoted passage makes it clear that pathos is closely related to ethos, but stronger in intensity.[14] The passage also indicates that the two types of arguments can be interspersed with one another, perhaps as a symphony moves from crescendo to diminuendo and back. As a result ethos and pathos can be difficult to distinguish from one another:

> Sed est quaedam in his duobus generibus, quorum alterum lene, alterum vehemens esse volumus, difficilis ad distinguendum similitudo; nam et ex illa lenitate, qua conciliamur eis, qui audiunt ad hanc vim acerrimam, qua eosdem excitamus, influat oportet aliquid, et ex hac vi non numquam animi aliquid inflandum est illi lenitati . . . (2.212)

But there is a certain similitude in these two styles, of which the one we require to be mild, the other vehement, which makes it difficult for them to be distinguished; for from that mildness, by which we are reconciled to the audience, it is necessary for something to flow to this fiercest force, by which we rouse the audience, and from this force, sometimes something of that mildness must be brought in.

When describing pathos and its effects, Cicero often employs fire imagery.[15] He compares rousing pathos in an audience to setting a fire (*De Or.* 2.190), and suggests the orator should himself burn with a flaming emotion ("te ipsum flagrantem odio") (*De Or.* 2.190); Antonius is described as setting the audience on fire with his oratory ("tantum incendium non oratione solum, sed etiam multo magis vi et dolore et ardore animi concitaras") (*De Or.* 2.197). The word *vis*, denoting vigor and energy, is employed throughout Cicero's discussion of pathos in order to demonstrate the force of this type of argument (*De Or.* 2.188; 2.191; 2.197; 2.212; 2.213). Cicero also characterizes pathos as having the harshness of strife ("asperitas contentionis") (*De Or.* 2.212); *contentio* is used to describe this type of argument several times (*De Or.* 2.212; 2.213; 2.214). These terms clearly refer not only to the nature of the speech itself, but to the manner of its delivery (especially "contentione actionis" at 2.214). The orator could only awaken emotions in the audience if he felt these emotions himself (*De Or.* 2.194–196). He could inflame the audience not only by the words themselves but also by his tone of voice: the use of pauses, crescendo and diminuendo; by his facial expression, and gestures (*De Or.* 2.194). Thus pathos, closely linked to ethos, is also associated with the delivery of the speech. Although the delivery, unfortunately, is unrecoverable, it is important to recognize its vital role in the presentation of pathos. Pathos is also closely linked to *elocutio*, since the style itself is supposed to evoke and, with a Roman audience, must have evoked certain emotions.[16]

In order to be able to rouse emotions, the orator must understand the thoughts and judgments of the jury (*De Or.* 2.186):

sic equidem cum aggredior in ancipiti causa et gravi, ad animos iudicum pertractandos, omni mente in ea cogitatione curaque versor, ut odorer, quam sagacissime possim, quid sentiant, quid existiment, quid exspectent, quid velint, quo deduci oratione facillime posse videantur.

Thus indeed when I approach a doubtful and important case, in order to deal with the minds of the jurors, I reflect with undivided attention and careful thought, in order to scent out as keenly as I can, what they perceive, what they think, what they expect, what they want, where they appear to be able to be led most easily by the speech.

If this was difficult for the orator, it is even more so for the modern commentator. In order to understand fully the emotional manipulation in a given Ciceronian speech, the commentator, like the orator, must understand the prejudices, likes, and dislikes which the jurors bring in from outside. These feelings may not be concerned with matters directly connected to the case; nonetheless the orator may play on them and try to make a connection. Take, for example, the case of Norbanus in *De Oratore*.[17] In addition to employing other techniques of rousing emotion, Antonius states: "sic et eorum dolorem, qui lugebant suos, oratione refricabam, et animos equitum Romanorum, apud quos tum iudices causa agebatur, ad Q. Caepionis odium, a quo erant ipsi propter iudicia abalienati, renovabam" (*De Or.* 2.199) ("thus with my speech I was both grating on the pain of those who were mourning their relatives and renewing the emotions of the Roman *equites*, before whom the case was being tried, to hatred of Quintus Caepio, from whom they themselves were estranged because of the courts.").[18] A further example is found in Cicero's first Verrine speech, where the orator plays on the jury's fears of a restructuring of the jury system if the judges did not convict Verres.[19] A third example occurs in the epilogue to the *Pro Sexto Roscio*, where Cicero alludes to the possible renewal of proscriptions.[20] If the jury is neutral, then the orator must rouse emotion by his speech alone, without help from the listeners' character, a more challenging task (*De Or.* 2.187).

In this dissertation, pathos will be differentiated from ethos as distinctly as possible. Ethos represents the portrayal of character, involving the milder emotion of sympathy, and pathos the stronger emotional reaction which the orator is attempting to produce in the audience. The emotion may be aroused by a portrayal of character, as for example, with Pompey and Marius. Where Cicero employs these former consuls to provoke intense feelings both of admiration and of patriotism, ethos has given way to pathos, and Pompey and Marius become fitting subjects for a discussion of emotional appeal. Emotion may also be aroused by the use of *evidentia*,[21] as it is with the evocation of Marius, by an appeal to patriotism, and appeals to Roman fears which are not directly linked to the case in question.[22] Since I characterize pathos as evoking an intense emotion in the audience, at the same time pathos is not always pitched at one single level of high intensity. Instead it is modulated and involves various levels of intensity and appeal. Its crescendoes are gradual, as recommended by Cicero (*De Or.* 2.213). Also, the audience itself is very important, since the orator's ability to rouse emotions in the audience is contingent upon his knowledge of them. Hence audience response becomes important, and Nisbet's approach here is instructive in any analysis of pathos.[23]

Lussky sees little pathos in the *Pro Balbo*, pointing out only four examples in the entire speech.[24] He suggests the reason for lack of pathos is the legal validity of the case.[25] But as Brunt indicates,[26] hostility to Balbus could outweigh legal considerations, and therefore Cicero has to incorporate both ethos and pathos into his speech in order to win over the hearts of the jurors. In fact a close examination of the speech indicates many more appeals than the four specified by Lussky.

The rousing of the emotions of the audience begins mildly with an appeal to the audience's feelings for Pompey.[27] Here pathos is barely distinguishable from ethos; in fact this passage can be looked at as an example of both ethos and of pathos. This does not indicate a weakness of ethos/pathos distinctions in rhetoric, but rather the strength of Cicero's skill as an orator: he is able to bind different types of arguments into a unified, almost seamless whole. The passage can be analyzed as pathos because one of its goals is to rouse emotion. However, since the emotion roused is mild and is built around Pompey's character, the passage can also be seen as an example of ethos. The mildness of emotion aroused indicates that pathos is not always vehement, especially at the beginning of a "pathetic" passage. Cicero reminds the audience of their approval for Pompey's speech of the previous day: "non opinione tacita vestrorum animorum, sed perspicua admiratione declarari videbatur." (2) (". . . was seen to be made clear not by your unspoken opinion, but by your evident admiration"). This tactic, discussed in chapter one,[28] follows the strategy suggested in *De Oratore*:

> Atque illud optandum est oratori, ut aliquam permotionem animorum sua sponte ipsi adferant ad causam iudices ad id, quod utilitas oratoris feret, accommodatam; facilius est enim currentem, ut aiunt, incitare quam commovere languentem; (2.185)

> And the orator must hope, that the jurors themselves, of their own accord, bring to the case some emotion that is applicable to what the interest of the orator proposes; for it is easier, as they say, to urge on a running horse than to set in motion a listless one.

Cicero intensifies the emotions of admiration and approval for Pompey by reiterating the general's qualities and achievements. At the same time Cicero makes an appeal to *amor* for himself by stressing his modesty and his gratitude to the audience, and the difficulty of speaking after such excellent orators as Pompey and Crassus (4).[29]

In section 5 Cicero begins an attempt to rouse feelings of *indignatio* in regard to the charges, which he portrays as completely unjustified. Balbus has committed no wrongdoing, the prosecution admits, according to Cicero, and yet Balbus' rights as a citizen are at stake as well as Pompey's reputation. Emotions are roused by elaboration, the use of parallel clauses, and anaphora: "Non enim furatus esse civitatem, non genus suum ementitus, non in aliquo impudenti mendacio delituisse, non irrepsisse in censum dicitur; unum obicitur, natum esse Gadibus." (5) ("For he is not said to have stolen his citizenship, nor to have falsely represented his family, nor to have concealed himself behind some shameless lie, nor to have insinuated himself into the census; he is reproached with one thing: he was born at Gades"). The four clauses beginning with "non" emphasize that no serious charge was brought against Balbus, and make the accusation that he was born at Gades (a rhetorical rephrasing of the prosecutor's charge) appear ridiculous by comparison. The anaphora is meant to provoke a negative emotive reaction, which slowly builds against the prosecutor throughout the speech.

Cicero encourages feelings of sympathy for his client by juxtaposing the accusation with a description of Balbus' illustrious background, emphasizing his earlier life, his noble family, and his energy in battle (5). At the same time, Cicero rouses odium against the prosecutor by suggesting he was wittingly trying to ruin an innocent man (Balbus) and a most distinguished commander (Pompey) (6).[30] The prosecutor is portrayed as framing the case in such a way that it is an attack on Pompey, a depiction that is certain to incur the hostility of the jury,[31] especially one which favored and approved of the general. The *indignatio* and *odium* towards the charges and the prosecutor and the *amor* towards Pompey play against and intensify each other. By depicting the charges as an unwarranted attack on Pompey, Cicero increases the sympathy felt for the man, and by increasing the sympathy for Pompey, Cicero intensifies the enmity towards the prosecutor. Here the "pathetic" strategy, of manipulating the audience into feelings of outrage towards the prosecutor and strong admiration towards Pompey begins to align itself with Cicero's "ethical" strategy, of presenting Pompey as a great, experienced military and political leader of tremendous *auctoritas* and the prosecutor as an inexperienced nonentity.

The first *ethica digressio* (9–16) provides Cicero with the opportunity to create a crescendo of emotion for Pompey.[32] The type of argumentation employed in this *digressio* is clearly "pathetic" rather than "ethical," and the *digressio* provides an excellent opportunity to point out the qualities which make the passage an example of pathos. Although the *digressio*, as with a passage based on ethos, is built around a *persona*, both the goal and the manner of presentation distinguish it from "ethical" argumentation. The use of questions, which Cicero answers with hyperbole, the piling up of his answers, the expansion so that Pompey is depicted against a global backdrop are all tactics which increase the emotional impact of the passage and clearly demonstrate that the goal of the passage is to rouse the emotions of the audience.

The *digressio* is divided into three parts, the first discussing Pompey's experience and character, the second providing two *exempla*, and the third part returning to the theme of Pompey, this time linking him to the Roman people and empire. This part attempts to refute the suggestion that Pompey could have acted either wittingly or unwittingly against the treaties. In the first part (9–10), a series of rhetorical questions loaded with hyperbole intensifies the admiration for Pompey. The young age at which he attained important military commands, the number of his triumphs (a topic which receives two comparisons: one to the achievements of his equals in age, the other to continents in the world), his large number of victories, are all geared to create approval in the audience:

> Ususne rerum? qui pueritiae tempus extremum principium habuit bellorum atque imperiorum maximorum, cuius plerique aequales minus saepe castra viderunt quam his triumphavit, qui tot habet triumphos quot orae sunt partesque terrarum, tot victorias bellicas quot sunt in rerum natura genera bellorum. (9)

> Experience in military service? In him whom the final period of boyhood held the beginning of service in wars and the highest commands, most of whose contemporaries saw military camps less often than he won triumphs over them, who had so many triumphs as there are countries and parts of the earth, won so many military victories as there are kinds of wars?

The above passage picks up on themes first introduced at the outset of the speech: Pompey's *usus*, and later in the digression his *ingenium*, his *pudor*, his *auctoritas* are all discussed. As well as demonstrating Pompey's *usus*, the above-quoted passage provides proofs of qualities that Cicero attributes to Pompey later in the digression.[33] For example, his youthful commands and large number of triumphs not only prove his *usus*, but also solidly demonstrate tremendous *ingenium*. The comparison to his equals in age reminds the jurors why he is worthy of *auctoritas* (not that Cicero needed to remind them of this). The references to the earth, continents, distant races, and kings broaden the scope until Pompey is seen not just in relation to Rome, but to the entire world:[34] "Quem provinciae nostrae, quem liberi populi, quem reges, quem ultimae gentes castiorem, moderatiorem, sanctiorem non modo viderunt, sed aut sperando umquam aut optando cogitaverunt?" (9) ("Whom have our provinces, whom have free peoples, whom have kings, the most remote races not only not seen who is a more self-controlled, more temperate, more venerable man [than Pompey], but neither imagined either in their hopes or dreams?"). This makes Pompey's achievements far more worthy of admiration since they are lauded and appreciated throughout the world, according to Cicero. It also increases Pompey's stature and prestige because he is recognized as being an outstanding man not just at Rome but throughout the world.

The orator then narrows the scope back to Rome while still maintaining an emotional intensity. He discusses Pompey's *auctoritas*, and in doing so employs a tactic to create emotional intensity that he uses extensively in his character portrayals: he links Pompey to the jury. He associates Pompey with the senate and

Roman people by reminding the jury of the distinctions they provided Pompey, who did not demand them (10). These actions of the senate serve as a validation of Cicero's praise of Pompey. They also provide an emotional link between the citizen jurors and Pompey, and form the basis for Cicero's following claim: that the lawsuit is not only an insult to Pompey but also to the senate and Roman people, and therefore also to them, the jury. This claim is an attempt to increase the feeling of indignation on the part of the jury towards the charges. The diction is emphatic; the emotional high-point coming in the final line with the word *turpe*—a strong, jarring term, and with *vobis* placed in the emphatic final position of the sentence.

Because style is so important in creating emotional intensity in these two sections, I will briefly comment on it here. The series of rhetorical questions which make up sections 9 and 10 relentlessly build a crescendo of emotion in a fine example of style assisting pathos. The alliteration in 9 of "qui . . . cuius . . . quam . . . qui . . . quot . . . quot . . . ." is somewhat relieved by the *variatio* provided by the anaphora in: "*An* pudor, *an* integritas, *an* religio . . . *an* diligentia . . . ." ("Have decency, or integrity, or religious scruples, or diligence . . ."). The hard *qu—cu* sounds return with *quem* repeated five times in a series of short clauses, somewhat relieved by the longer clause, "quem ultimae gentes . . .," followed by the alliteration of "quid . . . quae . . . quanta . . . cui . . . quod" in 10. The phrasing of the short questions and the harsh *qu—cu* sounds[35] mirror Cicero's indignation (and presumably the jury's growing indignation) at having to respond to the prosecutor's suggestion (as Cicero views it) that Pompey was somehow lacking. It must be remembered that *indignatio* would also be roused by Cicero's manner of delivery, by his facial expressions, gestures, and tone of voice.

The two *exempla* in the second section of the *ethica digressio* form a lull in emotion, a diminuendo,[36] meant to offer a suggestion to the jury as to how they should approach the case.[37] The *exempla* are cleverly placed immediately after a highly charged emotional passage in which the jury has been roused to indignation and told that it has been grievously insulted. The movement from an emotional peak to calm is not just stylistic *variatio*, but by giving the jurors a break and a chance to reflect, it also serves the rhetorical purpose of making them more receptive to suggestions about their behavior. The third section (13–16) begins with a question about Pompey: "Utrum enim inscientem vultis contra foedera fecisse an scientem?" (13) ("For do you claim that he acted in breach of the treaty unknowingly or knowingly?"). This passage picks up on the emotions of *amor* and *indignatio* aroused in the first part of the digression (9–10) and quickly intensifies them. Here one can distinguish pathos from ethos by the goal, again, but also, again, by the style, in particular by the emotive repetition of "O" in the invocations, by the emphatic presentation of the whole world's admiration for Pompey, and by the linking of patriotism and empire, with their strong emotional connotations, to Pompey.

The emotional rise begins with a series of invocations of the Empire, the Roman people, the renown of Pompey, and the tribes, and lands and seas of the Empire. They form a glowing tribute, with the first two comments about Pompey's renown framed on either side by the components of the empire:

> O nomen nostri imperi! O populi Romani excellens dignitas! O Cn. Pompei sic late longeque diffusa laus ut eius gloriae domicilium communis imperi finibus terminetur! O nationes, urbes, populi, reges, tetrarchae, tyranni,—testes Cn. Pompei non solum virtutis in bello sed etiam religionis in pace! Vos denique, mutae regiones, imploro, et sola terrarum ultimarum; vos, maria, portus, insulae, litora! Quae est enim ora, quae sedes, qui locus in quo non exstent huius cum fortitudinis tum vero humanitatis, cum animi tum consili impressa vestigia? (13)

> Alas for the glory of our empire! Alas for the excellent worth of the Roman people! Alas for the renown of Pompey, spread so far and wide that his glory is a household word to the very limits of the empire we all share! Alas for the nations, the cities, people, kings, tetrarchs, tyrants—witnesses not only to the courage of Pompey in war, but also of his religious scruples in peace! And you, voiceless tracts, I beseech you, and the soils of the farthest lands; you, seas, harbors, islands, shores! For what shore, what inhabited place, what spot is there which has not been imprinted by traces not only of the courage and indeed compassion of this man, but also of his intellect and judgment?

The passage is highly figurative and written in the high style, as is often found in passages appealing to pathos. The initial three emotional exclamations link Pompey to the Roman people and empire. *Nostri* includes the jurors, emphasizing the bond between them and Pompey. (An association, it should be pointed out, that the prosecutor could never share.) Each invocation is longer than the preceding one, and each provides more detail, the detail creating a gradual intensification of emotion. The plurality of *nationes, urbes, populi, reges, tetrarchae, tyranni* gives the impression of enormous masses both of common people and rulers who have witnessed Pompey's achievements. In the final two lyrical invocations, the human and geographical components of the empire become *testes* to Pompey's qualities. Cicero ends the invocation with a vivid metaphor bringing to mind Pompey's footprint imprinted in every place in the world, but also asserting that Pompey's influence is potent everywhere. This laudatory passage is similar to one in the *De Imperio Cn. Pompei*, which later becomes canonical for Pompey:[38]

> Testis est Italia . . . testis Sicilia . . . testis Africa . . . testis Hispania . . . testis iterum et saepius Italia. . . . Testes nunc vero iam omnes orae atque omnes terrae gentes nationes, maria denique omnia cum universa tum in singulis oris omnes sinus

atque portus. Quis enim toto mari locus per hos annos aut tam firmum habuit praesidium ut tutus esset, aut tam fuit abditus ut lateret? Quis navigavit qui non se aut mortis aut servitutis periculo committeret, cum aut hieme aut referto praedonum mari navigaret? (30–31)

Italy is a witness, Sicily is a witness, Africa is a witness, Spain is a witness, again and more often Italy is a witness. . . . Now indeed at this very time every region and every land, people, nation, and finally every sea, both as a whole, and every gulf and harbor in its individual shores is a witness. For what place on the whole sea coast has either had so strong a garrison that it was safe through these years, or was so removed that it was hidden? Who sailed who did not resign himself to the danger of either death or servitude, when he sailed either in winter or when the sea was full of pirates?

As the latter passage makes clear, the references to *maria, portus, insulae, litora* in the *Pro Balbo* would remind the audience of one of Pompey's major successes: ridding the seas of pirates.[39] This achievement was particularly dear to such *equites* as engaged in overseas trade. The description of these places thus evokes strong feelings in the audience as they make the associations between the places mentioned and Pompey.[40] The invocation of all the peoples who witnessed Pompey's courage in war and his piety in peace reminded the audience of all the general's foreign campaigns, which emphasize his glory.

This passage thus creates an intense feeling of admiration for Pompey for his glorious achievements, and one of indignation that he could be accused of wrongdoing. The passage also provides an emotional non-answer to the question Cicero poses at the beginning of the section: ". . . nos etiam in ipsa religione et legum et foederum conservanda qualis fuerit Cn. Pompeius dubitamus? Utrum enim inscientem vultis contra foedera fecisse an scientem? Si scientem,— O nomen nostri imperi!" (12–13) (". . . shall we, moreover, doubt the kind of man Gnaeus Pompeius was in maintaining respect for both laws and treaties? For do you want to say that he acted in breach of the treaty either unknowingly or knowingly? If knowingly—alas for the glory of our empire!").

Here the use of pathos fulfills two purposes. First, it enables Cicero to wriggle out of answering the question he poses, and secondly, it attempts to raise the emotions of the jury to such a pitch that they will not notice Cicero's evasiveness and instead will be won over before Cicero even begins discussing the actual merits of the case.[41]

The second half of this part of the *digressio* refutes the charge that Pompey unknowingly acted against the treaty (14–16). This refutation does not reach the same emotional peak as the previous one. The sarcastic rhetorical questions Cicero employs to answer the charge provide *variatio* and also rouse feelings of ridicule and strong indignation both towards the charges and towards the prosecutor. The end to this part forms another emotional rise by comparing the contemporary treatment of Pompey to the manner in which Romans of Cicero's day would regard him had he lived in an earlier Roman age (16). By hypothetically placing Pompey five hundred years in the past, Cicero tacitly equates him with the heroes of legend. This evokes the Roman feelings of respect for the past and the traditional Roman values the past represented.[42] Also effective is the invocation of the past without offering the names of specific men. This allows the audience to participate by imagining ancient heroes to whom they might compare Pompey.[43] By placing Pompey in a larger framework of Roman history, Cicero is able to present the idea that in the larger scheme of things no one should pay attention to accusations of Pompey violating the terms of the treaty.

As Cicero turns to the refutation of the prosecutor's arguments based on laws and treaties, he sometimes combines "pathetic" arguments with logical ones. One example, which follows, is worth noting because it consists of a "pathetic" argument which does not contain ethos. It is simply built upon the emotion of fear:

> atqui si imperatoribus nostris, si senatui, si populo Romano non licebit propositis praemiis elicere ex civitatibus sociorum atque amicorum fortissimum atque optimum quemque ad subeunda pro salute nostra pericula, summa utilitate ac maximo saepe praesidio periculosis atque asperis temporibus carendum nobis erit. (22)

> And yet if it will not be permitted for our generals, the senate, the Roman people to draw out, with proposed rewards, the bravest and the best of our allies and friends from states [with whom we have treaties], to undergo danger for our safety, we must inevitably lack the greatest benefit and often the most important protection in dangerous and stormy times.

The basis of this argument is rational, but by exaggeration, it actually attempts to create (or play on) a Roman fear of not being able to attract allies to fight for them in a desperate situation. The metaphor *asperis temporibus* introduces this emotive theme, and each time the fear is repeated it gains greater detail and acquires greater potency through resonance.[44] Here, as in the earlier passage, the orator is vague; no specific comparisons to historic instances are made. Again it is left to the audience to imagine the horrible circumstances under which allies would be needed.[45] The Gauls' sack of Rome in 390 B.C. and Hannibal's invasion of Italy in 218 B.C. are the instances that spring first to mind. More recently, only fifty years before the *Pro Balbo*, the Teutons, Cimbri, and Tigurini had attempted to invade Italy. The Romans lost a few battles before they defeated the German tribes under Marius, with the help of their allies and the Latins.[46] And at another time of great crisis, just seven years prior to the *Pro Balbo*, some allies—envoys from the Allobroges—provided invaluable assistance to the Roman state by giving Cicero written evidence that Catiline was fomenting an uprising.[47] In this passage Cicero is warning the jury that events will be different next time if generals are not permitted to enfranchise foreigners. That allies will be lacking is stressed by the use of the gerundive *carendum nobis erit* and its emphatic placement at the end of the sentence. The fear among Romans that there would be times of disaster when they would need to call on allies for help is a rational one. Cicero's corollary, that at such times Rome would not be able to obtain their help without enfranchisement is also rational within his frame of reference. He implies that supreme valor cannot be bought, and therefore other rewards, such as monetary ones, would not be sufficient.[48]

Cicero also employs pathetic arguments to give greater force to rational ones, as is demonstrated by the stirring description of the Gaditans. This passage comes after the rebuttal of the argument that the treaty is sacrosanct and Cicero's argument that there is nothing in the treaty to make it unlawful for a Gaditan to obtain Roman citizenship. The passage describes the Gaditans in such a way as to arouse a strong emotional reaction in the audience:

> Nunc vero quid ego contra Gaditanos loquar, cum id quod defendo voluntate eorum, auctoritate, legatione ipsa comprobetur? qui a principio sui generis ac rei publicae, id est ii ab omni studio sensuque Poenorum mentis suas ad nostrum imperium nomenque flexerunt; qui, cum maxima bella nobis inferretur, moenibus hostem excluserunt, classibus insecuti sunt, corporibus opibus copiis depulerunt; . . . quorum moenia, delubra, agros ut Hercules itinerum ac laborum suorum, sic maiores nostri imperi ac nominis populi Romani terminos esse voluerunt. . . . et hoc tempore ipsum populum Romanum, quem in caritate annonae, ut saepe ante fecerant, frumento suppeditato levarunt . . . (39–40)

> Now indeed, why should I speak against the Gaditans, when the very thesis which I am maintaining is proved by their goodwill, their prestige, by their legation itself? A people who have turned away from the source of their national existence and of their government, that is from their zeal and fellow-feeling for the Carthaginians towards our empire and our name; a people who, when the most important wars were being waged against us, shut out the enemies from their city walls, pursued them with their fleets, drove them off with their bodies, their resources, their troops;
> . . . whose walls, shrines, fields, our ancestors wanted to be the boundaries of our empire and of the name of the Roman people, just as Hercules made them the boundaries of his journeys and labors . . . and at this time, as they had often done before, they have supported the Roman people themselves at a time of high grain prices, with a supply of grain . . .

In this passage Cicero characterizes the Gaditans in terms of their goodwill both to his argument and to Rome. Cicero's case is also supported by the *auctoritas* of the Gaditans, a point he elaborates upon later (41–42). The term *auctoritas* implies that it is Gaditans of political weight and importance in their own city who have given thought to the issue and have sent the legation favoring Balbus. This group of Gaditans may be contrasted with the prosecutor, who is shown later to have no *auctoritas* at Gades (and, of course, none at Rome) (41). The embassy present at the trial acquires *auctoritas* through the *auctoritas* of the Gaditans who dispatched it.

Having established the worth of the embassy (ethos), Cicero then builds an emotive bond between the Gaditans and Rome. The passage at first is not fiercely intense and emotive, but is not *lene* either. Cicero picks up on the fears played on in section 22, this time providing more detail by reminding the Romans of past assistance Gades had given them. The loyalty of the Gaditans to Rome, both in past battles—particularly the Punic Wars, which carried potent emotional resonance with the Romans—and with present grain supplies, is described in graphic detail. Gaditan loyalty is portrayed as so strong that they turned away from their "natural" allies, the Carthaginians, who like them were of Phoenician descent, to support Rome.[49]

The linkage of Gades with Empire and Hercules, the mention of famous Roman military leaders whom the Gaditans had helped all serve to raise the emotional tenor of the passage. Hercules, worshipped by Romans as a god of military victory who had apotropaic powers, was the founder of the Ara Maxima, one of the oldest altars in Rome.[50] As Galinsky points out: "Herakles satisfied the personal cult needs that were left unfulfilled by the state religion and thus came to share in the same religious intensity that was accorded the oriental cults for exactly the same reason."[51] The hero-god is a fitting figure for Cicero to mention in this speech. Although Cicero does not draw a parallel in his speech, Pompey's triumphs and military successes encourage comparison to Hercules.[52] Both Pliny (*N.H.* 7.95–99) and Plutarch (*Pomp.* 45) draw parallels between the two. There are further connections of Hercules with the speech as a whole. The orator identifies Hercules with Gades as the endpoint of his journeys. Like Balbus, or the unnamed courageous foreigners Cicero describes throughout this speech, Hercules, although the son of a god, was also a foreigner in the sense that he had Greek origins[53] and helped save early Rome by a courageous act: a battle with the evil monster Cacus.[54] For his efforts Hercules was given the reward he desired, which was worship at the Ara Maxima.[55] This worship assimilated him into Rome by making him a part of its religious and cultural life; perhaps for a god this is the equivalent of being enfranchised.

Another, more powerful emotional passage is contained in the *agumentatio*: the *ethica digressio* on Marius (46–49).[56] Here there is a coalescence of ethos and pathos: Marius is presented both as an emotional icon and as an ethical *exemplum*. Marius is mentioned in several Ciceronian speeches, always as a positive example.[57] Often he is described as savior, or protector of the city or Empire.[58] In some speeches Cicero compares himself to Marius, in others, such as the *De*

Lege Manilia, he compares Pompey to the earlier general.[59] Marius had won favor with the *equites* for, among other achievements, his successes in the Numidian War,[60] and his building of the canal on the Rhone which facilitated commerce;[61] he found favor with all Romans for saving the city from a possible sack by Germanic tribes.[62] In 100 B.C. Marius put down unrest in the city during which C. Memmius, a candidate for the consulship, was murdered.[63] Although at this point Marius was not popular either with his contemporaries in the senate or among the people (in fact shortly afterwards he left Rome for Asia), in 56 B.C. in a Rome until very recently wracked by fighting between supporters of Clodius and those of Milo, senators and *equites* might look back with nostalgic longing at a strong man who had been able to quench rioting in the city. Cicero works on these emotions throughout this digression.[64]

The *digressio* is shorter than the earlier one on Pompey, but as in the earlier one, it also provides an appeal to *amor* and *indignatio*. The orator immediately places the prosecutor in opposition to Marius: "Possumusne igitur tibi probare auctorem exempli atque facti illius quod a te reprehenditur, C. Marium?" (46) ("Can we therefore satisfy you by offering as an authority for a case in point and for that course of action which you blame, the name of Gaius Marius?")

The *digressio* begins as a logical argument, with Marius providing a precedent and positive example of a general who offered citizenship to foreigners. The passage then moves to a brief ethical portrayal of the general: "Quaeris aliquem graviorem, constantiorem, praestantiorem virtute, prudentia, religione?"(46) ("Do you seek someone more important, more steadfast, more outstanding in terms of courage, of prudence, of piety?") These characteristics all illustrate the political, social, and moral weight of Marius and demonstrate why he has *auctoritas* as an *exemplum*. The words recall those used earlier to describe Pompey, who had been the *protégé* of the great general Sulla.[65]

Marius' grants of citizenship are then discussed: Cicero brings the citizenship case down to its barest bones, by stating that Marius had enfranchised Marcus Annius Appius of Iguvium and two cohorts from Camerinum and therefore Balbus ought not to be condemned. He is able to draw this parallel between Marius' enfranchisements and Pompey's not because of the similarity of the circumstances, which he admits later are completely different (49), but because of the similarities between the *auctoritas* of Marius and Pompey.

After this statement the passage progresses from ethos to pathos as Cicero employs *evidentia* to present a vivid depiction of Marius that is pure pathos.[66] Cicero works on the emotions of the jurors by summoning the image of Marius before them: "Exsistat ergo ille vir parumper cogitatione vestra, quoniam re non potest, ut conspiciatis eum mentibus, quoniam oculis non potestis . . ." (47) ("Therefore let that man appear in your imagination for a little while, since he cannot appear in person, so that you may observe him with your minds, since you cannot with your eyes . . ."). This passage begins in the same way as some of Cicero's *prosopopoeiai*,[67] but because Cicero does not impersonate Marius and does not use the first person, the passage cannot be considered a true one. Cicero imagines a defense speech Marius would deliver to Balbus' prosecutor, which he "delivers" in the third person. The imagined speech moves from litotes: "dicat se non imperitum foederis, non rudem exemplorum, non ignarum belli fuisse . . ." (47) ("Let him say that he was not unacquainted with the treaty, not unknowing of precedents, not ignorant of war . . .") to hyperbole: "si tanta bella attigisset, quanta gessit et confecit, si tot consulibus meruisset, quotiens ipse consul fuit . . ." (47) ("If only he had soldiered in as many wars as ones he had carried out and completed, if only he had served under as many consuls as times he himself had been consul . . .").

"Marius'" argument, with its focus on extensive practical experience and success, emphasizes the general's *auctoritas*, and presents a close parallel to Cicero's defense of Pompey earlier in the *Pro Balbo*. "Marius" reminds the jurors of his knowledge of treaties and wars, his experience and successes as a general, and the great number of consulships he had held. His "speech" concludes on an emotive but not highly intense note, with the declaration that there was no saving clause in the treaties with Iguvium and Camerinum (such as the one Balbus' prosecutor was invoking). Such a statement assumes inaccurately that if there was no saving clause in these two treaties, then there could be no saving clause in the treaty with Gades. The assumption is cunningly slipped in at the end of the "oration" (47). Furthermore, as mentioned above, Cicero makes clear later (48–49) that a saving clause was *not* the issue in either of Marius' cases. What Cicero is doing here, is giving Marius the kind of speech he would have delivered if the dead general were defending Balbus and not his own enfranchisements.

The passage moves from the *evidentia* to the *exemplum* of the citizenship case of Matrinius of Spoletum, which Marius won because of his great prestige. Cicero stated earlier that if Balbus is condemned, then Marius must also be condemned. Here pathos serves logos: the logical corollary of this is that if Marius is not condemned, then Balbus should not be condemned. This example demonstrates that Marius was not condemned, because of his prestige. The (not entirely logical) conclusion is not stated: therefore Balbus should not be condemned because of the prestige of Pompey, to whom Marius is implicitly compared in this speech. The circumstances, too, favor a parallel beween Marius and Pompey since both were consuls, generals, *populares*, had enfranchised foreigners, and had great *auctoritas*. Cicero's conclusion is possible because Pompey and Balbus have been linked so closely throughout the speech and because Cicero pleads the case as if Pompey were the one on trial. Instead of explicitly stating the conclusion, Cicero asks a question: why then should the generals be deprived of the right to reward bravery with citizenship?

The *ethica digressio* concludes with a stirring evocation of Marius that is a fine example of pathos. Cicero mentions his face, his voice, the blazing of his eyes, to bring the picture of Marius with greater vividness and clarity before the mind's eye of the audience (49). The detailed clarity works to rouse the emotions of the audience.[68] Cicero then evokes the achievements and memory of Marius. The emotional power of the passage derives partly from its style: the repetition of the *si* clauses in the protasis and the use and repetition of *valeat* add force to the rousing invocation, as do the short clauses which focus on Marius' outstanding *auctoritas* and achievements. But the pathos also derives from the power the memory of Marius had over the audience; hence it is an example of pathos being fueled by ethos, which in turn confirms the interpretation of ethos. Cicero ends the passage on a high emotional plane: "Sit hoc discrimen inter gratiosos civis atque fortis, ut illi vivi fruantur opibus suis, horum etiam mortuorum, si quisquam huius imperi defensor mori potest, vivat auctoritas immortalis." (49) ("Let there be this difference between influential citizens and brave ones, that the former, while living, enjoy their own influence, whereas of the latter even when deceased, if any defender of this empire can die, the authority is everlasting.") The three final words *vivat auctoritas immortalis* ring with pathos. The word *immortalis*, concludes the *digressio* with a resounding climax. One should think of the passion that would have been in Cicero's voice when he delivered these words. The subjunctive "Sit hoc discrimen . . ." suggests the role the jury must play in this: they can let Marius' authority live if they are swayed by his influence and acquit Balbus.

Towards the end of the *argumentatio* Cicero begins to arouse pity for himself and Balbus. Sympathy for Balbus is created by a description of the behavior of those who envy him: ". . . more hominum invident, in conviviis rodunt, in circulis vellicant; non illo inimico, sed hoc malo dente carpunt." (57) (". . . as humans will, they are jealous, at banquets they disparage him, in social circles they pull him to pieces; they gnaw at him not with unfriendly tooth, but with a bite of envy.").[69] The implication is that the envy is unjustly directed towards Balbus, who has never acted in such a way to attract it. The envy is also shown in a petty way, as malicious gossip, created by men who are not even enemies of the defendant, but of his friends. The unjustness of such behavior creates sympathy for Balbus, a sympathy heightened when contrasted with the defendant's own respectful and deferential behavior towards others. Although at one time in a position where he could have lorded it above others, he never offended anyone: "Versatus in intima familiaritate hominis potentissimi, in maximis nostris malis atque discordiis neminem umquam alterius rationis ac partis non re, non verbo, non vultu denique offendit." (58) ("Associated in deepest friendship with a very powerful man, at the time of our greatest evils and discord, he never offended anyone of the other way of thinking or on the other side, not by an action, nor by a word, nor even by a facial expression.") Here again there is considerable modulation and not just one high level of intensity.

The sympathy deepens to pity as Cicero describes his exile in such terms as to create pity for himself, by equating his *fatum* with that of the state, and by stating that he alone had to bear the weight of those times. Then he depicts Balbus' emotional and practical reactions to his exile: "Non modo non exsultavit in ruinis nostris vestrisque sordibus Cornelius, sed omni officio,—lacrimis, opera, consolatione,—omnes me absente meos sublevavit." (58) ("Not only did Cornelius Balbus not exult in my downfall and your mourning, but in my absence he supported my whole family with every service: with his tears, with his actions, and with his consolation.").

Such a description is geared to create pity (another aspect of pathos) in the audience for Balbus, for his showing such compassion to a man who was not on the same political side as his patron Caesar. It also offers a tacit example to the jury of how they could behave when faced with the ruin of a man unjustly accused: that is, react with compassion to him.

Balbus' behavior starkly contrasts with that of those who envy the defendant. Cicero intensifies the pathos by repeating that Balbus has no enemies of his own, but is attacked by the enemies of his friends. Moreover, such a statement creates animosity towards the prosecutor for cowardice. Cicero uses this moment also to remind the audience of an emotional part of Pompey's speech in which he told the prosecution to attack him if they wished, but not to attack Balbus in an unequal contest (59). This statement both places Pompey (and Balbus) in a noble light and the prosecutor in an ignoble one and recalls to the minds of the audience the feelings of pathos they had experienced during Pompey's speech.

At the same time as he works on the emotion of pity, Cicero continues to arouse odium against the opponents of Balbus. He declares once more that these opponents ought to fight their true enemies and not their adherents:

> Sed si qui sunt quibus infinitum sit odium in quos semel susceptum sit, quos video esse non nullos, cum ducibus ipsis, non cum comitatu adsectatoribus confligant. Illam enim fortasse pertinaciam non nulli, virtutem alii putabunt, hanc vero iniquitatem omnes cum aliqua crudelitate coniunctam. (62)

> But if there are those whose hatred against others, once incurred, is boundless, of whom I see there are some, let them contend with the leaders themselves, not with their retinue and attendants. For perhaps some will think the former obstinacy and others a virtue, but all will think the latter injustice mixed with some cruelty.

This time Cicero states outright how the audience ought to regard such behavior. The orator has suppressed such a conclusion until the third time the behavior is mentioned. By waiting, Cicero allows the audience to form their own idea about it (although with subtle guidance). His conclusion regarding the behavior—that these men are unjust and cruel—is one the audience has formed on their own, and thus Cicero's statement becomes a validation of the audience's own opinion.

Halfway through the peroration Cicero defends Balbus' relationship with Caesar. He makes a strong appeal to pity for Balbus with a poignant description of Caesar,[70] who, far away at the bounds of the Empire—which as Cicero is quick to point out are boundaries Caesar has helped create—will receive news of the trial:[71]

> Sed quoniam C. Caesar abest longissime, atque in iis est nunc locis quae regione orbem terrarum, rebus illius gestis imperium populi Romani definiunt, nolite, per deos immortalis, iudices, hunc illi acerbum nuntium velle perferri, ut suum praefectum fabrum, ut hominem sibi carissimum, non ob ipsius aliquod delictum, sed ob suam familiaritatem vestris oppressum sententiis audiat. (64)

> But because Gaius Caesar is very far away, and is now in those places which in terms of region, define the boundaries of the earth, and in terms of his military exploits define the boundaries of the empire of the Roman people, members of the jury, do not, by the immortal gods desire this bitter message to be brought to him, that he may hear that his chief engineer, that a man most dear to him, has been ruined by your judgment, not because of some fault of his own, but because of his friendship with him.

The grief of Caesar makes vivid the picture of a decision against Balbus merely on the basis of his friendship with the general, especially since Caesar is working so hard abroad to help Rome by enlarging its empire.

Cicero closes the description of Caesar at 64 with a direct appeal to the judges for pity for Balbus ("Miseremini eius . . ."), emphasizing again that the man has committed no crime, but is in court merely because of a point of law. This flattering suggestion that the jurors' sense of *humanitas* has appeased them is an appeal to their feelings of fairness.[72]

As Cicero states in the *De Oratore* (2.310) about pathos in general, the pathos in this speech pervades it like the blood in one's body.[73] The pathos is heightened throughout the peroration, one of the two traditional places one finds pathos, but it also appears in the *digressio* on Pompey, which partly serves as a *narratio*, and several times in the *argumentatio*. Neumeister sees a gradual intensification of pathos in each speech individually throughout the speeches which he studies,[74] and indeed the pathos in the *peroratio* of the *Pro Balbo* is intense, but not necessarily more so than in the *ethica digressio* on Marius, which is found in the *argumentatio*. Rather than one steady increase of pathos through-out, one finds in the *Pro Balbo* a series of crescendos and diminuendos, with the peroration concluding on a crescendo.

The emotions played upon in this speech are liking and admiration (for fig-ures such as Pompey, Marius, Caesar, the Gaditans, and Cicero himself), hatred, pity, and fear, with admiration and hatred being the predominant ones. In some cases pathos is so interlocked with ethos that it is difficult to separate the two, as with the portrayals of Balbus (especially), Pompey, and Marius. One of the challenges of such a study as this is to differentiate between the two. It was found that style often helps to indicate the type of argument. Pathos is often associat-ed with the "high" style, particularly when Cicero is discussing an important fig-ure such as Pompey or Marius. Stylistic techniques such as invocations and ques-tions help raise the emotional tenor of passages. In addition diction and the phrasing of sentences help to inflame emotion in the audience. In the *digressio* on Marius, the use of vivid depiction, geared to rouse strong emotions, places those passages firmly in the pathos camp. The linkage of characters such as Pompey and Marius with strong emotional ideas, such as patriotism and empire also distinguish pathos from ethos, as does the use of hyperbole when coupled with the stylistic tactics. Another important technique Cicero employs in rous-ing emotion is the linkage of Pompey and Caesar with the good of Rome, and therefore with the good of the jury. This allows him to intensify feelings of indignation on the part of the jury by making them feel personally involved in the case. It also heightens feelings of admiration for Pompey and Caesar because their achievements were on behalf of Rome. A point worth noting is that in some cases there is pathos and no ethos at all, as seen when Cicero plays upon the fears of Romans regarding the security of Rome. And often pathos is used to help buttress a shaky rational argument, as with the depiction of the Gaditans.

Chapter Three
Inventio: Logos

IN THIS CHAPTER I EXAMINE RATIONAL ARGUMENTATION IN THE *PRO BALBO*.[1] I analyze the types of rational arguments Cicero employs, the structure of the enthymemes, with particular attention to the premises (both stated and unstated) and the conclusions (stated and unstated). The purpose is to determine to what extent the arguments Cicero employs are truly rational and to what extent he manipulates them to give the appearance of rationality. I also attempt to determine whether these arguments are relevant to Balbus' case, and if not, why they are introduced. In instances where a brief pathetic argument is tied into a longer rational one, it makes sense to examine both together in this chapter.

As Cousin notes,[2] the overall structure of argumentation in the speech can be reduced to two major issues: first, could Pompey give the citizenship grant legitimately? and secondly, could Balbus legitimately accept it? The answer to these questions is provided by "ethical," "pathetic," and rational arguments. The rational arguments are spread throughout the *argumentatio*, and consist of enthymemes and *exempla*.

The *argumentatio*[3] opens with a major premise designed to demonstrate that Pompey enfranchised Balbus legally: "Nascitur, iudices, causa Corneli ex ea lege quam L. Gellius Cn. Cornelius ex senatus sententia tulerunt; qua lege videmus rite esse sanctum ut cives Romani sint ii quos Cn. Pompeius de consili sententia singillatim civitate donaverit" (19). ("Judges, Cornelius' case arises from that law which Lucius Gellius and Cnaeus Cornelius carried, in accordance with the decision of the senate. We see that by that law it has been properly enacted that those men are Roman citizens, whom Gnaeus Pompeius enfranchised singly according to the wishes of his council.")

The citation of the law appears to give validity to Pompey's action. But it is unlikely that the prosecutor's argument was that Pompey acted illegally by enfranchising Balbus without an enabling law. It is more likely that the argument focussed on the second issue predominantly:[4] that Balbus could not legitimately accept Roman citizenship, and because of that, Pompey made a mistake in bestowing it. Cicero twists this argument to imply that the prosecutor meant that Pompey had not followed proper Roman procedure. By misrepresenting the prosecutor's intentions, Cicero makes a strong rebuttal to an argument that the prosecutor had not made, doubtlessly with full realization that the jury would not want to find Pompey at fault. Cicero's argument here, therefore, is a manipulated rational one.[5]

The minor premise follows: "Donatum esse L. Cornelium praesens Pompeius dicit, indicant publicae tabulae. Accusator fatetur . . ." (19) ("Pompeius states in your presence that Lucius Cornelius was enfranchised, the public records declare it. The prosecutor admits it . . ."). Especially after the "[a]ccusator fatetur," one expects the conclusion: therefore citizenship was given legally to Balbus. Cicero lets the audience draw that conclusion on its own.[6] Letting the juror think through the syllogism to reach the conclusion on his own is an important rhetorical technique. Because the juror makes the associations himself, the conclusion then appears to him to be his own, and not one "imposed" by the speaker. As Quintilian points out, a juror more readily believes something he thinks he has figured out himself (*Inst. Or.* 9.2.71). This is because a juror listens with critical faculties on full alert to any statements from either party in a given case, but when coming to a decision on his own, he appears simply to fill in the gaps in logic left by defendant and prosecutor. A juror more readily trusts his own instincts, possibly because he believes himself to be less biased than the parties directly involved with the case. In this instance, instead of a conclusion Cicero presents an objection by the prosecution, that no individual from a federated state could become a Roman citizen unless the state had given its consent ("populus fundus factus esset").

Cicero rebuts this objection first by ridiculing the prosecutor: "O praeclarum interpretem iuris, auctorem antiquitatis, correctorem atque emendatorem nostrae civitatis . . ." (20) ("Here is a magnificent interpreter of the law, pomoter of antiquity, improver and amender of our constitution. . ."), and then by misinterpreting the prosecutor's objection: "qui hanc poenam foederibus adscribat, ut omnium praemiorum beneficiorum nostrorum expertis faciat foederatos!" (20) ("since he attaches a punishment to treaties in such a way that he deprives our allies of all our rewards and benefits!"). The prosecutor assuredly did not assert that federated states could not have any share in rewards and favors, but only that the man's original community must give permission Pro before Roman citizenship could be granted. Such a distortion makes the prosecution seem ridiculous and by becoming a premise in a later argument, gives Cicero more ammunition for his rebuttal. Again, this is a manipulated rational argument. It should be pointed out in light of these reoccurring manipulated arguments that Cicero spoke last of three orators,[7] and as final speaker he may presumably not have been expected to provide a technically sound, rational argument, but rather concentrate on his strength, which was stirring pathos.

Finally Cicero also refutes the "consent" objection with rational argumentation. "Quid enim potuit dici imperitius quam foederatos populos fieri fundos oportere?" (20) ("For what could be more inexperienced to say than that allied people must give consent?") becomes the premise; simply stated: it would be very ignorant to declare that *foederati* must give consent.[8] His first proof is that "giving consent" (when applicable) is not applicable only to *foederati*, but also to all free people. This means that the issue of consent does not depend upon whether Gaditans were *foederati* or not, and therefore not upon the stipulations of the treaty.[9] This point becomes important later when Cicero is discussing the terms of the treaty (32–37). The argument, rather unjustly, is also meant to demonstrate the ignorance of the prosecutor. It is, however, unlikely that the prosecutor said that *foederati* alone must give consent, which Cicero implies his opponent meant.

Cicero then elaborates upon the term *fieri fundi* with a mistaken etymology.[10] If the Romans adopted a law, and then *socii* or *Latini* adopted it, then the law settled down on solid ground in that state. The true purpose of this ostensible explanation is to make *socii* and *Latini* appear interchangeable in a discussion of *fundi fieri*. This becomes clear in section 21 where Cicero illustrates some types of situations in which a state is able to give consent to Roman laws with examples of Latin states.

The *fundus fieri* point forms the legal crux of the case and is the major issue on which Cicero and the prosecutor differ.[11] From the energy Cicero devotes to rebutting specific allegations, it is probable the argument that the Gaditans ought to have given consent to the *lex Cornelia Gallia* formed a substantial part of the prosecutor's argument[12] (and not an attack on Pompey, as Cicero declares earlier [6—7]).[13] Because of the importance of this issue, Cicero argues in several different ways throughout the *argumentatio* against the necessity of Gaditan consent to the *lex Cornelia Gallia*. Here he puts forward the important and reasonable contention that the object in giving consent was not that Roman law should be weakened, but that a state could adopt and benefit from a Roman law. Since the jury was entirely Roman, this point would be easily accepted.

He then provides some examples of instances in which another state could *fundus fieri* (21). The first is the *lex Furia*, regarding the testator's right to bequeath, the second example is the *lex Voconia*, which forbade instituting women as heirs in certain cases.[14] Cicero adds there were several other laws dealing with civil matters; of these the Latins adopted the ones they wanted. It is clear that these instances were quite different from Rome bestowing citizenship upon an individual. In the two *exempla*, the adoption of the law by the Latins would not affect Rome. Cicero next provides the example of the *lex Julia*, a law which concerned citizenship.[15] Under this law a Latin or allied state could obtain Roman citizenship for all its own citizens, but only if it first "gave consent" ("qui fundi populi facti non essent civitatem non haberent"). Because this law dealt with citizenship and required the consent of the Latin or allied state, it no doubt played an important role as an analogy and precedent in the prosecutor's case.

As Brunt and Reid indicate, there is a major distinction between Balbus's case and the situation of states such as Naples and Heracleia under the *lex Julia*. Since the *lex Julia* affected entire communities, the entire community had to agree before adopting the law:

> . . . the *lex Julia* of 90, which enacted that the citizens of all the then loyal Italian communities were to become Roman citizens provided that those communities adopted the law. This might have suggested that the enfranchisement of foreigners by Rome required the consent of the communities to which they belonged. However, this provision in the *lex Julia* concerned the grant of citizen rights not to individuals who could accept it personally for themselves alone, but to whole communities, whose separate existence as states was to be extinguished, with the result that all their citizens would become Roman, whether or not they had individually consented: in this case therefore the consent of the communities was to be obtained, given that it was the purpose of the law to reward and maintain their loyalty and that it would thus have been absurd for Rome to have imposed their incorporation in the Roman states: Rome was making an offer, which they were free to reject and which two cities nearly did reject.[16]

In the absence of an actual law detailing precisely the circumstances under which a state must give consent, one is left with Cicero's arguments. An examination of the *lex Furia*, the *lex Voconia*, and the *lex Julia* makes it apparent that these are laws which would affect the entire community in which they were adopted. The case of Balbus can be distinguished from the above, since the citizenship grant applied to one individual only and not to the entire city.[17] Whether Balbus adopted Roman citizenship or not would not have the same major impact upon his community as enfranchisement of the whole community. From this it seems most likely that a city had to give consent only when a law affected it as whole community.[18]

In his argumentation, Cicero does not focus on this aspect of the argument. Instead, he differentiates between other states' ability to adopt Roman laws which may benefit them, and these states' inability to refuse laws which Rome passes regarding herself. By refusing the *lex Cornelia Gallia*, Gades would be doing more than refusing a benefit, it would be infringing on Rome's sovereignty, that is, Rome's right to control who her citizens were.[19] The repetition of the word *noster* in the following passage emphasizes this point:

Cum aliquid populus Romanus iussit, id si est eius modi ut quibusdam populis, sive foederatis sive liberis, permittendum esse videatur ut statuant ipsi non de *nostris* sed de suis rebus, quo iure uti velint, tum utrum fundi facti sint an non quaerendum esse videtur; de *nostra* vero re publica, de *nostro* imperio, de *nostris* bellis, de victoria, de salute fundos populos fieri noluerunt. (22)

When the Roman people have enacted something, if it is of such a kind that it seems [to the Roman government] certain peoples must be permitted, whether bound to us by treaty or free, to decide themselves—not about *our* interests but about their own interests—which law they wish to use, then it appears we ought to inquire whether they have given consent or not; but indeed regarding our republic, our empire, our wars, victory, welfare, they did not want peoples to [have the option of] giving consent.

Given the differences between Balbus' situation and that of cities adopting the *leges* mentioned above, and given the argument about Rome's sovereignty, it is most likely that Gades did not have to "give consent" for Balbus' citizenship grant to be legitimate. Unfortunately without the actual text of the treaty, it is impossible to say so with absolute certainty.

The next section (22–26) forms the proof for the premise that the object of *fundus fieri* was not to weaken the Roman legal system, but to benefit the state that adopted a Roman law. Cicero argues that requiring consent from Gades in cases such as Balbus' would both weaken the Roman state and provide no benefit to the allied state. He begins with the distortion of the prosecution's argument first seen in 20.[20] This distortion forms the first proof of what Rohde calls an argument *quid eventurum sit*:[21]

Atqui si imperatoribus nostris, si senatui, si populo Romano non licebit propositis praemiis elicere ex civitatibus sociorum atque amicorum fortissimum atque optimum quemque ad subeunda pro salute nostra pericula, summa utilitate ac maximo saepe praesidio periculosis atque asperis temporibus carendum nobis erit. (22)

And if it will not be permitted for our generals, the senate, the Roman people to draw out, with proposed rewards, the bravest and the best of our allies and friends from states [with whom we have treaties], to undergo danger for our safety, we will necessarily lack the greatest benefit and often the most important protection in dangerous and stormy times.

The idea that the only way to encourage allies to fight for Rome is by offering them citizenship, is a reasonable argument to make to an audience that does not believe that valor may be bought with a mercenary army. But Cicero has shifted the prosecutor's argument since the latter did not state that the senate and Roman people could not offer rewards, or even that they could not specifically offer citizenship, but simply that Balbus' enfranchisement was illegal because of the lack of official Gaditan consent. Because it attempts to rebut an argument the prosecutor did not make, Cicero's premise is on tenuous ground. The apodosis is therefore also dubious because the champion could still hope for citizenship.

In the proof, Cicero broadens the argument to include other allied states, such as Massilia and Saguntum (23). This argument from analogy is calculated to increase the gravity of the issue, by having it include allied states in general and not just one city. This tactic of universalization is one that Cicero also employed in his ethical argumentation.[22] The analogy argument is also an excellent example of the interweaving of rational and pathetic arguments. The cities Cicero chooses to name also would have a strong emotive effect on the audience. Massilia had friendly relations with Rome dating back to early times, and is said to have helped Rome (at a time of very great need) to pay the ransom when the Gauls sacked her.[23] Saguntum was an ally of Rome before and during the time of the Punic Wars, another period which had great emotional resonance for the Romans.[24] By linking Gades with these two allies from the same general geographical area, who had helped Rome during her worst crises, Gades is imbued with the same emotional coloring. The position of the word *Gades* between these two allies emphasizes the association. Association is another tactic utilized in "ethical" argumentation, which Cicero employs for this rational/pathetic argument.[25]

Cicero then turns to demonstrate that the requirement of the consent of the individual's original community to the citizenship law would not provide an advantage to that community either. By distorting the interpretation of a law that actually would give a community more control over itself, Cicero makes it appear the opposite: ". . . in socios vero ipsos, et in eos de quibus agimus foederatos, iniuriosum et contumeliosum est iis praemiis et iis honoribus exclusos esse fidelissmos et coniunctissimos socios quae pateant stipendiariis, pateant hostibus, pateant saepe servis." (24) (". . . certainly in regard to the allies themselves and those with whom we have treaties, whom we are dealing with now, it is unjust and insulting that the most loyal and friendly allies should be absolutely shut out from those rewards and those honors which are accessible to members of tributary states, to our enemies, and often to slaves").

With this argument *a minore* (*de Inv.* 1.30.49; *Top* 23.68), the supposed inability of individuals of allied states to acquire Roman citizenship is compared unfavorably with the ability of *stipendarii*, enemies, and slaves to be enfranchised. This argument distorts the issue at stake. First, it is assumed again that the prosecutor was arguing that *foederati* should not be allowed to be enfranchised.[26] Secondly, whether or not slaves and enemies can achieve citizenship is irrelevant to the issue of Gades giving consent. The *a minore* argument distracts the audience from these points, and on first reading appears reasonable. Once this argument is accepted, the obvious conclusion to it is that if slaves and enemies, who have fewer rights than *foederati*, are able to acquire citizenship, then the *foederati* should certainly be able to.

An argument from analogy caps the proofs, with Cicero declaring that requiring states to give consent for grants of Roman citizenship would be the same as these *foederati* having laws forbidding their citizens to accept Roman citizenship. This comparison enables him to conclude that no one will risk danger to help Rome when a reward is forbidden (*interdicto* (26)). The comparison, of course, is not valid, since it assumes in every case that the state would not give consent for the individual to acquire Roman citizenship, and that the individual would realize this and not perform brave deeds for Rome:

> Atqui nihil interest, iudices, utrum haec foederati iura constituant, ut ne cui liceat ex iis civitatibus ad nostrorum bellorum pericula accedere, an, quae nos eorum civibus virtutis causa tribuerimus, ea rata esse non possint; nihilo enim magis uteremur iis adiutoribus, sublatis virtutis praemiis, quam si omnino iis versari in nostris bellis non liceret . . . quemquam fore putatis qui se opponat periculis non modo nullo proposito praemio, sed etiam interdicto? (26)

> And it makes no difference, judges, whether states bound to us by treaty establish these laws, in order to forbid anyone of their own citizens to undertake dangers in our wars or whether those benefits which we have bestowed upon their citizens because of courage can have no validity; for with rewards for courage removed, we would no more employ them as helpers than if it were altogether forbidden for them to take part in our wars . . . for whom do you think would face danger not only with no reward proposed, but with it actually forbidden?

In sections 27–31, Cicero turns to the rights of Roman citizens to acquire citizenship in another state. These sections provide an argument by analogy (and *a fortiori*)[27] against the Gaditans' ability to "give consent." A Roman was free to accept the citizenship of another state without the approval of Rome: "Iure enim nostro neque mutare civitatem quisquam invitus potest, neque si velit mutare non potest, modo adsciscatur ab ea civitate cuius esse se civitatis velit." (27) ("For by our law it is neither possible for anyone [of our citizens] to change his citizenship against his will, nor if he wishes to change it not to be able to, as long as he is received by that state of which he wishes to be a citizen").[28] A change of citizenship could be brought about either by adoption by the state, or by a right of subsequent return (*postliminium*).[29] Cicero provides a hypothetical example of a Roman adopted by Gades, then as proof provides several examples of

Roman citizens who became attached to other cities: Quintus Maximus, Gaius Laenas, Quintus Philippus, Gaius Cato, Quintus Caepio, and Publius Rutilius (28). A further example is provided of the *postliminium* type: Gaius Publicius Menander, a freedman who was given permission to go to Greece and then return to Rome without losing his Roman citizenship (28). The six *exempla* add weight to the argument, and give it apparent credibility. These *exempla*, however, only demonstrate that *Romans* can change citizenship without Roman approval.

The conclusion to this argument is posed in the form of a question: "Quodsi civi Romano licet esse Gaditanum sive exsilio sive postliminio sive reiectione huius civitatis . . . quid est, quam ob rem civi Gaditano in hanc civitatem venire non liceat?" (29) ("But if a Roman citizen may become a Gaditan, either by exile or by the right of return or by the rejection of this state . . . what reason is there why it should not be permitted for a Gaditan citizen to acquire our citizenship?"). Again this is an example of Cicero letting the audience reach the conclusion on its own.[30]

The conclusion is not valid, however, since one cannot assume that all states have the same type of citizenship laws as Rome. Indeed, Cicero unwittingly proves this in the digression which follows, in 29–30. In this digression he states that Roman citizens may be citizens only of Rome: that is, if a Roman citizen takes on the citizenship of another state, he loses his Roman citizenship. Citizens of other states, such as Athens, Rhodes, and Sparta, however, may be citizens of more than one state.

This conclusion, that Gaditans are able to become Romans of their own accord because Romans are able to become Gaditans is further supported by the argument that the more closely the state was tied to Rome by "societate amicitia sponsione pactione foedere" (29) ("by alliance, by friendship, by promise, by agreement, by treaty") the more closely it could share in "beneficiorum, praemiorum, civitatis" ("privileges, rewards, and citizenship"). This statement cannot be justified any more than the point it is meant to support. In fact, Cicero completes this sentence with *videtur* which indicates he is not speaking in the world of hard facts. The conclusion, which is not logically supported by the proof, is that Rome is able to enfranchise anyone in the world it wishes.[31]

This group of sections concludes with an elaboration and an emotional appeal to Roman patriotism, in which the right to retain or renounce citizenship is linked to fundamental Roman rights: "Haec sunt enim fundamenta firmissima nostrae libertatis, sui quemque iuris et retinendi et dimittendi esse dominum." (31) ("For these are the firmest foundations of our freedom, that each man is his own master in retaining or giving up his citizenship.") The importance of new citizens to Rome is stressed with several *exempla* reaching back to the time of Romulus: the Sabines, inhabitants of Latin towns, of

Tusculum, of Lanuvium, the Sabines again, the Volscians, and the Hernicians. None of these peoples, according to Cicero, infringed any treaty by becoming Romans. The antiquity of the *exempla* lends the argument weight and importance. The argument, however, has the same weakness as the argument *a fortiori* cited above, since it assumes that the rights of the Gaditans are the same as those of various Italian groups.

The emphasis Cicero places in this group of sections[32] on the inability of Romans to be stripped of citizenship against their will contains an implicit allusion to Balbus, whom, according to Cicero, the prosecutor desired to strip of his citizenship. (The prosecutor presumably saw it differently: in his opinion, Balbus wasn't really a Roman citizen because he acquired franchise in an illegitimate manner.) Cicero's argument implies that Balbus is no longer a citizen of Gades, since he is now a Roman citizen, and therefore Gades has no jurisdiction over him.[33]

In the following group of sections (32–37), Cicero refutes a series of arguments made by the prosecutor. By "asking" the prosecutor rhetorical and leading questions, pretending to voice the prosecutor's responses, and breaking into indignant interjections, this section of the *argumentatio* takes on a livelier tone.

The prosecutor argued that various peoples, such as the Cenomani, the Insubres, the Helvetii, and the Iapudes, had made treaties with Rome in which there was a saving clause ("in foederibus exceptum est") (32) which did not allow their citizens to be made Roman, and such a clause was also to be understood in regard to Gades. The saving clause among the aforementioned tribes has caused speculation among scholars. Reid suggests that such a clause was demanded by the tribes themselves rather than by the Romans, in order that these tribes might protect their nationality.[34] Brunt considers the clause perplexing:

> It is puzzling that this clause was inserted in any of these treaties. At whose instance? The Romans had no reason to tie their own hands, and the barbarians could hardly have expected Rome to make a practice of enfranchising their nationals. But perhaps some deserters to Rome had been given franchise, and Rome conceded there would be no more such grants.[35]

Scullard believes the clause has to do with land assignations: "The practical bearing of this stipulation probably was to exclude natives from land assignations made by the Roman government in Cisalpine Gaul."[36] The question this raises is why the tribes would ever refuse permission in this case. It is unlikely that the stipulation came at the insistence of the tribes, since the treaties were made with the Cenomani, Insubres, and Iapudes after they had been defeated in battle by the Romans, and were not in a position to make demands. Therefore the clause had to benefit the Romans in some way, but possibly at the same time it throws a fairly meaningless bone to defeated but distant tribes. Hence it is most likely that Scullard's interpretation is the correct one.

Cicero rebuts the prosecutor's argument with an *in utramque partem* argument.[37] First, he concedes that certain tribes such as the Cenomani, the Insubres, the Helvetii, and the Iapudes did have such clauses in their treaties, but he adds that such a clause was not specifically spelled out in the Gaditan treaty, and therefore did not exist in respect to Gades (32). Such an argument is probably a valid one, since these four are the only known cases of such a clause. In addition, these four cases all concern tribes and not urban communities,[38] such as Gades. Cicero makes an argument that at first glance may appear logical: "Quod si exceptio facit ne liceat, ubi *non sit exceptum*, ibi necesse est licere." (32) ("But if an excepting clause makes it impermissible, where there is no excepting clause, then it is necessary that it is permissible."). This statement, however, contains a fallacy, since it does not take into account the fact that there may be another reason to make enfranchisement illegal.

Cicero then argues the second part of his *in utramque partem* argument. He adds that even if such a clause did exist, the *lex Gellia Cornelia* would have been able to overrule the saving clause (32, 33). He employs arguments *ex definitione*[39] in a three-pronged proof. First, there is no clause in the *lex Gellia Cornelia* which renders it invalid against a *sacrosanctum* treaty.[40] Second, the Gaditan treaty is not *sacrosanctum*, since it was not passed by the *comitia populi* or the *concilium plebis* (33, 35). Third, there is no law relating to the treaty which contains an *obtestatio* or a *consecratio* (33).[41] Reid believes that Cicero's first proof is very questionable.[42] The second proof is reasonable, since there are other ancient sources which agree with the contention that a treaty must be ratified by the people.[43] The third proof follows from the second and is just as strong.[44] It regards the lack of a clause of consecration enacted by the people. If the treaty itself was not brought before the people, it is even more unlikely that a law regarding an *obtestatio* or a *consecratio* would have been.

Cicero's argument that the treaty with Gades is not sacrosanct causes him to digress and stress that he is not attempting to prove that the treaty is invalid: "Nec vero oratio mea ad infirmandum foedus Gaditanorum, iudices, pertinet"; (34) ("Nor indeed, judges, does my speech lead to the invalidation of the treaty with the Gaditans.") and "Quod cum magis fide illius populi, iustitia nostra, vetustate denique ipsa quam aliquo publico vinculo religionis teneretur" (34) ("But because it was kept more by the faith of that people, by our righteousness, and lastly by its long existence than by any public fetters of religious sanctity"). Although the treaty is not sacrosanct it does have the merit of the Gaditans, the *auctoritatem senatus*[45] and the *opinionem vetustatis* behind it (34). It is important that Cicero let both the jury and the Gaditans present know that he is not attempting to jettison the treaty entirely, since this could have bilateral repercussions, and therefore make it more difficult for the jury to accept his argument.

After this digression Cicero presents further arguments as to why, even if the treaty had been made sacrosanct by the Roman people, it would not make adoption of Roman citizenship illegal for Gaditans. He bases his major premise upon a clause of the Gaditan treaty:[46] "Maiestatem populi Romani comiter conservanto." (35) ("Let them uphold the majesty of the Roman people in an obliging manner"). This phrase, that the Gaditans must uphold Roman sovereignty is found in *foedera iniqua*, that is, in treaties with states which have lost their sovereigny and must obey Rome.[47] A *foedus aequum*, on the other hand, which indicates that the state retained its sovereignty (theoretically, at least), would not contain such a clause.

Cicero easily rebuts the prosecutor's suggestion that *comiter* means the same thing as *communiter*.[48] He does so with another *in utramque partem* argument. The first part disputes the prosecutor's interpretation of the word, and is backed up with an example of correct usage in an argument *ex definitione*.[49] In the second part of the argument, Cicero demonstrates that even if the word *comiter* did mean *communiter*, as the prosecutor insisted, it still does not affect Cicero's argument, since nothing was said about upholding the greatness of Gades. The prosecutor's argument suggests that he saw the difficulty to his case posed by the "Maiestatem populi Romani comiter conservanto" clause.

The minor premise is that Roman greatness cannot be upheld if the Romans are not able to give rewards for bravery (37). The unspoken conclusion is that the enfranchisement of Balbus had helped maintain Roman greatness, and therefore Pompey had legitimately bestowed Roman citizenship upon the Spaniard. The minor premise appeared earlier in the *argumentatio* in the context of treaties not meant to diminish Roman power (20, 22). Here it is seen that in addition to the earlier argument, such an idea is incorporated in the treaty itself, by means of the *maiestatem* clause. The repetition of the minor premise reminds the jury of the earlier arguments about Roman greatness and strengthens this one.

Cicero makes a neat transition to his next argument by asking why he was arguing as if the Gaditans were his opponents. He then employs that hypothetical scenario to summarize and repeat all his preceding arguments (38). This summary emphasizes all the more the argument Cicero puts forth in the following group of sections (39–44): that the Gaditans, by their approval for Balbus, have actually given consent to the Cornelian Gellian law. This statement is the second part of an *in utramque partem* argument whose first part was presented at the beginning of the *argumentatio*. Cicero spent much of the *argumentatio* arguing that the Gaditans did not have to "give consent" to the Gellian Cornelian law. Now he demonstates that although they were not required to "give consent," their behavior towards Balbus demonstrates that they have thoroughly approved his enfranchisement, and so have given consent by implication.

The orator begins by stating that the Gaditans agree with the point he is making: "id quod defendo voluntate eorum, auctoritate, legatione ipsa comprobetur . . ." (39) ("the very thesis which I am maintaining is proved by their goodwill, their prestige, by their legation itself"). The actual point is unclear. Before clarifying it ("id, quod"), Cicero launches in on an emotional digression about the Gaditan loyalty to Rome (39–40). In addition to an ethical description of the Gaditans, Cicero mentions some of the most prestigious Roman *maiores*: the Scipiones, the Bruti, the Horatii, the Cassii, the Metelli together with Pompey, as examples of commanders whom the Gaditans had aided. Cicero also reminds the Romans that the Gaditans had helped them out with a supply of grain. This digression contains a convergence of modes of argument and is intended to increase the feeling of good will towards the Gaditans, thus giving more force to the rational arguments Cicero will make in 41 and 42.

The argument in 41 is a repetition of the argument *a minore* made in 24: it is unjust if the *stipendarii* of Africa, Sardinia, and Spain are entitled to Roman citizenship, but the people of Gades are not. In 24 Cicero had argued this with the stress on the dangers to the Roman state if the Gaditans were not able to acquire Roman citizenship. Presumably he won over the jury with these arguments *quid eventurum sit*, which were based on Roman self-interest. Such arguments prepare for the acceptance of the slightly altered argument in 41. In 41, the emphasis is on the Gaditan reaction to such an interpretation of their treaty: ". . . non foedus sibi nobiscum ictum, sed iniquissimas leges impositas a nobis esse arbitrabuntur" ("they will not think that a treaty has been made with us, but that the most unjust laws have been imposed by us"). This statement leads to the proofs of the minor premise, presented before the minor itself. Such an arrangement of the argument allows the jury to come to the conclusion on their own, rather than being told by Cicero.

The first proof that the Gaditans accepted Balbus as a Roman citizen is that they had appointed Balbus as their guest-friend in Rome (41, 42).[50] As both Kaden and Sherwin-White note, such an appointment meant that the Gaditans no longer regarded Balbus as a Gaditan, but as a Roman.[51] Cicero's second proof is the presence of the Gaditan envoys, who support Balbus (42). The third is that Gaditans in their own senate had criticized and fined the prosecutor and shown concern for Balbus (41, 42). Such actions of active support for Balbus, Cicero states in the minor premise, are the same as Gades "giving consent" to his Roman citizenship. Technically, this is not so, since there is a difference between adopting a law and post factum agreement to something which was done without prior consent. (A common rhetorical tactic is to argue in favor of intent when the letter of the law is against one [*de Inv.* 1.17; 2.116–143; *Top.* 96].)

Nonetheless, the overall argument clearly demonstrates that Balbus had the support of his city behind him, and whether or not consent was obtained in the first place, the city was happy to have him as a Roman citizen. To emphasize this point, Cicero indicates the benefits that Gades had received from Balbus, and from Caesar, Balbus' patron: "summa in eam civitatem huius rogatu studia et beneficia contulerit" (43) ("he [Caesar] conferred the greatest devotion and benefits upon that state at the request of this man").

A transition to the following group of sections (45–51) is provided by the assertion that the legal point of this case has never been in any doubt. This assertion leads to several examples of generals who have bestowed citizenship on allies in battle. Cicero introduces this argument with the premise that the most skilled interpreters of treaties are those who have commanded armies and waged wars. Cicero paved the way for the audience's acceptance of this premise by his praise of Pompey at the beginning of the speech (11–15). When discussing Pompey, Cicero asserted that his experience in the battlefield and in public affairs made it impossible that he should mistakenly bestow citizenship.[52]

Cicero then provides two proofs by analogy for his premise. The first example is that of Quintus Scaevola, the augur (consul 117 B.C.), who although he was a great jurist, referred clients to the *praediatores* (brokers) Furius and Cascellius for advice regarding the law of mortgaged properties (45). The second example is that of Cicero himself, who consulted Marcus Turgio regarding water rights on his land at Tusculum (45). These examples demonstrate that in certain specialized areas, experts in the field are best equipped to provide accurate advice. The *exempla* implicitly make the suggestion that Pompey is as much an expert in the field of treaties as Furius, Cascellius and Turgio were in their given areas. In fact, Pompey's administrative rearrangement of the Eastern seaboard of the Mediterranean in 63 to 62 B.C. gave him considerable expertise in foreign affairs. The implication by analogy in the *exempla* is given in a restatement of the major premise: Roman commanders are the most qualified to judge about treaties. Here, instead of testing the case on actual legal grounds of Balbus' enfranchisement in 72 B.C., Cicero brings up Pompey's military and administrative achievements, both of which provided him with expertise in treaty relations with foreign countries and also contributed to his tremendous personal *auctoritas*.

In an argument *de locis extrinsecus assumptis de testimoniis*,[53] Marius is offered as a precedent (46): he is the best example of such a commander. He enfranchised Marcus Annius Appius of Iguvium, and two whole cohorts from Camerinum, which had a *foedus aequum* with Rome. The latter is an implicit argument *a fortiori*: if Rome could enfranchise individuals from states with which Rome had a *foedus aequum*, then she should be able to do the same with a state such as Gades, with which Rome had a *foedus iniquum*. Neither of these examples presents a true parallel to Balbus' case, as Brunt notes: ". . . even the recital of precedents for the grant of citizenship by generals to foreigners who had been valiant in Rome's service (46–51) . . . hardly touches the prosecutor's case."[54] Both of these towns are Italian, not Spanish. In the case of the cohorts from Camerium, there was some controversy as to the legality of the enfranchisement at the time, and even Marius himself seemed to realize it was not quite legal, given his comment that he did not hear the law because of the noise of arms.[55] It is likely that Marius enfranchised the cohorts without an enabling law such as the *lex Cornelia Gellia* under which Pompey bestowed citizenship upon Balbus.[56] As such it is rather a weak example of a legitimate bestowal of citizenship.

The conclusion to this premise becomes the minor premise: if Balbus is condemned, then Marius must be condemned. Again, as in the case of Pompey, the appeal is to personality rather than to laws. The conclusion assumes that Pompey's citizenship grant to Balbus was made under exactly the same circumstances as the citizenship grants by Marius. The statement is followed by the example of Matrinius of Spoletium, a Latin colony (48). The circumstances of this bestowal of citizenship were also completely different from those of Balbus.[57] Matrinius' prosecutor argued that the enfranchisement was invalid because the colonies under the Appuleian Law,[58] which permitted Marius to enfranchise Matrinius, had never been founded. Cicero himself states that Matrinius' case had no resemblance to that of Balbus (49). The conclusion to this example is that Marius won his case because of his prestige (49). Several points are implied here. The first harkens back to the minor: if Balbus is condemned, then Marius also must be condemned. But Marius was acquitted. The logical corollary is that Balbus must therefore also be acquitted. The second implied point is that if Marius won his case because of his prestige, then surely Pompey (to whom Marius is implicitly compared) should win the present case because of his prestige.

From a legal standpoint the examples of Marius' citizenship grants are weak. The arguments are shored up by the emphasis on pathos, discussed in the previous chapter,[59] and especially on Marius' *auctoritas*, and by the unstated conclusions mentioned above. The legal arguments may even be purposely weak, to demonstrate that Marius was able to enfranchise people under questionable circumstances. (And if he was able to do so under weak circumstances, then how much more valid would Pompey's enfranchisement be!)

The argument by analogy to Marius concludes with a restatement of one of the themes of the speech: that commanders ought to be able to reward the bravest in battle.[60] Cicero reinforces the argument by analogy to Marius with six more examples of commanders who had bestowed citizenship for courage on the battlefield (50–51). These examples gain weight by their sheer numbers. The first is Pompey *pater*, who enfranchised Publius Caesius, then Marius (again) and the cohorts of Camerinum, third is Publius Crassus who enfranchised Alexas of Heraclea, fourth Lucius Sulla who bestowed citizenship upon Aristo of Massilia and nine slaves of Gades, fifth Quintus Metellus Pius, upon Quintus Fabius of Saguntum, and lastly Marcus Crassus, upon a man of Avennio.[61] In 51 Cicero adds some other enfranchisements Pompey made,[62] only one of which was of a Gaditan. The generals presented as precedents in bestowing citizenship are all highly prestigious Romans, whose actions carried great *auctoritas*. None of these "precedents," however, bears any resemblance to Balbus' case, with the exception of the enfranchisement of Hasdrubal of Gades by Pompey. Even the grant by Sulla to Gaditan slaves would not, since slaves were not considered citizens, and therefore did not require the Gaditans' consent. Cicero concludes with a quote from Ennius regarding an exhortation by Hannibal (51).[63] This suggests an argument *a minore*: if even Rome's worst enemy would enfranchise someone who fought on his side, then surely Rome must do the same. It provides no legal example, but a strong emotional one.

This argument from the *exempla* of various important generals is followed by Cicero's promise of further precedents offered by the decisions of jurors, of the Roman people, and of the Senate (52–56). These examples seem to encompass all the Roman people, setting them against the prosecutor.

The first precedent is the case of Marcus Cassius, for whom the Mamertines claimed restitution (*repetitio*) in 64 B.C.[64] Cicero is vague about the precise facts of the case. The prosecution withdrew the charges, so the jury did not reach a verdict, contrary to Cicero's assertion earlier in 52. Cicero makes the dropping of the case a point in his favor by stating that the prosecution let go the case after they learned that the jury was going to vote in Cassius' favor. The only evidence to support this view is the supposition that if the prosecution dropped the case, it must have been because they did not think they could win it. In any event speculation is irrelevant since Cassius' case appears to bear little resemblance to that of Balbus. In the former the town as a whole (*Mamertini*) were seeking restitution, whereas in Balbus' case it was a single prosecutor. This difference, however, may be the entire point behind Cicero's mentioning of Cassius' case. Sherwin-White suggests that Gades would have had to go through the process of *repetitio* if it wanted to claim back Balbus.[65] The difference between Cassius' and Balbus' cases emphasizes the point that the Gaditans as a whole, as Cicero had shown earlier, were not opposed to Balbus' enfranchisement, as the Mamertines opposed that of Cassius.

Cicero concludes his first example with the repetition of the argument[66] that no one enfranchised by the Romans had ever been prosecuted or condemned because his former city had not "given consent" or been prevented from assuming Roman citizenship by a treaty (52).[67] This argument is entirely irrelevant here in terms of being legally probative.[68] It has little to do with the Cassius example, but nonetheless the argument gains force through repetition. It is also effective because of the importance Romans placed on precedents.[69] In addition it appeals to Roman chauvinism, in that no Roman is going to admit that the laws of Rome are inferior those of any other state, whatever its status.

The second example, the verdict of the Roman people (53–54), has even less to do with Balbus' case. There is no indication that any treaty with the Latins had any resemblance whatsoever to that with Gades.[70] Indeed Cicero gives us no details about the Cassian and Cominian treaties. He makes an argument *a minore*:[71] if it is possible for people to acquire Roman citizenship by litigation under the Servilian Law, then it ought to be possible for those who fight on Rome's behalf. "An lingua et ingenio patefieri aditus ad civitatem potuit, manu et virtute non potuit?" (54) ("Could the right of admittance to the state lie open by means of oratory and talent but not by means of military service and courage?"). He draws an example from the jury: Lucius Cossinius of Tibur, the father of one of the jurors, won his citizenship through the prosecution of Titus Caelius. The argument *a minore* implies that the only difference between Lucius Cossinius' enfranchisement and that of Balbus is that Cossinius obtained his from a jury while Balbus received his from a general.

But in making this argument, Cicero manages to twist facts a little. The treaty with the Latins, which he invokes, dates to 493 B.C (Livy 2.33.9; Dion. Hal. 6.95.2). He mentions it in order to be able to call the Latins *foederati* later in section 54. Sherwin-White makes the following comment about this:[72]

> Apart from Lavinium it is incorrect to speak of the Latins as *foederati* . . . After casually referring to Cassian treaty he (Cicero) goes on to treat the Latins of a later day as if they enjoyed the same status as the Prisci Latini. For the purposes of his case he slips in the phrase 'hanc Latinis, id est foederatis, viam ad civitatem populi iussu patere passi sunt.' What better proof could there be than this rhetorical malpractice that the Latins were not *foederati* in the normal meaning of the term?

Cicero pretends that the Latins are *foederati* in order to make his example of the Latins seem relevant to Gades and Balbus. The *exemplum* is also an appeal to antiquity and to the *mos maiorum*. The Servilian Law to which Cicero refers is, if Levick is right, the *lex Servilia Glaucia*, which allowed only Latins to receive citizenship as a reward for successful prosecution for *repetundarum* cases.[73] Thus Cicero is manipulating facts again to make his argument appear to be relevant for Balbus and Gades.

As with the example of the jurors' decision, this second example, that of the people's decisions, concludes with a suggestion that consent did not have to be given for the Servilian Law by the Latins. This decision of the people has absolutely nothing to do with Balbus' case.

The third example consists of a decision of the Senate to enfranchise priestesses from Greece and one from Velia to conduct the rites of Ceres[74] (55). Cicero follows the ancient examples of the Greek priestesses with a more recent one: Valerius Flaccus enfranchised Calliphana of Velia.[75] Together, the two examples, one ancient and one more recent, emphasize the lengthy period of time over which the Romans have consistently enfranchised foreigners. At the same time, the second example makes the same point as the two previous ones: the Velians did not give their consent, nor did the enfranchisement violate their treaty with Rome. As with the other examples this one is not relevant to Balbus and Gades. By his comparison Cicero is implicitly assuming that the treaties of Velia and Gades are the same. At the same time, he presents no precise information about these treaties. Although an analysis shows the weakness of his argumentation, Cicero's arguments gain force not by their validity, but by sheer repetition. It was unlikely that the jury was sufficiently informed on the details of this legislation to make the necessary discriminations.[76] In *De Oratore* (1.171–185), Cicero stresses the importance of the orator knowing the law and here in the *Pro Balbo* Cicero demonstrates that as well as being capable of using the law, he is also quite capable of abusing it.

In sections 56 to 59 Cicero turns to a *refutatio* of the prosecution's arguments against Balbus. The "ethical" and "pathetic" aspects of these arguments have been studied in the previous chapter. In this chapter the rational aspects of Cicero's rebuttal will be examined.

Cicero begins with the repetition of a statement he has made several times in this speech: "Intellego, iudices, in causa aperta minimeque dubia multo et plura et a pluribus peritissimis esse dicta quam res postularet." (56) ("I know, judges, that in this cut and dried case, about which there is no doubt at all, many things have been said by several very experienced men, more than the matter was generally thought to require"). He then explains the overkill by drawing attention to the prejudice which has arisen against his client. The prosecutor criticized Balbus for his wealth, his house, his admission into the *tribus Clustumina*, and his adoption by Theophanes. Perhaps because the real reasons for Balbus' prosecution are not found in the legal realm, Cicero can argue against the prosecution in a similar manner, not bound by strict legal proof either.

The first criticism is refuted by an attack on the premise Balbus acquired his wealth through corruption. According to Cicero, it was acquired through careful management. This statement becomes an assumption for the following rebuttal of extravagance. Cicero simply denies the extravagance charge, stating that the prosecution was able to cite no specific charges. An unstated assumption is that a man who acquired wealth through careful management was unlikely to be a spendthrift.

The accusation of overreaching himself by acquiring a house previously owned by some of the most prestigious Romans (not a legal offense, but prejudicial against Balbus) is easily rebutted. Cicero demonstrates that the prosecutor had omitted from his enumeration of previous owners a freedman, Sotericus Marcius (56).[77] The rebuttal is framed as an argument *a minore*. The assumption Cicero makes is that if an ex-slave could own such a house then surely ownership would not be overreaching for such a man as Balbus. This assumption is faulty since it is possible that both the freedman and Balbus were exceeding their proper spheres, as the Romans saw them. In addition, the prosecutor's point probably had more to do with the history of the house, that is, the illustrious previous owners (Quintus Metellus and Lucius Crassus), rather than the inherent qualities of the building. If that is so, Cicero's strategy is to appropriate and modify the prosecutor's actual accusation.[78] The criticism of Balbus' admission to the *tribus Clustumina* is refuted with the statement that it was acquired legally, and with an argument *a minore*: the grounds of Balbus' entry to the *tribus Clustumina* are not as invidious as those of men who could reach a higher grade in the Senate through successful litigation (57). The criticism of his adoption by Theophanes is rebutted by an argument *ex factis*: the adoption merely enabled Balbus to inherit the property of his own relatives (57).[79]

Cicero openly attacks the prejudice against Balbus with two arguments. The first is an argument *ex rebus personis attributis ex victu*.[80] Here Balbus' friendship with Caesar is stressed: "Versatus in intima familiaritate hominis potentissimi, in maximis nostris malis atque discordiis . . ." (58) ("Associated in deepest friendship with a very powerful man, at the time of our greatest evils and discord"). The second is an argument *ex factis*, in which Cicero recalls Balbus' kindness to himself during his exile: "omni officio,—lacrimis, opera, consolatione,— omnis me absente meos sublevavit."[81] (58) ("in my absence he supported my whole family with ever service: with his tears, with his actions, and with his consolations") Mention of Balbus' aid during the exile provides the transition from *refutatio* to *peroratio*, with an emotional crescendo.

In 59 Cicero expresses his gratitude to Balbus, which serves as a preamble for an enthymeme: the jurors love and hold dear the champions of Cicero's welfare. Balbus championed Cicero's welfare. Therefore they should be grateful to Balbus. (Unstated but obvious is how they should do this: with an acquittal.) This enthymeme is followed by another one, whose second part and conclusion is left unspoken: Balbus is attacked not by his own enemies, but by the enemies of Pompey. The jurors have been prepared by Cicero from the beginning of the speech for this assumption. Indeed, as Cicero states (59), Pompey himself made this accusation in his speech earlier. The unstated, but logical corollary is that if the jurors attack Balbus by voting against him, they will also be attacking Pompey.

Cicero then turns to Balbus' relationship with Caesar. In an argument *a fortiori* he argues that if he himself, who had been exiled, was able to reconcile with Caesar, so should the jurors, who had not suffered so badly. In this way Cicero turns a potentially embarrassing situation to his advantage, with a demonstration of his own virtue. (Interest in the well-being of the state caused him to overcome differences with Caesar (60).) Balbus' friendship with Caesar is elaborated upon in an argument *ex rebus personis attributis ex victu* (63) (*De Inv.* 1.35). "Quid enim est cur non potius ad summam laudem huic quam ad minimam fraudem Caesaris familiaritas valere debeat?" ("For what reason is there why his friendship with Caesar should not rather give strength to the highest praise for this man rather than the least loss?").

Theoretically all the arguments are summed up in the *peroratio* (*De Inv.* 1.98). In this speech, as Rohde notices, the orator omits some: "Item *Pro Balbo* 28.64 omissis ceteris argumentis eos tantum viros enumerat, quorum auctoritate in argumentione nisus erat" ("Likewise at *Pro Balbo* 28.64, after having omitted the other arguments, he lists only the men whose authority (as precedents) he relied upon in the *argumentatio*.")[82] The treaty and consent arguments had been reiterated during the arguments from the precedents provided by the decisions of the jurors, senate, and Roman people, so Cicero probably did not think it necessary to repeat them here. In addition, Cicero no doubt wanted to focus on the "precedents" set by former generals (64), and those established by former jurors, the senate, and Roman people. Although these arguments are actually weak, since the precedents are not true parallels, they would carry most weight with the jury because they appear to set the whole Roman world on the side of Balbus, with the prosecutor as the sole opponent.

In conclusion I shall present a brief assessment of the main arguments based on logos. In his use of logos in the *Pro Balbo*, Cicero makes a two-pronged attack: the first consists of the argument that Pompey's enfranchisement was legal, and the second that Balbus was legally entitled to accept. The first is bolstered by the *lex Cornelia Gallia*, which gave Pompey permission to enfranchise individuals. To support the second, Cicero presents an array of arguments. Some of these arguments are quite rational while others are irrational, and still others are manipulated rational arguments, an exaggerated interpretation and rebuttal of arguments it is highly unlikely the prosecutor made. He rebuts the argument that the Gaditans would have had to give consent to the enfranchisement with several points. First, Cicero makes a distinction between cases in which states were allowed to give consent, as for example the adoption of the *leges Furia*, *Voconia*, and *Julia*. Here the major distinction, reasonably enough, appears to be that the latter laws all concern the community as a whole, where Balbus' enfranchisement for the most part, affected an individual. Cicero also argues that states could give consent only in instances where Rome's interests were not at stake.

Cases of enfranchisement, he argues reasonably enough within his frame of reference, were a matter of national security, since Rome had needed in the past, and would need in the future, the assistance of allies. It is worth noting that to bolster this legal argument Cicero employs pathos to play on the audience's fears. The national security argument is a manipulated rational one since Cicero equates the prosecutor's position with the enfranchisement of allies being completely forbidden.

In a questionable rational argument, Cicero states that since Romans could obtain citizenship elsewhere without Rome's consent, other nations therefore did not require their state to consent to their citizens becoming Roman. This argument suffers from the weakness of assuming other nations had the same laws about citizenship as Rome did. (In fact Cicero inadvertently informs us there were differences in citizenship laws, since other states allowed dual citizenship while Rome did not.) In a stronger argument Cicero mentions that states which did have the right to give consent to their citizens' enfranchisements by Rome, such as some Gallic tribes, all had that right expressed in a treaty. Gades, on the other hand, had no such clause in its treaty and in addition the treaty was *iniquum*. Perhaps the most dangerous argument in the speech is that the Gaditan treaty had never been enacted by the *comitia populi* or the *concilium plebis* and therefore was not *sacrosanctum*, and therefore even if it contained a consent clause, the treaty could be overridden by the *lex Cornelia Gellia*. Cicero is quick to point out that even if Rome was not legally required to uphold the Gaditan treaty, it was morally bound to do so. This leads one to wonder: if, following Cicero's logic here, the Gaditan treaty *did* contain a consent clause (as Cicero has just hypothetically suggested, although he argues earlier it did not), would Rome be morally, if not legally bound to uphold it? It seems that Cicero's arguments here can be turned against him. This is a weakness in Cicero's argumentation: in isolation his arguments make sense, but sometimes when one attempts to place them together in a coherent whole, they do not fit together rationally. But perhaps this is a weakness more easily spotted when one reads a speech, and can turn back and forth and reread, than when one hears a speech. In any case, Cicero moves on to argue that the Gaditans had in spirit, if not officially, given a kind of consent to Balbus' enfranchisement by their various actions, such as making him their guest-friend.

Characteristic of Cicero's rational argument in this speech is his willingness to seek out every possibility and argue that no matter how one looked at the case, the outcome was the same: the enfranchisement was legal. In fact, this *in utramque partem* argumentation is the most pervasive type of rational argument found in the *Pro Balbo*.[83] It appears throughout the *argumentatio*: Cicero argues that Gades does not have to give consent (20, 32), and later (32, 33) that even if the treaty did have a clause requiring consent, the *lex Gellia Cornelia* would have overridden it. Then, with a third alternative, he adds (39–44) that the Gaditans had in a sense given their consent to Balbus' enfranchisement. The prosecutor's contention that *comiter* meant *communiter* is also rebutted with an *in utramque partem* argument.

Two other argument types frequently employed are *a fortiori* and *a minore*. In addition Cicero makes great use of precedents and *exempla*. These precedents often have little similarity to the circumstances of Balbus' case, and for the most part seem to acquire their strength as precedents through the *auctoritas* of the enfranchiser, as for example, in the precedent of Marius. Certain techniques, such as universalization and association, seen in both ethical and pathetic argumentation, also are employed in rational argumentation. One of the most interesting techniques is the posing of conclusions in the form of questions (or suppressing them altogether), which allows the jury to form the conclusion in its own mind. Perhaps since legal technicalities are only a pretext for the case against Balbus, Cicero is not completely bound by them. Hence, much of the "logical" argumentation consists of appeals to skewed precedents, to authoritative leaders, and the *mos maiorum*.

Chapter Four
Dispositio

THE ARRANGEMENT OF ARGUMENTS CANNOT BE IGNORED IN ANY STUDY OF a speech whose purpose is persuasion. In order to persuade one must not only have the right arguments, but one must know in what order to present them, and how to develop them. An argument made in the wrong place in a judicial speech, at a place where the jury is not ready to accept it, or an argument clumsily developed, can lose the case for the orator. To emphasize the importance of *dispositio*, Quintilian compares composing a speech to sculpting a statue (*Inst. Or.* 7. Pr. 2):

Nec inmerito secunda quinque partium posita est [i.e. dispositio], cum sine ea prior nihil valeat. Neque enim quamquam fusis omnibus membris statua sit, nisi conlocetur, et si quam in corporibus nostris aliorumve animalium partem permutes et transferas, licet habeat eadem omnia, prodigium sit tamen.

Nor is [arrangement] placed second of the five parts of oratory without cause, since without it the previous one is worthless. For nor is there a statue although all its limbs have been cast, unless the limbs have been placed together, and if you were to interchange and transfer some one part of our bodies or of other animals with another, although it would possess all the same limbs, it would nevertheless be a monster.

This striking comparison demonstrates the importance of arrangement.[1] In sculpting a statue the placement of limbs is dictated by aesthetics, which are in turn dictated by the natural world. A sculptor creates a statue of a man or woman to be as lifelike as possible. The purpose of a forensic speech is to persuade; therefore persuasion dictates the arrangement of the speech.[2] Arguments are not all equally convincing; with clever placement, the orator can ensure that a stronger argument wins over the audience first, and then he can place weaker arguments after strong ones, where the former will gain strength from the stronger ones.[3] In his rebuttal a defense advocate can also isolate and rearrange arguments presented by the prosecution,[4] and sometimes he appropriates and reverses them.[5] In addition to the strength and weakness of arguments in themselves, the feelings of the audience may affect the potency of an argument. The audience will have different attitudes about various arguments, players and issues in the case. Particularly in a case such as Balbus', where there is a strong feeling of hostility towards the defendant, the orator must be careful to prepare his audience for the arguments, so that when the arguments are presented, the audience accepts them. Otherwise he may unwittingly further alienate the jurors.

In my analysis of the arrangement of the speech, I first examine the *dispositio* of the *Pro Balbo* as a whole, in order to provide a broad overview before presenting a brief synopsis of *inventio* and tackling the placement and development of groups of arguments. Of particular interest here is why Cicero organizes his arguments in a certain order, and what effect the specific *dispositio* has. Finally, I examine the arrangement of arguments within the individual sections. The main concern is Cicero's pyschological preparation of his audience to accept his arguments by the blending and arranging of the different *genera* of arguments, and by the manner in which he develops the individual arguments.

The overall general structure of the speech is bipartite, a structure that Cicero employs in other speeches.[6] The first part of the *Pro Balbo* concerns Pompey and addresses the question of whether he could legally enfranchise Balbus.[7] The second part tackles the issue of whether Balbus could legitimately accept the citizenship grant. The speech may be divided according to the traditional divisions of the speech,[8] with some variations, since it is not a textbook example. This has caused difficulties for scholars analyzing the speech.[9] This does not mean that the *Pro Balbo* is a defective speech.[10] As Neumeister and Stroh have pointed out, the traditional rhetorical divisions presented merely suggestions for the orator.[11] Hence the rhetorical guidelines are merely guidelines, not rigid rules.[12] In some speeches, such as the *Pro Milone*, the orator follows these guidelines. In others, such as the *Pro Balbo*, he does not. In each case, the orator is governed by the case at hand.[13]

In the *Pro Balbo* the only division scholars (except for Reid) agree upon is that of the *exordium*. Differences of opinion appear immediately afterwards, where one would normally expect the *narratio*. In fact, we do get a very short *narratio* in sections 5 and 6. A detailed statement of facts is not necessary because Cicero is speaking third, and to repeat material that Crassus and Pompey had doubtless gone over (particularly Pompey, under whom Balbus had served), would be boring and hence counterproductive.[14] Classen observes that

Cicero never provides a *narratio* when his speech is one of several defense speeches.[15] Since Cicero normally spoke last,[16] this makes sense.

Cicero ends his brief *narratio* with: "Donatus igitur est ob eas causas a Cn. Pompeio civitate" (6) ("He was granted citizenship, then, by Gnaeus Pompeius for these reasons"). This sentence provides a brief transition to a discussion of the accusations (6–7), which Cicero must present now, in order to justify his *ethica digressio* (9–16) about Pompey.[17] As mentioned in chapter one, Cicero defends his *digressio* on Pompey with the statement that the prosecutor had attacked the general, and Pompey had asked Cicero to defend him.[18] This statement justifies the digression and gives it an air both of legitimacy and of a *refutatio*, since ostensibly Cicero is answering the prosecutor's doubts about the legality of Pompey's action. In fact the *digressio* takes the place of a longer *narratio* and it functions as a *praemunitio*. Cicero employs *praemunitiones* in other speeches, such as the *Pro Cluentio*, *Pro Caelio*, and *Pro Milone*.[19] In all of these speeches diminishment of *invidia* plays a large role in the defense strategy, and in each speech a major part of the speech is devoted to a *praemunitio*. Its purpose is to win the goodwill of the jurors, and this purpose demonstrates why the digression must be placed here and not between the *argumentatio* and the *peroratio,* which is the normal place for the *ethica digressio*.[20] That would not work at all, since Cicero uses the *digressio* to influence the jurors before they hear the true legal points of the case. Between the *ethica digressio* and the *argumentatio*, Cicero addresses the prejudice felt for Balbus (18–19). This is placed after the *digressio* for obvious reasons, and before the *argumentatio* in order that any sympathy obtained might influence the jurors' impressions of the legal issues. The *argumentatio* begins in section 19 and runs until 59. It is interrupted in sections 46–49 by the *ethica digressio* of Marius. This second digression is placed here instead of at the end of the *argumentatio* in order to build the jury's emotions, and to prepare for the argument developed from 50–55: that all of the Roman world sided with Pompey's interpretation of the law. The digression would not have worked as well if Cicero had placed it in the normal position at the end of the *argumentatio*, because reference to Marius would be anticlimactic[21] after Cicero's emotive declarations regarding other generals, juries, the senate, and the Roman people. The following sections, 56 to 59, should be considered a *refutatio* and thus part of the *argumentatio* because in them Cicero refutes charges the prosecutor made against Balbus. These refutations are placed right at the end of the *argumentatio*, after the jury has been won over by other arguments. A *peroratio* (59–65), containing the usual appeals to pity, concludes the speech.

The structure of the speech, therefore is not a textbook replica of the *dispositio* advocated by rhetorical handbooks, but rather a functional adaptation of arrangement to the situation, including both the circumstances and issues surrounding the case, and the fact that Cicero speaks as third and last defense advocate. The use of two *ethicae digressiones* is the most striking feature in the overall structure of the speech.

Before embarking on my analysis of the *dispositio* of groups of arguments, I shall present a brief recapitulation of the *inventio* in the *Pro Balbo*. We have seen that Cicero's major arguments in ethos are the substitution of Pompey for Balbus as a defendant, the reliance upon the *auctoritas* of Pompey to rebut the notion that he could have made an illegal enfranchisement, the attempt to diminish the *invidia* against Balbus, in particular by the close association of Balbus with more powerful figures such as Pompey, Caesar, and Cicero, and indirectly with the good of the republic, and finally the depiction of the prosecutor as an ignorant and incompetent person. In pathos Cicero rouses strong emotions of admiration for Pompey and Marius, and binds these feelings with patriotism and chauvinism; at the same time he rouses Roman fears about the protection of the republic, indignation against the prosecutor, and feelings of pity for Caesar and Balbus. Cicero's main proofs in logos are that the *lex Cornelia Gellia* permitted Pompey to enfranchise Balbus, that the Gaditans did not have the legal right to consent to the enfranchisement, and even if they did have such a right, their behavior as shown by their appointment of Balbus as guest friend indicated that they had in fact given a kind of consent. In addition Cicero presents several precedents (unfortunately none completely analogous) for enfranchisement.

Perhaps most interesting in a study of *dispositio* is how Cicero develops and arranges groups of arguments. In the *Pro Balbo* Cicero places his strongest argument of the entire speech first: his ethical argument regarding Pompey. Here he is following his own advice, as presented in *De Oratore* (2.313):[22]

> res enim hoc postulat, ut eorum exspectationi, qui audiunt, quam celerrime succurratur; cui si initio satis factum non sit; multo plus sit in reliqua causa laborandum; male enim se res habet, quae non statim, ut dici coepta est, melior fieri videtur. Ergo ut in oratore optimus quisque, sic in oratione firmissimum quodque sit primum, dum illud tamen in utroque teneatur, ut ea, quae excellent serventur etiam ad perorandum;si quae erunt mediocria, nam vitiosis nusquam esse oportet locum, in mediam turbam atque in gregem coniciantur.

> for a case demands this, that the expectations of those who are listening be satisfied as quickly as possible; if at the beginning the expectations are not satisfied, the rest of the case will require much more work; for a case goes badly which, as soon as it begins to be spoken, does not immediately appear to become better. Therefore just as in regard to the orator, the best should go first each time, so in regard to a speech, whatever argument is the strongest should go first, provided that nevertheless that precept is held in each, that those arguments which excel should be kept for the peroration; if there are unremarkable arguments, (for there

must be no place for bad ones), they should be placed together in the middle of the crowd and the flock.

Cicero does not wait until the *argumentatio*, but begins persuading the audience at the very outset of the *exordium*. This is similar to a tactic described by McClintock, in which the orator begins to offer proofs in the *narratio*, and thus catches the audience unawares.[23] The jury does not expect to hear arguments until the *argumentatio*,[24] at which point they will be on their guard to weigh and judge contentions put forth by the orator. By sliding into his argument in the *exordium*,[25] especially by presenting statements he knows the jury already agrees with, and then guiding them from there to his own position, the orator is able to persuade the audience without their realizing they are being persuaded.[26]

The "ethical" argument employed by Cicero regarding Pompey actually consists of two arguments, arranged in A B A fashion. The first argument Cicero presents openly: that someone as experienced as Pompey could not possibly have made a legal mistake in enfranchising Balbus. The second argument is not one he can present openly, so he places it within the context of an *exemplum* of Quintus Metellus (11). This argument contends that the jurors should not question the legality of anything done by a man of great prestige. Cicero links this contention to the present case by asking whether they should examine everything Pompey has done in the minutest detail. He follows this with another *exemplum* along the same lines, that of the venerable Greek man at whose trial the jurors objected to his having to take an oath (12). Immediately afterwards he places a pathetic appeal (13), and returns to the idea that it was impossible for Pompey to do anything illegal (13–16). The sandwiched "B" argument is not referred to again in the speech. By touching on the idea that the jurors should not pay too close attention to legal details and then retreating back to his first argument, Cicero plants a seed in the jurors' minds, but does not dwell on it.[27] The placement of this argument before the tackling of the actual legal arguments is meant to influence how the jury listen to those arguments.[28]

Cicero moves from the *ethica digressio* on Pompey to his address on *invidia*. Because *invidia* is such a vital element of the case, the arrangement of Cicero's arguments concerning it is important. *Invidia* played an important role in another Ciceronian speech, the *Pro Cluentio*.[29] In it Cicero tackles the issue of *invidia* head-on, but his reasons for doing so in that speech are different from his reasons in the *Pro Balbo*. In the *Pro Cluentio* he mentions *invidia* in the first paragraph of the *exordium*. Cicero deals with the *invidia* there because it was one of the major arguments of the prosecution,[30] and he must rebut it before the audience will accept his arguments on the actual charges. In the *Pro Balbo* *invidia* was also one of the strongest prosecution arguments, but the differences in the feelings of *invidia* against the two men dictated different strategies.[31] In Cluentius' case, there was a feeling of prejudice against the defendant because it was believed he had bribed judges in an earlier trial; that is, because he had done something wrong. By arguing that Cluentius had not done anything wrong, and that it was in fact Oppianicus who had bribed the jurors, Cicero is able to assuage the ill will against Cluentius and redirect it towards Oppianicus. The feelings against Balbus, however, had nothing to do with any wrongdoing on Balbus' part; instead they consisted of jealousy, and therefore were stronger and more visceral.[32] Balbus was highly successful; he had risen to a high position of power through his association with Caesar, and had accumulated a great deal of wealth. This was enough to encourage envy in others; but in Balbus' case the jealousy was intensified because he was a foreigner. Roman prejudice against foreigners can be seen in other speeches, where Cicero plays on these feelings.[33] Cicero could not begin the speech by talking about a man the jurors disliked to such a degree. And when Cicero does mention the *invidia*, he keeps his address short and moves immediately afterwards to Pompey, producing a sandwich effect. In the *Pro Balbo*, the intensity and the nature of the *invidia*, therefore, dictate the placement of the address against it and the internal arrangement of the address itself.

As in the *Pro Cluentio*, the passage on *invidia* in the *Pro Balbo* is placed before the legal arguments. Cicero does not approach the *invidia* issue directly. Instead he slides into the address by emphasizing that he must mention something which pertained to all of the jury in common: "de communi condicione *omnium nostrum*" (18) ("a circumstance which affects one and all of us"). This statement raises a moment of anticipation and curiosity until Cicero satisfies it with "deprecandae malivolentiae causa" (18) ("in order to ward off a cause of spitefulness"). The linkage of the issue of *invidia* with the jury is stressed in the following sentence: "Si quo quisque loco nostrum est, iudices, natus, aut si, in qua fortuna est nascendi initio constitutus, hunc vitae statum usque ad senectutem obtinere debet . . ." (18) ("If each one of us, judges, is bound to keep right up to old age that position in life in which he was born, or whatever position fortune established for him at birth . . .") With the clause that begins "if all whom good luck, or their own work, or industry have helped or made illustrious were to be punished for it" (18), Cicero is equating Balbus with hard-working, industrious men. This argument is arranged in general terms, so that the jury will agree with it before Balbus' name is even mentioned. After Cicero does mention Balbus' name, he reminds the jury that in many cases virtue, talent, and human feeling have been rewarded. This contention equates Balbus with these virtues, and assumes his present position is a direct result of these qualities.[34] It also makes his high position seem less of an anomaly, since many others have been rewarded for such virtues. This entire argument is phrased in terms of qualities of character rather than personality. Cicero does not ask the jury not to hate Balbus. Rather, he asks them not to hate talent, industry, human feelings, and courage (19), a request they are more likely to grant. After this reminder, Cicero expresses his fear regarding the jealousy of the jurors. This admission of fear is more effective here near the conclusion of the plea. Cicero employs his address on *invidia* to present Balbus' good qualities. By presenting these qualities as a response to the prosecutor's appeal to *invidia*, they appear as a defense rather than a boast, and as such would be less likely to alienate the jury. The address concludes with the request that if the jury decides Balbus' case is solid, that they should regard Balbus' good qualities as a help rather than a hindrance to the case. In this passage Cicero focuses on the good qualities of Balbus and makes no attempt to refute the negative qualities the prosecutor has stressed in his speech. He saves the refutation until after he feels the audience has been persuaded (59).

The attack on *invidia* is followed by the legal arguments. Cicero places a strong argument first by mentioning the *lex Cornelia Gellia* under which Pompey enfranchised Balbus. As mentioned in chapter three,[35] it is highly unlikely that the prosecutor suggested that Pompey lacked the legal authority to enfranchise Balbus. Cicero states that the prosecutor himself acknowledged this point (6). By placing an uncontested contention as the first argument, Cicero wins the confidence of the jury and begins his legal defense on solid ground.[36] He moves from this point to the "consent" argument. This was the prosecutor's strongest legal point and Cicero must refute it. Cicero rephrases the prosecutor's contention (19), then ridicules the prosecutor (20),[37] before moving to refute his argument. He begins this refutation with an explanation of cases in which "consent" could be given by allied states, and then presents three examples (the *lex Furia*, the *lex Voconia*, and the *lex Julia*). Cicero distinguishes the *lex Julia* from the *lex Cornelia Gellia*, thereby destroying this rather weak argument by the prosecutor. Cicero does not bring up the point that the *lex Julia* could not validly be used as an example for Gades giving consent because it did not apply to *foederati* but to Latins.[38] This enables him to employ the same confusion between Latin and *foederatus* and utilize the same law against the prosecutor. Cicero completes this argument with the conclusion that Rome was allowed to make laws which concerned her own *res publica*.

This leads to an argument based on emotion[39] (fear) in which Cicero asks what would happen if Rome was not able to recruit allies in times of need (22–24). In the middle of this argument, Cicero makes another insulting comment about the prosecution. If Cicero was successful in rousing the jury's fears in 22–24, and the latter accepted Cicero's arguments, then they would be more susceptible to the insults directed at the opposition in 25. The jury's acceptance of the insults and belief in the prosecutor's ignorance would then affect their

reaction to Cicero's remaining legal arguments. The less confidence the jury had
in the prosecutor, the less confidence they would have in his arguments. The
result would be more confidence in Cicero. One of Cicero's major tactics in the
Pro Balbo is to destroy the credibility of the prosecutor, and the *dispositio* helps
him accomplish this. Insults are liberally sprinkled throughout the legal arguments. The insults also provide another function: their entertainment value
helps divert from the possible tedium of long, dry legal arguments. The orator
must be very careful not to bore the jury with lengthy legalistic arguments (especially about a case the jury might think not very important). In *Brutus* (200),
Cicero presents an amusing but instructive portrait of a bored jury: "Videt osc-
itantem iudicem, loquentem cum altero, non numquam etiam circulantem,
mittentem ad horas, quaesitorem ut dimittat rogantem" ("He sees a juror yawn-
ing, speaking to another, sometimes even wandering around, sending someone
to find out the time, asking the president of the court for an adjournment."").
Cicero overcomes this potential problem with the careful arrangement of his
arguments.

After the insult in 25, Cicero returns to his legal argument, stressing the
danger to Rome if the prosecutor's case were accepted. He suggests in 26 that
there was no difference between whether *foederati* were able to forbid their citizens to fight on Rome's behalf or whether Rome's enfranchisements were
invalid. This analogy is a weak argument which gains strength from the emotional one placed before it. If Cicero managed to rouse the jury's ire with his
arguments in 22–24, then the jurors would be more willing to accept the analogy without close scrutiny.

The transition to the next argument is provided with another insult of the
prosecutor. The prosecutor is accused of ignorance for suggesting that *liberi*
could give consent as well as *foederati*. Instead of addressing this issue, Cicero
discusses change of citizenship laws for Romans. As mentioned in chapter
three,[40] Cicero's argument here is entirely irrelevant to the present case. Cicero
attempts to make it appear relevant by bringing Gades into the argument, with
the analogy of a Roman citizen seeking Gaditan citizenship. Cicero's conclusion:
". . . rem universam, nullam esse gentem ex omni regione terrarum neque tam
dissidentem a populo Romano odio quodam atque discidio neque tam fide
benivolentiaque coniunctam, ex qua nobis interdictum sit ne quem adsciscere
civem aut civitate donare possimus" (30) ("that it is a universal principle, that
there is no people from any region of the earth, whether so at variance with the
Roman people because of some hatred and discord, or united by such trust and
good-will, from whom it is prohibited for us to be able to admit or enfranchise
one of its citizens"), implies he has rebutted the argument that free people have
the right to "give consent." The conclusion, however, does not follow from the
"proofs." The argument is weak, but concludes with a rousing appeal to patri-

otism, which is geared to distract the audience from the irrelevance of the legal argument.

The following sections (32–37) contain the heart of Cicero's legal arguments. They are placed in the middle of the speech, after Cicero has alleviated some of the hostility towards Balbus and aroused some contempt towards the prosecutor. Although these are some of the strongest arguments in the whole speech, Cicero did not place them first for the reasons stated above, and also because a gradual increase is more effective. As Quintilian states,[41] when there are a series of arguments about a single point, it is far more effective to have them build to a crescendo.[42] Had Cicero started with this argument, the others, such as those about Rome's citizenship laws, would have been anticlimactic.

The first contention in this set of sections is strong. Cicero does not dispute the prosecutor's statement that certain tribes have a saving clause in their treaties with Rome requiring each tribe to "give consent" before a tribesman may be granted Roman citizenship (32).[43] He uses the prosecution's argument against it, by stating that since there was no saving clause in Gades' treaty, the Gaditans did not have to "give consent" (32). The second argument, that the *lex Cornelia Gellia* could override such a saving clause (32), is perhaps weaker.[44] It is followed by an insult to the prosecutor deprecating his knowledge of Gaditan and Roman jurisprudence (32).

The third argument, that the Gaditan treaty is not sacrosanct because it has not been passed by the people or the plebs (33), is the strongest argument in the entire speech. This argument undercuts all of the prosecution's arguments except the one that *liberi* could "give consent." The fourth argument, which states that the treaty is not sacrosanct because of any invocation of the gods or a clause of consecration (33), is somewhat anticlimactic. The third argument is linked to the fourth and repeated more clearly and concisely after the latter: "de iis, cum populus Romanus nihil umquam iusserit, quicquam audes dicere sacrosanctum fuisse" (33) ("do you dare to say something was sacrosanct regarding those people, when the Roman people never ordered anything [regarding them]").

The argument that the treaty is invalid since it was not passed by the Roman people requires a "clarifying" passage immediately afterwards to explain that it is not really invalid. In this instance Cicero wants to have his cake and eat it too. On the one hand, he wants the jury to realize that the treaty is not truly legally binding. But at the same time he doesn't want the jury (or Rome) to disregard it completely, since that would cause major bilateral problems with Gades and would alienate the Gaditans who were present to support Balbus.

Careful *dispositio* enables Cicero to get around this logical inconsistency. He does so by presenting an emotional argument detailing all the assistance that Gades had given Rome during the Punic Wars, at a time of dire necessity to Rome, and when the rest of Spain was on Carthage's side. This argument is followed by a moral one, which builds the emotional one: since Gades had assisted Rome at a time of such great need, Rome had a moral commitment to respect the treaty even though the legal obligation was not there (34). In other words, *mores* could govern Roman external relations where *leges* did not. This passage is followed by one stressing that the treaty with Gades is not legally binding. It is followed by a second reassurance to the jurors and the Gaditans: "Neque ideo est Gaditanorum causa deterior" (35) ("Nor is the case of the Gaditans weaker on that account") and an admonition to the prosecutor: "Sed isti diputationi hic certe nihil est loci" (35) ("But there is certainly no room for that debate here"). Here Cicero wants to have his cake and eat it too. By this point he has argued convincingly that the treaty is actually invalid, but that the Romans ought to recognize it for moral reasons, even though the treaty is not legally binding.[45]

Because this is a delicate matter, Cicero now moves to the second part of the *in utramque partem* argument: that even if the treaty had been voted upon by the Roman people and was therefore legally binding, there was no necessity for the Gaditans to give consent. Again the arrangement of the arguments comes to Cicero's assistance. Because the jurors already believe that the treaty is not legitimate, it is easier for them to accept this argument. This argument is supported with strong proofs: the phrase "maiestatem populi Romani comiter conservanto" (35) ("let them willingly preserve the sovereign power of the Roman people.") indicates that the treaty was *iniquum*. The second argument, regarding the meaning of the phrase *comiter*, is equally strong, and naturally leads to Cicero's hypothetical argument about how the interpretation of the treaty would not affect Cicero's case even if the prosecutor's definition of the word *communiter* were correct.

The summary of legal arguments presented in the following section (38), is placed in the middle of the *argumentatio* rather than at the end, where one might expect it. This summary is more useful at this point in the speech than it would be at the end. It repeats and briefly sums up the major arguments concerning Gades' inability to give consent, before Cicero goes on to present the second part of the *in utramque partem* argument: that Gades in fact had given a kind of consent.

This latter argument is made all the more potent by the juxtaposition with section 38, where Cicero responds to a hypothetical Gaditan demand for the return of Balbus. Cicero states he does not have to argue against the Gaditans, since they do not want the return of Balbus. Cicero declares this point bluntly: "Nunc vero quid ego contra Gaditanos loquar, cum id quod defendo, voluntate eorum, auctoritate, legatione ipsa comprobetur?" (39) ("Now indeed, why should I speak against the Gaditans, when the very thesis which I am maintaining is proved by their goodwill, their prestige, by their legation itself?"). Rather than elaborating on this argument at once, Cicero sets it aside for the moment, and instead intersperses another theme: the tremendous loyalty the Gaditans had demonstrated to Rome during times of war.[46]

The theme of Gaditan loyalty, although legally irrelevant, is an important "ethical" and emotional argument.[47] The argument appears three times (25, 34, 39) in the *Pro Balbo*, each time interwoven with legal arguments, and is gradually intensified and elaborated upon.[48] The description in 39 is the culmination: their loyalty was so intense that it caused the Gaditans to abandon the Carthaginians, who Cicero claims were the founders of the city. The Gaditans also shut out the Carthaginians from their city, and fought them on sea and land. Cicero elaborates copiously on the Gaditans, spending far more time on praising them and describing how they helped Rome, than he does on the initial argument he wants to prove. This description is interrupted at the beginning of section 40 with a calling upon some of the most illustrious (but dead) Roman commanders as witnesses for the defense. The idea is that all these men: the Scipiones, the Bruti, the Horatii, the Cassii, and the Metelli would be on the Gaditans', and hence Balbus', side, if they were alive. Then Cicero returns to the praise of the Gaditans, this time for actions they have undertaken at the present time.

The praise is designed to heighten the jury's approval to such a point that they accept Cicero's rather weak legal argument at the beginning of section 39. The implicit argument in Cicero's praise of the Gaditans is that Rome owes a debt to Gades for its loyalty, and after all Gades had done for Rome, the least the jury could do is acquiesce in this one minor issue, which after all the Gaditans themselves want, and acknowledge that the enfranchisement was legal. Cicero never explicitly voices this argument. Instead, after describing in vivid detail all that Gades had done for Rome, Cicero compares the Gaditans with the citizens of Africa, Sardinia, and Spain, who are able to be enfranchised, although they are tributary.

Cicero then returns to the contention he introduced at the beginning of 39: that the Gaditans had in fact given consent. It is only at this point, after he has roused strong feelings of approval for the Gaditans with the two emotional themes discussed above, that Cicero elaborates on the consent argument. He begins with the strongest argument: that the Gaditans have made Balbus their guest-friend at Rome. Cicero then states he will present the *tessera hospitalis*: tangible proof that Balbus was their guest-friend; he offers the testimony of highly placed envoys, and informs the jury that the Gaditan senate had sided with Balbus in the present dispute.

Having presented the evidence, Cicero attempts to persuade the jury that this evidence indicates the approval of the Gaditans (42). He suggests, through the use of rhetorical questions, that the Gaditans could not have given more formal consent than by making him their guest-friend, than by fining the prosecutor, and by sending envoys to testify. The actual answer to the rhetorical question, is yes, the Gaditans could have given more formal consent by actually passing a decree in the Gaditan senate, if indeed they believed they had the right to give consent.

Despite the weakness of this argument, or perhaps because of it, Cicero immediately launches a personal attack on anyone who disputes it: "Etenim quis est tam demens quin sentiat ius hoc Gaditanis esse retinendum . . ." (43) ("And indeed who is so demented that he does not perceive that this right must be retained by the Gaditans?"). Cicero then skillfully moves the argument towards Balbus, and the benefits he is able to confer on Gades, and then to Caesar, and the benefits he has offered them. By creating a feeling of benevolence towards the Gaditans first, and introducing Balbus by way of his aid for Gades, Balbus is seen in a favorable light, and benefits from the jury's goodwill towards the Gaditans. This group of sections would not have worked nearly so well if Cicero had begun with Balbus' good works towards Gades. Section 43 concludes with the linkage of Balbus to the Gaditans: "Itaque et adsunt principes civitatis et defendunt amore ut suum civem, testimonio ut nostrum, officio ut ex nobilissimo civi sanctissimum hospitem, studio ut diligentissimum defensorem commodorum suorum" (43) ("Therefore the leaders of that state both are present and defend him by their affection as their own citizen, by their testimony as one of ours, by their duty as one who from being a very noble citizen is now a most venerable guest-friend, and by their zeal, as a most diligent defender of their own interests"). Having associated the two, Cicero moves back to the Gaditans, stressing their loyalty to Rome, and assuring the court the question in issue has never been at doubt. That statement, repeated several times throughout the speech, concludes this group of sections on a strong note.[49]

Cicero now turns from the consent issue to precedents. In section 45, the idea of precedents is introduced in a round-about fashion, with a rhetorical question: "Quos igitur prudentissimos interpretes foederum . . ." (" Who, therefore, [do we think are] the most skilled interpreters of treaties . . ."). Cicero answers the question with: "eos profecto, qui iam imperia ac bella gesserunt" ("Those, of course, who have already held command and waged wars"). He then offers two analogies, one concerning himself, and sums up with the conclusion that commanders are better interpreters of treaties than jurists. The arrangement of the section is straightforward and acquires the appearance of rationality from the *dispositio*, although the analogies themselves are not truly analogous and the conclusion is dubious.

This discussion of commanders in general serves as an introduction to Gaius Marius, who is the first precedent (46–49). It also helps that Marius was long dead. This passage is an excellent example of Cicero's technique of interweaving rational, ethical, and pathetic arguments. He begins with an ethical argument, stressing Marius' important qualities of character: "graviorem, constantiorem, praestantiorem virtute, prudentia, religione" (46) ("more important, more steadfast, more outstanding in terms of courage, of prudence, of piety"). Immediately afterwards Cicero moves to rational arguments, informing the audience about Marius' actions in enfranchising various people. He concludes the rational argument, by suggesting through a rhetorical question, that Balbus' enfranchisement was every bit as legitimate as those brought about by Marius (46). This is followed by a long, vivid passage about Marius which is designed to rouse strong emotions in the audience (47). This passage emphasizes Marius' experience, and knowledge of treaties and the laws of war, but with language that arouses emotion. As Cicero describes the trial of Matrinius of Spoletium, the argument is rational. In 49 Cicero concludes "Nihil habet similitudinis ista accusatio . . ." ("that indictment has no resemblance [to this one]") and then returns to a pathetic argument, with a rousing description of Marius, and an exhortation to the jury to let him have the same power now.

Ostensibly, the purpose of this *digressio* is the analogy between Marius's legitimate ability to enfranchise Matrinius and Pompey's legitimate ability to enfranchise Balbus. More precisely Cicero is interested in drawing a parallel between the prestige of Marius, which actually won him the case, and that of Pompey. He wants to suggest to the jury that it should be won over by Pompey's *auctoritas*, just as the jury at Matrinius' trial was won over by Marius'*auctoritas*. By discussing Marius, Cicero is able to return to the *auctoritas* theme, which he spent so much time on at the beginning of the speech. By framing the theme around Marius Cicero intensifies the feelings of the audience and also creates variety.

One could ask why Cicero placed this passage on Marius here, and not with the material on Pompey before section 19 and the consent arguments. The *digressio* on Marius is far more effective here after the main legal arguments. It provides a change after the long and dry legal arguments of sections 19 to 44. It is suitable for the latter part of the *argumentatio* because the subject matter of Marius can rouse the emotions of the audience more readily than the consent arguments, something which is important as the orator moves towards the *peroratio*.[50] This placement also enables Cicero to present the *auctoritas* ideas about Pompey at the beginning, move away from them and deal with other issues at the commencement of the *argumentatio*, and then return to them (in the guise of Marius, who for Cicero represents a hallowed legend).[51] This has given the audience time to absorb the ideas, and then come back to them.

Cicero manages to phrase and arrange this argument in such a way that it appears to be a new one, based on precedent. Actually, it is the same argument which he presented at the outset of the speech. Cicero begins with his most effective *exemplum*, Gaius Marius (45–49), then goes on to add six more examples

(50): Gnaeus Pompeius Strabo, Gaius Marius (again), Publius Crassus, Lucius Sulla, Quintus Metellus Pius, and Marcus Crassus. The first, fourth and last of these are linked directly to Pompey: the first, Gnaeus Pompeius Strabo is his father; Pompeius Magnus was Sulla's *protégé*; in fact Plutarch states it was Sulla who named him "Magnus"; the final *exemplum*, Marcus Crassus, was a close associate of Pompey and co-defender of Cornelius Balbus.[52] This citation of precedents is a rational argument, but it is buttressed by ethos. Pompeius Strabo is characterized by "rebus Italico bello maximis gestis" ("having undertaken the greatest military exploits in the Italian war"), Quintus Metellus Pius as "vir sanctissimus et summa religione ac modestia" ("a most venerable man of the greatest piety and moderation"), and Marcus Crassus as "homo . . . gravitate et prudentia praestans" ("a man outstanding in dignity and practical judgment"). The praiseworthy qualities of character attributed to these men make them more worthy of credibility as precedents.

As Cicero links Pompey Magnus to these precedents, he repeats the five names, plus Marius' for effect: "Hic tu Cn. Pompei beneficium vel potius iudicium et factum infirmare conaris, qui fecit quod C. Marium fecisse audierat, fecit quod P. Crassum, quod L. Sullam, quod Q. Metellum, quod M. Crassum, quod denique domesticum auctorem patrem suum facere viderat?" (51) ("Here you are attempting to invalidate the benefaction or rather the judgment and act of Gnaeus Pompeius, who did what he had heard Gaius Marius had done, he did what Publius Crassus, what Lucius Sulla, what Quintus Metellus, what Marcus Crassus, and finally what he had seen an authority in his own household, his own father, doing"). The arrangement of these names in this second sentence is not fortuitous. Pompey Strabo is placed in the emphatic final position (changed from first in the previous section), the only person elaborated upon in this reiteration of generals. He is not identified by name, but by his relationship to his son. After these six, Pompey becomes an *exemplum* himself, as Cicero lists other, unchallenged enfranchisements Pompey had made: "Neque vero id in uno Cornelio fecit; nam et Gaditanum Hasdrubalem ex bello illo Africano et Mamertinos Ovios et quosdam Uticensis et Saguntinos Fabios civitate donavit" (51) ("Nor indeed did he do that with reference to Cornelius alone; for he enfranchised both Hasdrubal of Gades after that African war and the Ovians, the descendants of the Mamertines, and some Fabii of Utica and Saguntum").

After this list of legal precedents, Cicero reintroduces the argument based on pathos that he has been building since 22: that those who face danger on behalf of Rome deserve to be enfranchised. This strongly emotional argument gains resonance each time it is repeated, and it also gains strength from the preceding enumeration of eminent precedents.[53] Cicero strengthens this argument by quoting Ennius, at the time Rome's most revered epic poet, on Hannibal.

Here both Ennius and Hannibal himself, Rome's worst enemy and the man who invaded Italy, become examples of how Rome should treat courageous and outstanding foreigners. Ennius was a foreigner who received Roman citizenship; Hannibal an excellent general who considered men who fought on his side fellow citizens: "Hostem qui feriet, erit, inquit [Hannibal], mihi Karthaginiensis, quisquis erit" (51) ("'The man who strikes the enemy will be a Carthaginian to me, whoever he may be,' he said"). Hannibal, as well as providing a historical precedent, carries various emotional connotations, which Cicero has been working on throughout the speech. His name reminds the audience of a time when Rome was in grave danger and in great need of courageous allies; his name in fact becomes a confirmation of the necessity of enfranchising allies. At the same time, in the statement given him by Ennius, by his actions towards his own troops, he shows the Romans how they should behave towards brave allies. Sections 51 and 52 demonstrate the dexterity with which Cicero can interweave ethical, logical and emotional arguments.

The transition to the following group of arguments consists of a summing up of the qualities of the generals listed in 45–51. They are all "imperator[es] summ[i] et sapientissim[i] homin[es], clarissim[i] vir[es]" who have demonstrated their "interpretationem iuris ac foederum" (52). Such a description is an appeal to *auctoritas*. Then Cicero turns from specific individuals (certain illustrious military commanders) to whole classes of people: jurors, the entire Roman people, and the Senate. This is a reversal of Cicero's normal arrangement of arguments. In this case, however, it is far more effective, since by moving from specific to general Cicero seems gradually to encompass all Rome, and bring it over to his side. The arguments themselves are not very strong, as noted in the preceding chapter. What gives them strength is their numbers.

The rebuttal of the prosecutor's accusations against Balbus' personal life (56–59) is placed right before the *peroratio* (59–65). One might have expected this *refutatio* earlier, before the *digressio* on Marius. Cicero's arrangement, however, allows him to build up goodwill and emotion among the jurors with the "pathetic" and "ethical" arguments from 45–49. This puts the jurors in a better frame of mind to accept the rebuttal arguments on Balbus' character. As Cicero points out in *De Oratore* 2.178: "Nihil est enim in dicendo, Catule, maius, quam ut faveat oratori is, qui audiet, utque ipse sic moveatur, ut impetu quodam animi et perturbatione, magis quam iudicio aut consilio regatur" ("Now nothing in oratory, Catulus, is more important than to win for the orator the favor of his hearer, and to have the latter so affected as to be swayed by something resembling a mental impulse or emotion, rather than by judgment or deliberation"). This is the tactic Cicero employs in both places in the *Pro Balbo* where he tackles the prejudice against Balbus.[54] By placing arguments about Balbus directly after emotional and pathetic arguments that have influenced the jury favorably, Cicero obtains a more favorable hearing for his client.

Cicero arranges the rebuttal material in such a way as to provide a smooth transition to the *peroratio*. The defense of Balbus' lifestyle leads to the passage about Balbus' help to Cicero's family during his exile (58), which raises the emotional tenor of the passage, and allows Cicero to expand on this theme (59), before offering a defense of his own behavior in accepting the role of advocate for Balbus (60–62). Before he concludes his *apologia* for defending Balbus, Cicero begins to interweave arguments about the senate's honoring of Caesar, which provides the groundwork for the appeal to *miseratio* in 64. Mention of Caesar leads to a reminder of Balbus' close association to the general, and then to an appeal for pity for Caesar (rather than for the defendant, Balbus). The associations work cleverly: first Caesar is linked to the senate and Romans in general, with the reminder of their approval (the thanksgiving of an unprecedented number of days), and then he is linked to Balbus, thus providing a connection between the Spaniard and the jurors. Cicero then sums up the generals whom he used as precedents in the *argumentatio*, followed by the senate and Romans, and judges in other citizenship cases. His suggestion that the jurors would do better to err with these precedents rather than to be guided by the prosecutor (64) picks up the argument he had made by analogy in the reference to Metellus in 11.[55] In 64, however, Cicero makes the argument outright, since by this point he has no doubt won the jury over to his side. The speech concludes on a high note, with the impression that all the illustrious generals, as well as Pompey, are on trial.

Throughout this speech Cicero relies on the careful arrangements of his argument to effect persuasion. The most prevalent techniques are the interweaving of ethical, pathetic, and rational arguments. This interweaving is seen most effectively in the two digressions, which provide a melding of the three, in particular of emotional and character-based arguments. These intertwining arguments are employed to bring about ready acceptance of rational arguments. "Pathetic" arguments are also often closely used without "ethical" ones in conjunction with rational arguments, especially when the rational argument is weak. Another prevalent tactic is the sprinkling of amusing, biting insults throughout the speech directed at the prosecutor. These lower the prosecutor in the estimation of the jurors and provide a entertaining relief from dry legal arguments. Although generally short, the insults have a cumulative effect through resonance. Resonance is also used to build on the fears of Romans regarding the availability and willingness of allies to serve Rome in times of need, and to impress on the jurors the loyalty of Gades. In general the resonance works through repetition of the argument in question at various points throughout the speech, with increasing elaboration. As a whole, the *dispositio* of the speech is masterly: each argument is carefully arranged and placed in a certain position to effect the most persuasive power possible.

Chapter Five
Elocutio

IN THIS CHAPTER, I AM PRIMARILY CONCERNED WITH THE EFFECT OF STYLE upon rhetoric and persuasion; that is, with how the diction and stylistic techniques Cicero employs maneuver arguments and guide the listeners to accept his propositions. Of particular interest is the association between style and "ethical," "pathetic," and rational argumentation. In *De Oratore* 2. 120, Cicero states that the orator seeks two objectives in a case, the first being what to say, and the second how to say it. Through practice, the orator can achieve the first; it is in the second that the orator demonstrates his divine power and excellence (*oratoris vis illa divina virtusque cernitur*).

The most important element in deciding which style to use is propriety: ". . . semperque in omni parte orationis ut vitae quid deceat est considerandum; quod et in re de qua agitur positum est et in personis et eorum qui dicunt et eorum qui audiunt" (71) ("As always, in every respect with oratory as with life, it is necessary to pay close attention to propriety, and this depends on the matter being prosecuted, and on the character both of those who are speaking and those who listen").[1] Laurand states[2] that both the *Pro Balbo* and the *Pro Tullio*, as speeches dealing with civil matters, are written in the plain style, although the *Pro Balbo*, which addresses issues of public law, is less in the plain style than the *Pro Tullio*.[3] Cicero employed this style for less important matters, and in *Orator* he offers the *Pro Caecina* as an example of a speech written in this style (101).

Like the *Pro Caecina*, the *Pro Balbo* concerns matters which would not at first glance be considered of the highest importance to the state.[4] In the case of Cornelius Balbus, the issue was a citizenship grant to a foreigner.[5] Too elevated a style would be completely inappropriate for such a subject, especially when the defendant was not of Italian stock and intensely disliked.[6] Using a grand style in these circumstances would simply add to the existing feeling that Balbus was overreaching himself.[7]

As Cicero is quick to indicate in *Orator*, however, he employs all three styles in many of his speeches (69, 74, 103).[8] According to the orator, the different parts of the speech demand different styles: the *argumentatio* requires the plain style, for too flowery language would make the audience suspicious that the wool was being pulled over their eyes; the *exordium* requires the medium style, the *peroratio*, where emotions are roused, the grand.[9] A study of the *Pro Balbo* demonstrates that Cicero employs a variety of styles in this speech. As a whole the plain style predominates, but the other two styles are also found. The *exordium*, for example, contains intricate, highly crafted and complex sentences, and the *peroratio* also rises to the medium style. But one also finds a variety of styles within the *argumentatio*. The style here ranges from simple, straightforward passages, to Cicero's ironical legal instruction of the prosecutor, to passages of full-blown eloquence.

Because of the length of the speech, it is impossible to present a study of every sentence. Therefore I have proceeded eclectically. I have chosen to analyze the entire first two sections because of their importance and intricacy. It is here that Cicero makes his first impressions on the audience, and it is vital for him to win them over. His remarkable aptitude with style assists him in making a persuasive case. Because of the interesting variety of style in the *argumentatio*, I have chosen several passages from that part of the speech. Here I demonstrate the differences in style and attempt to determine their purpose. Because I discussed the passage on Pompey in great detail in chapter two, on Pathos, I only include a brief selection in this chapter. It is in the passages on Pompey, as well as the *digressio* on Marius—that is, the parts of the speech dealing with two very important men, that Cicero rises to the grand style. Finally, I analyze a passage from the *peroratio* which is characteristic of that part of the speech as a whole.

The beginning of a speech is very important, since the orator must win the goodwill of the audience. As Laurand notes, the first sentence of a speech may be the best crafted in the whole work: "On n'a qu'a prendre au hasard n'importe quel exorde, on verra que la première phrase est une période, et c'est presque toujours une des plus soignées de tout le discourse, soit pour la regularité du parallelisme rythmique, soit pour le choix des clausules. . . ."[10] As one of his two examples, Laurand chooses the introductory sentence to the *Pro Balbo*.[11] Whether it is the best-crafted sentence in the entire speech is debatable, but it certainly is carefully constructed:

> Si auctoritates patronorum in iudiciis valent, ab amplissimis viris L. Corneli causa defensa est;
> si usus, a peritissimis;
> si ingenia, ab eloquentissimis;
> si studia, ab amicissimis et cum beneficiis cum L. Cornelio, tum maxima familiaritate coniunctis.[12]

> If the prestige of advocates holds weight in judicial trials, then Lucius Cornelius'
> case has been defended by the most distinguished men, if experience holds weight,
> then by the most skilled, if natural ability, then by the most eloquent, if devotion,
> then by very close friends and those associated with Lucius Cornelius by benefits
> and the greatest familiarity.

Cicero begins several of his speeches with conditional sentences.[13] The *Pro Archia* and the *Pro Balbo*, however, are the only ones extant which employ a series of parallel conditional clauses. The introductory sentence to the *Pro Balbo* is not a true periodic sentence, since the meaning is not withheld until the final part of the sentence. The first conditional clause, however, is periodic, since the sense is withheld until the words *defensa est*.[14]

The four clauses are parallel, but they are not perfectly balanced as to number of words or syllables. The use of ellipsis in the second and third clauses shortens these two clauses, reducing them to the most essential elements, and emphasizing these elements. The length of the fourth clause contrasts with the previous ones, and especially with the second and third. The fourth clause begins, as do the second and third, with only the essential ideas expressed and the remainder ellipsed. Indeed in this final conditional clause, Cicero could have stopped after *ab amicissimis* but instead effects a surprise *variatio* by extending the clause. The word *studia* is followed not just by one attribute (*a/ab* plus a single, superlative word), like the other clauses, but by two: a superlative noun with *a/ab* and a long participial phrase which functions substantively: *amicissimis et cum beneficiis cum L. Cornelio, tum maxima familiaritate coniunctis*. The placement of *coniunctis* at the end of the sentence achieves a periodicity for this last condition, just as periodicity was achieved for the first. The deliberate imbalance of the apodosis of this fourth conditional clause prevents the sentence from being too symmetrical, a technique noted by Gotoff in the *Pro Archia*.[15]

The use of anaphora in the repetition of *si* at the beginning of each conditional clause and the homoeoteleuton of *-issimis* at the end of the superlative adjectives characterizing Balbus' defenders stresses Pompey's and Crassus' excellence: ampl*issimis* . . . perit*issimis* . . . eloquent*issimis* . . . amic*issimis*. . . . This is a clear instance of *elocutio* assisting *ethos*. The homoeoteleuton is modified somewhat by *variatio*, with the last terms characterizing the relationship between defenders and Balbus: benef*iciis* and coni*unctis*.

The imbalance in the length of each conditional clause, in particular the brevity of the two middle clauses, creates a straightforward tone, far different from the sonorous, measured tone produced in the series of clauses at the outset of the *Pro Archia*.[16] The length of the fourth conditional clause in the *Pro Balbo*, especially the participial phrase within it, emphasizes that phrase and the *beneficia* and *familiaritas*.

The style of this introductory sentence, however, is not divorced from the rhetoric of the speech. This first sentence introduces some of the major themes: the *auctoritas* and experience (*peritissimis*) of Pompey, and the close friendship between Pompey and Balbus (*amicissimis . . . maxima familiaritate coniunctis*). The *amplificatio* of the theme of friendship, although with *variatio*, doubly stresses the connection between Pompey and Balbus.

In contrast to the lengthy first sentence, with its series of conditional clauses, the second sentence is short, consisting of a rhetorical question which Cicero answers himself:

> Quae sunt igitur meae partes?
> Auctoritatis tantae quantam vos in me esse voluistis,
> usus mediocris,
> ingenium minime voluntati paris.

> What therefore is my role? I have as much influence as you desire me to have, moderate experience, a natural ability in no way equal to my goodwill.

The question is a clever way for Cicero to bring himself into the speech. The technique of posing a question gets the audience mentally involved. Merely listening to someone making statements is a passive undertaking. When a question is asked, the audience obtains the opportunity to take a more (mentally) active role by formulating their own answer, and then feel satisfaction when the answer is mirrored by that of the orator. In this case it also allows them to arrive at an answer more flattering to Cicero than the one he gives them with false modesty.

The lengthy third sentence is paratactic rather than periodic. The sentence is broken down into a series of short phrases, with signposts to anticipate phrases or clauses to follow. *Tantae* anticipates *quantam*, *auctoritas* anticipates the other three qualities Cicero employed to describe the other defense speakers. The first part of this sentence provides an interesting combination of *repetitio* and apparent contrast. The qualities by which Cicero had assessed Crassus and Pompey: *auctoritas*, *usus*, and *ingenii*, are repeated with reference to Cicero, but *studia* is replaced by *voluntas*. This repetition emphasizes the themes.[17] A contrast arises between Cicero's assessment of these qualities in Pompey and Crassus, and himself. Whereas Pompey and Crassus are characterized as *amplissimis*, Cicero is coy about his own *auctoritas*: "Auctoritatis tantae, quantam vos in me esse voluistis" ("As much influence as you desire me to have"). Pompey and Crassus are *peritissimi*, while Cicero claims his *usus* is *mediocris*, and while Pompey and Crassus are *eloquentissimi*, Cicero states his *ingenium* is not at all equal to his *voluntas*. The clauses of the first part of the third sentence are not completely parallel to those of the first sentence, because Cicero compresses the third and fourth qualities into a single clause. This *variatio* prevents the sentence from becoming too predictable.

The following sentence consists of two antithetical clauses which briefly explain why Cicero's *ingenium* is not at all equal to his *voluntas*. A comparison is set up between the debt owed by Balbus to Pompey and Crassus (*hunc debere*) and the debt owed by Cicero (*debeam*) to his client:

> Nam ceteris a quibus est defensus hunc debere plurimum video;
> ego quantum ei debeam, alio loco;

> For I see that this man [Balbus] owes a great deal to those others who defended him; how much I owe to him, I will describe elsewhere.

While the debt is compared, the recipients of the first debt *(ceteris)* are contrasted with the ower (*ego*) of the second, the latter placed first in its clause—even to the point of preceding the subordinating conjunction *quantum*—in order to indicate the contrast.[18] The word order of the *nam* clause more or less reveals the direction of the clause with the word *debere*; full understanding is held back until the final word (*video*). The *ego* clause is periodic, with complete understanding withheld until the final word.

> principio orationis hoc pono,
> me omnibus, qui amici fuerint saluti et dignitati meae,
> si minus referenda gratia satis facere potuerim,
> praedicanda et habenda certe satis esse facturum.

> Here at the beginning of my speech I assert this: to all those who were friends to my welfare and dignity, if I will not have been able to recompense them sufficiently, I will certainly satisfy them by proclaiming and acknowledging my gratitude.

The opening words of the following clause (*principio orationis*) provide an antithesis to the closing words of the previous one (*alio loco*). This antithesis implies a contrast, but with clever use of *praeteritio*, Cicero actually employs this clause to explain a little more about the debt mentioned in the preceding one. *hoc pono* anticipates an infinitive clause, which is introduced by *me. omnibus, qui amici fuerint*. . . informs the audience that Cicero means more than Pompey here, as will become clear later in the speech. *saluti et dignitati meae* is a low-key, elliptical way for Cicero to refer to his exile and recall, by focusing on the two aspects of his existence which had been, in his view, most threatened.[19] The placement of *me omnibus* side by side emphasizes those who stood by Cicero (at least in his own mind) in his time of need. To achieve this effect, Cicero varies the arrangement he used in the first sentence of the speech (*si* placed first followed by the protasis and then apodosis) by placing *me* before the *si* clause instead of after it.[20] *omnibus* proves the unanimity of Cicero's supporters and perhaps suggests their number was large.

The structure of the sentence as a whole is careful and much more effective than if Cicero had placed the *si* clause immediately after *pono*. The placement of the *me omnibus qui* . . . clause before the *si* clause creates far more drama. The placement of the *si* clause in the middle gives the least emphasis on Cicero not having made adequate repayment. By focusing attention on those *amici* who helped him, Cicero stresses the key ideas of friends and the admission of indebtedness to friends. The reference to friends who assisted him also provides a transition to a discussion of Pompey, as does the antithesis between today (*principio orationis*) and yesterday (*hesterno die . . . in dicendo*).

The following sentence deals entirely with Pompey:

Quae fuerit hesterno die Cn. Pompei gravitas in dicendo, iudices,
quae facultas,
quae copia,
non opinione tacita vestrorum animorum,
sed perspicua admiratione
declarari videbatur.

Gnaeus Pompey's dignity in speaking yesterday, judges, his capability, his ability, were seen to be declared not by your silent opinion but by your manifest admira-
:ion.

The use of anaphora in the first three clauses of this sentence (*quae . . . quae . . . quae*) combined with the elipsis in the second and third clauses, is reminiscent of the first sentence (*si auctoritas . . . si usus, a peritissimis, si ingenia, ab eloquentissimis . . .*), and stresses Pompey's qualities:*gravitas . . . facultas . . . copia*. The isocolon in the qualities, each word consisting of three syllables, is further brought out by the isocolon in the second and third clauses. A further parallelism may be seen between this sentence and the introductory sentence: both begin with a fairly lengthy clause, followed by two clauses shortened by ellipsis and thus containing only the essential ideas, followed by an even longer clause explaining the quality/qualities ascribed to Pompey and/or Crassus. The structure of *cum . . . tum* in the first sentence of the speech is mirrored by *non . . . sed* in this one, although the sense of the two sentences provides contrary notions: *cum . . . tum* being inclusive, while *non . . . sed* is contrasting. The contrast is picked up by the antithetical words *tacita* and *perspicua*, which are artistically arranged in chiastic order of noun adjective, adjective noun: *opinione tacita . . . perspicua admiratione*. The contrast is also contained in *opinone* (inside the head) and *admiratione* (facial expression outside the head). This sentence is more or less periodic because of the placement of *admiratione* third from last.

In the following sentence, Cicero continues to focus on Pompey. The praise becomes more specific as Cicero expands on Pompey's military and legal knowledge, as well as his character. The arrangement of the clauses prevents the list of qualities from becoming monotonous.

> Nihil enim umquam audivi quod mihi de iure subtilius dici videretur
> nihil memoria maiore de exemplis,
> nihil peritius de foederibus
> nihil inlustriore auctoritate de bellis,
> nihil de re publica gravius,
> nihil de ipso modestius,
> nihil de causa et crimine ornatius;
> ut mihi iam verum videatur illud esse
> quod non nulli litteris ac studiis doctrinae dediti
> quasi quiddam incredible dicere putabantur,
> ei qui omnis animo virtutes penitus comprehendisset
> omnia quae faceret *recte providere.*[21]

For I have heard nothing, ever, which seemed to me more accurately stated about the law, nothing that demonstrated a greater recollection of precedents, nothing that demonstrated more experience in regard to treaties, nothing that showed a more illustrious authority about war, nothing more weighty about the republic, nothing more modest about oneself, nothing more elegant about a case and a charge, that now the saying, which some men dedicated to literature and philosophical studies believed almost incredible, seems to me to be true: that for the man who contains all the virtues in his soul, everything he does proceeds advantageously.

The above sentence is long and periodic, the most ornate sentence in the speech so far. The intricate artistic arrangement of its components can be compared to that of Vergil or Horace. The anaphora of the word *nihil,* which appears seven times, is emphatic.[22] The use of *nihil* and the comparative is even more emphatic than the superlative alone. In the last three clauses *de* is placed immediately after *nihil,* creating in each case an emphatic spondee with the following syllable.

The clauses beginning with *nihil* are arranged in an alternating order. When the elements *enim umquam audivi quod mihi* and *dici videretur* are ignored, the first clause consists of *nihil, de* and noun, adverb. The third clause consists of the same grammatical elements, this time arranged chiastically: *nihil,* adverb, *de* and noun. The fifth clause is arranged like the first: *nihil, de* and noun, comparative adverb. The sixth and seventh are the same except for minor variations: the sixth has a pronoun (*ipso*) instead of a noun, and the seventh contains two nouns (*de causa et crimine*).

The second clause has somewhat different components; it contains *nihil* and a noun modified by an adjective directly following it, and *de* and another noun. The fourth clause has the same components, with the following arrangement, chiastic to the second clause: *nihil*, adjective (this time preceding the noun it modifies), noun, *de* and noun.

The sentence begins with three disyllabic words followed by *audivi*, which, with its long vowels, slows down the sentence. The series of *nihil* clauses delays the *ut*, which introduces the result clause. The *mihi videatur* in this clause is verbal echo of the *mihi videretur* in the second clause of the sentence. The *iam* stresses *verum*, which is bracketed between *mihi* and *videatur*. A break after *verum* further emphasizes this word. Cicero builds anticipation as to what exactly is *verum* by delaying the answer to the final word of the final clause.[23] In between he builds up to the answer with subordinate clauses. The last clause, placed in the most emphatic position in this lengthy sentence: *omnia, quae faceret recte procedere*, contains a major argument of the speech.

The stylistic care Cicero has put into this sentence is not merely for aesthetic purposes. He has two major goals: as to the first, the *exordium* is supposed to delight the audience and win their goodwill. The complex arrangement, with the chiastic order within the clauses, the interlocking arrangement of the clauses, the combination of repetition and variety are doubtless intended to delight the ear of the audience[24] and make them more receptive to words they are hearing.[25] This effect helps the second purpose of the sentence, which is more directly rhetorical. Here, before the *argumentatio* has even begun, Cicero is, in disguised fashion, introducing the arguments he will later make, persuading the audience in a suggestive manner.[26]

This technique, remarked on by McClintock and Neumeister in regard to other speeches,[27] is effective. The *exordium* was meant to please, and by combining this purpose with that of persuasion Cicero is able to insinuate his arguments into the minds of the jurors.[28] The style of the sentence has a functional purpose: it is meant to wrap the argument in a pleasing covering, and thereby help persuade. It is also worth remarking that Cicero does not use this elaborate style when discussing Balbus, but rather when he talks about Pompey. This is an example of appropriateness of subject. Pompey is worthy of a more elaborate style; Balbus is not. Another point worth making is that in the *argumentatio*, arguments are meant to be made in plain style, lest flowery language rouse the suspicions of the jury. Here in the *exordium* Cicero can get away with dressing up the argument in elaborate style since ostensibly it is not an argument.

We have seen that the style in the *exordium* is sustained on a high level. In the *argumentatio*, in contrast, the style is varied. I have chosen passages from the *argumentatio* which reflect this variety. In my chapter on pathos I discussed in detail the following passage (13) praising Pompey. But since the passage is an important one, it is worthwhile examining it once more with respect to style:

O nomen nostri imperi! O populi Romani excellens dignitas! O Cn. Pompei sic late longeque diffusa laus ut eius gloriae domicilium communis imperi finibus terminetur! O nationes, urbes, populi, reges, tetrarchae, tyranni,—testes Cn. Pompei non solum virtutis in bello sed etiam religionis in pace! Vos denique, mutae regiones, imploro, et sola terrarum ultimarum; vos, maria, portus, insulae, litora! Quae est enim ora, quae sedes, qui locus in quo non exstent huius cum fortitudinis tum vero humanitatis, cum animi tum consili impressa vestigia?

Alas for the glory of our empire! Alas for the excellent worth of the Roman people! Alas for the renown of Pompey, spread so far and wide that his glory is a household word to the very limits of the empire we all share! Alas for the nations, the cities, people, kings, tetrarchs, tyrants—witnesses not only to the courage of Pompey in war, but also of his religious scruples in peace! And you, voiceless tracts, I beseech you, and the soils of the farthest lands; you, seas, harbors, islands, shores! For what shore, what inhabited place, what spot is there which has not been impinted by traces not only of the courage and indeed compassion of this man, but also of his intellect and judgment?

This selection is an excellent example of style assisting pathos. The series of four invocation raises the emotional tenor of the passage. Each of the four is longer than the preceding clause, and the focus moves from empire to the Roman people to Pompey, then linking Pompey with empire, and finally the focus moves to the whole world, which is also linked to Pompey. The diction of the invocations elevates the passage, in particular the references to *excellens dignitas*, *laus*, and *gloria*. The fourth invocation personifies *nationes* and *urbes*, by calling them witnesses, and this personification is strengthened by the address to the various geographical areas of the world in the following sentences. *Vos* is placed in the emphatic first position of the fifth sentence, and is repeated at the beginning of the final clause of this sentence also an emphatic position, stressing the personification. The use of *elaboratio* in *mutae regiones* and *sola terrarum*, and later *maria, portus, insulae, litora* emphasizes the vast geographical extent of Pompey's military successes. The rhetorical question with its series of relative clauses marked by the anaphora of *quae . . . quae . . . qui* also stresses this. The passage concludes with the vivid metaphor *impressa vestigia* which brings to mind the imprint of Pompey's foot as well as his influence throughout these regions. The passage as a whole is characterized by figurative language, no doubt meant to rouse feelings of patriotism and admiration for Pompey.

The following passage (22–23) is less artistically elaborate than both the sentences from the *exordium*, with their intricate word arrangements, and the passage praising Pompey, but nonetheless demonstrates a careful craftsmanship:

Atqui si imperatoribus nostris, si senatui, si populo Romano non licebit propositis praemiis elicere ex civitatibus sociorum atque amicorum fortissimum atque optimum quemque ad subeunda pro salute nostra *pericula*,[29] summa utilitate ac maximo saepe praesidio *periculosis* atque asperis temporibus carendum nobis erit.

Sed, per deos immortales, quae est ista societas, quae amicitia, quod foedus, ut aut nostra civitas careat in suis *periculis* Massiliensi propugnatore, careat Gaditano, careat Saguntino, aut, si quis ex his populis sit exortus qui nostros duces auxilio laboris, commeatus *periculo* suo iuverit, qui cum hoste nostro comminus in acie saepe pugnarit, qui se saepe telis hostium, qui dimicationi capitis, qui morti obiecerit, nulla condicione huius civitatis praemiis adfici possit?

And yet if it will not be permitted for our generals, the senate, the Roman people to draw out, with proposed rewards, the bravest and the best from states of allies and friends, to undergo danger for our safety, we will have to be deprived of the greatest benefit and often the most important protection in dangerous and stormy times.

But, by the immortal gods, what is that association, what is that friendship, what is that treaty, that either our state in its dangers will lack a Massilian champion,[30] will lack a Gaditan champion, will lack a Saguntine champion, or, if anyone has come forward from these peoples who has assisted our military leaders with his hard work, or helped our supply convoys at his own private risk, who has often fought against our enemy in hand to hand combat, who has often opposed the spears of the enemy, who has battled for his life, who has thrown himself in the path of death, can he under no circumstances obtain the reward of Roman citizenship?

This passage is another excellent example of the use of *elocutio* to assist persuasion. Although less so than the *exordium*, the style here is more elaborate than one might expect in the *argumentatio*, and this is no doubt due to the fact that this passage is appealing to the audience's emotions. The first sentence is a conditional in which three protases share the same apodosis. The anaphora of *si* at the beginning of each protasis emphasizes the broadening of the condition. The condition moves from potential inability of generals in the field to that of the *Senatus Populusque Romanus* at home to offer rewards to foreigners.[31] The absurdity of tying the hands of generals, senate, and people is stressed, and *non licebit* is placed early in the sentence to create a paradox, and even an impossibility.

In addition to the rhetorical reasoning for the placement of the finite verb, there is also a grammatical reason: the interposition of *non licebit* separates the datives at the beginning of the protasis (*imperatoribus nostris, senatui, populo Romano*) from the ablative (*propositis praemiis*). In addition, the ablative, which is instrumental, must go with *elicere*, and is set, like an adverb, immediately in front of it. The use of a future more vivid rather than a future less vivid bestows greater immediacy upon the condition; an immediacy that is intensified most forcefully by the use of the passive pariphrastic: *carendum nobis erit*. Here the gerund corresponds to *non licebit* in the protasis.

The idea of danger that such a situation will entail is drummed in by the repetition of the word *pericula/periculosis* and a synonym: *asperis temporibus*.[32] The words of danger are juxtaposed with words of safety: *salute nostra pericula* and *praesidio periculosis*. The brave foreigner is placed in the middle of the sentence, balanced by the Roman generals, senate, and Roman people and the three words of danger at the end of the sentence. The placing of *fortissimum atque optimum quemque* squarely between the two iconically expresses what such a man will be doing: standing as a bulwark between Rome and danger. Cicero also employs elaboration to describe this man and the states from which he comes. In regard to the state, Cicero employs the standard phrase *sociorum atque amicorum*;[33] in regard to the man, *fortissimum* would suffice, but Cicero adds *optimum*, which indicates bravery for the best reasons. The use of two nouns interposed by *atque* creates a balance between *sociorum atque amicorum* and *fortissum atque amicorum*.

The argument which Cicero introduces in this first sentence is a strong emotional one that will resonate throughout the speech. In the second sentence Cicero elaborates upon this argument, using what Neumeister calls "honing."[34] Cicero employs style to create an emotional tone right at the start with his invocation of the gods: *Sed, per deos immortales*. Such a tone is heightened by the employment of short clauses and anaphora: *quae est ista societas, quae amicitia, quod foedus* . . . and *careat . . . careat . . . careat* . . . . The use of the second person *ista* "that [association] of yours" is a contemptuous reference to the prosecutor and his misconceived notions of Roman—Gaditan bilateral relations (*societas, amicitia, foedus*).

Despite the short clauses, however, the sentence is complicated. It ends as a result clause, which answers the question asked in the three first clauses (just as the preceding sentences had three protases and only one apodosis): what kind of *societas, amicitia, foedus* is it that these bad consequences should follow? The *aut* immediately after the *ut* signals an "either . . . or" situation. The first result is that Rome will lack a champion in dangerous times. The second *aut* introduces a more complicated result, since a conditional clause follows: that even if a champion does come forward, he will not be enfranchised. The question that Cicero poses in this sentence is the one he would rather have the jury answer than the question they are meant to:[35] as to whether Pompey legally enfranchised Balbus. The question Cicero poses here is quite different: if a foreigner has helped Rome, is he never to be offered the reward of citizenship for his action? Cicero knows the answer the audience will give to this question.

Diction is just as important to this sentence as it was to the preceding one. *Periculum* is repeated twice; the first time it is used in conjunction with Rome, the second time it refers to the danger the hypothetical foreigner takes on to assist Rome. The use of *nostra civitas* is emphatic; the subject could have been contained in the verb by using *careamus*. *Nostra*, however, is employed for rhetorical and stylistic reasons. The word is employed three times: *nostra civitas . . . nostros duces . . . hoste nostro*. This repetition emphasizes the difference between Romans and others—either potential allies or enemies; it also illustrates a progression from state center to inside the Roman frontier to outside the frontier.

This sentence becomes increasingly more vivid and dramatic as it progresses.[36] It begins with a criticism of an alliance that disallows foreigners from becoming citizens, and moves to mention three allied states—all in the western Mediterranean—by name: Massilia, Gades, and Saguntum. A man is pictured as arising from one of these states: *ex his populis exortus* and helping the Roman generals: *nostros duces auxilio laboris*. The help becomes increasingly detailed as the man is pictured helping Roman supplies: *commeatus periculo suo iuverit*, and fighting Roman enemies: *qui cum hoste nostro comminus acie saepe pugnarit*, and facing the weapons of the enemy, fighting for his life, and risking death: *qui se saepe telis hostium, qui dimicationi capitis, qui morti obiecerit. . . .*[37] The anaphora of *quis/qui*, which appears six times, stresses the man carrying out these risky undertakings.

Each activity described is more dangerous than the preceding one, resulting in an intensification not only of the danger, but of the emotions aroused in the audience as they listen.[38] The final, most dangerous activity, that of facing death, is juxtaposed to the apodosis: *nulla condicione huius civitatis praemiis adfici possit* and makes even the idea of such a refusal seem an outrage. Again, Cicero employs his technique of posing a question because he wants the jury to see the unfairness of the situation (as Cicero has framed it), and to come to the appropriate answer (ostensibly) on their own.[39]

Two themes are interlinked in this passage: the first, which appeals to Roman self-interest, is the danger to Rome if foreigners are forbidden citizenship; and the second, which appeals to a sense of fairness, is that if a man risks his life for Rome, he deserves to be enfranchised.[40] The style in which these ideas are cloaked helps to drive them home, embed them in the audience's mind, and make them feel strongly that what Cicero is saying is right.

In the following passage, also from the *argumentatio* (32–33), the style is quite different from the previous passage. It should be noted that the subject material is also quite different. In the previous passage, Cicero was discussing Rome's security and brave foreigners who risked their lives for Rome. In the following passage Cicero is dealing with dry legal points. Here the style helps bring alive a passage that otherwise might be considered dull.

"Exceptum," inquit, "est foedus, SI QUID SACROSANCTUM EST." Ignosco tibi, si neque Poenorum iura calles (reliqueras enim civitatem tuam) neque nostras potuisti leges inspicere; ipsae enim te a cognitione sua iudicio publico reppulerunt. Quid fuit in rogatione ea quae de Pompeio a Gellio et a Lentulo consulibus lata est, in quo aliquid sacrosanctum exceptum videretur? Primum enim sacrosanctum esse nihil potest nisi quod populus plebesve sanxit; deinde sanctiones sacrandae sunt aut genere ipso aut obtestatione et consecratione legis aut poenae, cum caput eius qui contra fecerit consecratur. Quid habes igitur dicere de Gaditano foedere eius modi utrum capitis consecratione an obtestatione legis sacrosanctum esse confirmas? Nihil omnino umquam de isto foedere ad populum, nihil ad plebem latum esse neque legem neque poenam consecratam esse dico. De quibus etiam si latum esset ne quem civem reciperemus, tamen id esset quod postea populus iussisset ratum, nec quicquam illis verbis SI QUID SACROSANCTUM EST exceptum videretur, de iis, cum populus Romanus nihil umquam iusserit, quicquam audes dicere sacrosanctum fuisse?

[The prosecutor] says, "The treaty has been excepted by the phrase 'if anything is sacrosanct.'" I forgive you, if you neither understand Carthaginian laws (for you had left your city) nor were able to become acquainted with our laws; for these laws themselves, by means of a public trial, held you back from acquiring knowledge of them. What was there in that bill regarding Pompey which was proposed by the consuls Gellius and Lentulus, in which anything sacrosanct [in a treaty] would seem exempt [from the bill]? For first, nothing can be sacrosanct except for what the people or the plebs have enacted. Second, penal clauses must be placed under divine sanction either by the type itself, or by an invocation of the gods and by an execration contained in a law or bringing punishment, when the civil rights of him who has acted against it are surrendered. Therefore what do you have to say of such a kind about the Gaditan treaty? Can you point out anything made sacrosanct by either the invocation of the gods to punish the offender contained in the law or by an execration bringing human punishment? For I say that nothing at all was ever enacted regarding this treaty by the [Roman] people, nothing by the plebs, nor was a law or a punishment consecrated. Even if it had been enacted regarding some people that we should not enfranchise any citizen, nevertheless that which the [Roman] people had decided upon would afterward be valid, nor would there appear to be any saving clause made by the words "if there is anything sacrosanct," do you dare to say anything has been made sacrosanct regarding them, when the Roman people never enacted anything?

The tone of this passage is that of a teacher (Cicero) instructing a student (the prosecutor), with Cicero playing the role both of the prosecutor and of himself.[41] Cicero begins by impersonating the prosecutor in a minor kind of *prosopopoeiia*, and voicing the prosecutor's contention that the treaty with Gades had a saving clause. The sentence given to the prosecutor is brief. The *inquit*, placed second (in its normal position), informs the audience right away that they are hearing the prosecutor's argument.

Cicero's response is merciless. The *ignosco* is placed first in the sentence, in the most emphatic position. The word is withering and patronizing, suggesting that the prosecutor's argument is so ridiculous that it does not even merit an answer. The *si* introduces an explanation; the first *neque* signals there will be another one. The two *neque* clauses are not parallel either in number of words or grammatical features. The first *neque* clause contains a finite verb (*calles*); the second a finite modal verb (*potuisti*) and an infinitive (*inspicere*). The one parallel, insofar as the terms are analogous, is between *iura* and *leges*; and *Poenorum* is contrasted with *nostras*. Here Cicero could have easily achieved balance, had he so desired, by using *potuisti* and the infinitive *callere* and employing *Poena* (*iura*) instead of *Poenorum* in the first neque clause. Likewise in the protasis, the verb in the first condition is second person singular, active (*reliqueras*), while in the second it is third person plural, active (*reppulerunt*). Again, had Cicero wished to create a balance, he could have. The deliberate imbalance, however, has a rhetorical purpose: it creates more interest, since constant balance is mechanical and boring.[42]

Cicero's response does not even answer the prosecutor's argument. Rather, he uses the contention as a springboard to insult his opponent and to remind the jury that it had been a long time since the prosecutor had been in Gades and that he had been stripped of Roman citizenship. It also allows Cicero to stress again that the prosecutor knew little law, whether Gaditan or Roman. Thus the instructional style of this passage effectively brings across to the jury an unflattering and outright insulting "ethical" portrayal of the prosecutor. This passage also demonstrates the effective intertwining of style and "ethical" and rational arguments.

Cicero then poses a somewhat different question,[43] directed at the prosecutor: "quid fuit in rogatione ea, quae de Pompeio a Gellio et a Lentulo consulibus lata est, in quo aliquid sacrosanctum exceptum videretur?" The *ea* in the first clause points forward to the relative pronoun *quae* in the second; and the *in quo* in the third clause refers back to the *quid* in the first. The clauses are short, the language simple, and the sentence structure of Cicero's legalese is hypotactic. Cicero's rephrasing of the question is more technical than the "prosecutor's." Where the "prosecutor" had simply said "Exceptum est foedus . . .,"Cicero gives more information: "in rogatione ea, quae de Pompeio a Gellio et a Lentulo consulibus lata est." By presenting more detail, such as naming the two consuls who moved the bill and stating what the bill concerned (*de Pompeio*), Cicero presents himself as more precise and a greater legal authority. This characterization is cleverly and yet simply accomplished through the conversation he attributes to the prosecutor and himself.

Cicero's answer is presented simply and logically. The words *primum* and *deinde* mark his two points. The placement of the infinitive phrase *sacrosanctum esse* early in the sentence emphasizes it. The *deinde* clause contains more complicated ideas than the first clause, but the structure of the sentence is clearly signaled by sign-posts. The positioning of *deinde*, subject, main verb is straightforward. The *aut . . . aut* indicating an either . . . or introduces a bipartite construction, the second component of which is also further broken down into two components signaled by the third *aut* in the sentence. This third phrase contains an ablative noun followed by a clause consisting of *cum caput eius . . . consecratur* interrupted by a relative clause, introduced by *qui*. The employment of relative clauses in this passage is deliberate. Cicero could have used other grammatical methods to impart his information to the jury, but relative clauses are simple and straightforward, and an excellent stylistic tool for presenting complicated legal arguments. In fact the use of relative clauses is common in legal texts.

Cicero then poses two more questions in a row, again directed at the prosecutor. The shortness of the questions provides variety after the long sentence preceding. The first question links the last question Cicero posed, about the *lex Cornelia Gellia*, with the argument the prosecutor had made about the Gaditan treaty: "Quid habes igitur dicere de Gaditano foedere eius modi?" The question is straightforward; the most notable feature is the placement of *eius modi* in the emphatic final position. This is the point Cicero will contest in his response. The second question is more precise, the *utrum . . . an* forcing the prosecutor to choose one of the two responses offered by Cicero.

The response to this question is emphatic; each of the first three words adds more force to the preceding one: "Nihil omnino umquam. . . ." In this sentence Cicero is also careful not to achieve complete symmetry between the two clauses. In the second clause *omnino umquam* is omitted; in the first *latum esse* is ellipsed. *Nihil* is preferred to *ne* in the second clause because it is more emphatic. These two clauses are followed by a somewhat complicated mixed contrary to fact condition.[44] The quoting of a proviso of the twelve tables ("id esset quod postea populus iussisset ratum, . . .")[45] imparts greater weight, loftiness and apparent precision[46] to Cicero's statement. In the final two clauses of the sentence Cicero switches back to the indicative as he poses a question to the prosecutor. But he does not simply use *dicis*, he employs the emphatic *audes dicere*, suggesting that the prosecutor's behavior is outrageous, and also implying that the prosecutor is trying to put one over on the jury. The word *audes* carries emotional force, suggests that Cicero himself feels outrage at the prosecutor's behavior, and is geared to rouse emotion in the jury.

This passage is meant to refute the prosecutor's argument that there was a saving clause in the treaty to which the *lex Cornelia Gellia* was subject. Cicero's use of style in this passage assists in his refutation. By means of the questioning and "answering" of the opposition Cicero is able to put words in the prosecutor's mouth, which, when compared with the words Cicero himself uses regarding the *lex* and the saving clause, make the prosecutor seem less knowledgeable.[47] In particular, precision of diction and quoting of laws make Cicero seem an expert on the issues. In addition, Cicero uses words designed to rouse emotions in the jury and bring them over to his side.

The following passage is also from the *argumentatio* (35). It is fairly simple in style, as indicated by the straightforward arrangement of the clauses, and is perhaps closer to the previous example than the first passage selected from the *argumentatio*:

Ita Gaditana civitas, quod beneficiis suis erga rem publicam nostram consequi potuit, quod imperatorum testimoniis, quod vetustate, quod Q. Catuli, summi viri, auctoritate, quod iudicio senatus, quod foedere, consecuta est; quod publica religione sanciri potuit, id abest; populus enim se nusquam obligavit. Neque ideo est Gaditanorum causa deterior; gravissimis enim et plurimis rebus est fulta. Sed isti disputationi hic certe nihil est loci. Sacrosanctum enim nihil potest esse, nisi quod per populum plebemve sanctum est. Quodsi hoc foedus, quod populus Romanus auctore senatu, commendatione et iudicio vetustatis, voluntate et sententiis suis comprobat, idem suffragiis comprobasset, quid erat, cur ex ipso foedere Gaditanum in civitatem nostram recipi non liceret? Nihil est enim aliud in foedere, nisi ut "PIA ET AETERNA PAX SIT." Quid id ad civitatem? Adiunctum illud etiam est, quod non est in omnibus foederibus: "MAIESTATEM POPULI ROMANI COMITER CONSERVANTO." Id habet hanc vim, ut sint illi in foedere inferiores.

Thus what the Gaditan state was able to obtain by means of its services to our state, what by means of the witness of our generals, what by long duration, what by the sponsorship of Quintus Catulus, a most eminent man, what by the judgment of the senate, what by treaty; what could be sanctioned by public religious rites, that is missing; for the public never put itself under an obligation. Nor for that reason is the Gaditan case weaker; for it is strengthened by many weighty matters. But there is certainly no place for that debate here. For nothing can be sacrosanct unless it has been enacted by the people or the plebs. But if this treaty, which the Roman people approved, with the authority of the senate, with the commendation and judgment of antiquity, with their own will and opinion, had likewise approved it with their votes, what reason would there be in the Gaditan treaty itself why it would not be permitted for someone to be received into citizenship in our state? For there is nothing in the treaty other than "let there be pious and eternal peace." What has that to do with citizenship? Moreover, joined to that is a clause which is not found in every treaty: "Let them willingly preserve the sovereign power of the Roman people." That has this force: that they are the inferior party in the treaty.

The sentence structure of this passage is somewhat less complicated than that of the previous one. Subordinate clauses are short, which makes them easier for the audience to follow. The first sentence is one of the longest in the passage. It is more or less periodic; the main verb (*consecuta est*) appears at the end of the sentence. The most notable feature of this sentence is the anaphora of the word *quod*, which appears seven times in this first sentence. The first six *quod* clauses explain how the Gaditan state acquired its benefits: through its help to Rome, by the testimony of Roman commanders, through passage of time, through the sponsorship of Quintus Catulus, by the judgment of the senate, and by the treaty. The first clause refers to actions taken by Gaditans; the others all refer to Roman reactions to these benefits. The second to sixth clauses arguably form a crescendo; each is more important than its predecessor: the approbation moves from nameless Roman commanders to precedents, to a famous Roman general, to the senate, and finally to the treaty. The seventh clause follows logically from the sixth, and stands in contrast to the preceding ones: there was no enactment founded on a sacred public obligation. In a last clause, Cicero repeats the final *quod* clause in slightly different words. The use of *enim* suggests he is explaining the *id abest*, as in fact he is, but the repetition also stresses the lack of obligation.

In the first *quod* clause, *beneficiis suis* is balanced by *rem publicam nostram*; *suis* contrasts with *nostram* and *erga* separates the two phrases. The word order is A B A B (noun, possessive adjective, noun, possessive adjective). The placement of *id abest* at the end of the sentence emphasizes the lack of obligation. The use of *nusquam* instead of *numquam* in the last clause of the sentence is also emphatic.[48]

Several short sentences follow the lengthy first one, providing *variatio*. The first of these is bipartite; it consists of a statement and proof; *deterior* is placed in the final emphatic position. Juxtaposed with it is *gravissimis*, the first word of the following clause. In the following two sentences, Cicero drives home his argument that nothing can be sacrosanct except what has been enacted by the Roman people; *nihil* appears twice.

Having made his emphatic argument, Cicero now allows a hypothetical, past contrary to fact condition. In the protasis, a relative clause picks up some of the themes from the first sentence in the passage, and varies them slightly: *auctore senatu, commendatione et iudicio vetustatis, voluntate et sententiis suis comprobat* . . . . The treaty has the *voluntas* and *sententiae*[49] of the Roman people, but not, in contrast, their *suffragia*. But if it did have their *suffragia*, as Cicero's hypothetical question runs, what in it (note the emphatic ex *ipso* foedere) would disallow a Gaditan to receive Roman citizenship? Cicero answers the question himself by repeating two clauses. The first, "pia et aeterna pax sit" has nothing to do with citizenship, as Cicero makes clear by the rhetorical question following it. Then he delivers his punch: a second clause, which proves the treaty is unfavorable to Gades. "Adiunctum illud etiam est, quod non est in omnibus foederibus: MAIESTATEM POPULI ROMANI COMITER CONSERVAN-TO." The structure of this sentence is periodic; the treaty clause is left until the end of the sentence, and the last word of the treaty is the verb. In case any member of the audience missed the significance of this treaty clause, Cicero spells it out in the following sentence: "Id habet hanc vim, ut sint illi in foedere inferiores." The most important word in the sentence, *inferiores*, is placed in the final position, as was *deterior* earlier in the passage.

This passage is an excellent example of a smooth transition from one argument to another. It was most important for the orator to create smooth transitions, so that his speech did not sound like one long list of arguments.[50] By presenting the hypothetical situation, which flows so smoothly from his refutation of the sacrosanctity of the treaty, Cicero is able to edge into the argument that the Gaditan treaty is an unfavorable one, and from there to his *comiter conservanto* argument.

The following passage is from the latter part of the *argumentatio* (51). Here as Cicero moves towards the end of the *argumentatio* a rise in emotion is apparent together with a rise in style, indicated, for example, by the longer clauses, the quoting of Ennius, and the use of diction:

> Etenim cum ceteris praemiis digni sunt qui suo labore et periculo nostram rem publicam defendunt, tum certe dignissimi sunt qui civitate ea donentur pro qua pericula ac tela subierunt. Atque utinam qui ubique sunt propugnatores huius imperi possent in hanc civitatem venire, et contra oppugnatores rei publicae de civitate exterminari! Neque enim ille summus poeta noster Hannibalis illam magis cohortationem quam communem imperatoriam voluit esse: "Hostem qui feriet, erit, inquit, mihi Carthaginiensis, Quisquis erit." Cuius civitatis sit id habent hodie leve et semper habuerunt, itaque et cives undique fortis viros adsciverunt et hominum ignobilium virtutem persaepe nobilitatis inertiae praetulerunt.

And indeed not only are those men who defend our republic with their own hard work and danger worthy of all other rewards, but also they are certainly most worthy of being enfranchised by that state on whose behalf they submit to danger and weapons. And if only those who are champions of this state everywhere could acquire this citizenship and assailants of this republic could be expelled from the state! Nor indeed did that great poet of ours want that exhortation of Hannibal's to be Hannibal's own rather than common to every general: "The man who strikes the enemy will be a Carthaginian to me, whoever he may be." Of whose state he may be generals consider trifling today and have always considered trifling, and thus they have received brave men from everywhere as citizens and very often they have preferred the courage of low-born men to the idleness of high-born.

Cicero places the clause describing foreigners' brave actions in the final position of the first sentence, and that position for the *pro qua* clause also gives greater clarity to the sentence. Nonetheless the sentence is carefully arranged, with the *cum* clause looking ahead to the *tum* clause and the *tum* clause carrying more weight.[51] In addition the *ea* points to *qua*. Both clauses are followed by relative clauses introduced by *qui*, which complete the preceding *cum* or *tum* clause. There is also a resonance of ideas between the *cum* and *tum* clauses through the use of *digni sunt* in the first clause and *dignissimi sunt* in the second. This is strengthened by the style of the sentence, particularly by the repetition of sounds in *cum* and *tum*, *ceteris* and *certe*, *digni sunt* and *dignissimi sunt*. There is also a contrast presented in the first relative *qui* clause between <u>suo</u> *labore et periculo* and <u>nostram</u> *rem publicam*. The word order is possessive adjective, noun, noun; possessive adjective, noun: A B B; A B. The foreigner's side is elaborated, receiving two nouns. *Nostram* emphasizes that these foreigners were risking their lives for a state that was not their own. The risks the foreigners were taking is stressed by the repetition of the word *periculo/pericula*. In the last clause of the sentence the danger is emphasized through the use of hendiadys in *qua pericula ac tela*.

The following sentence repeats the idea of foreigners fighting on behalf of Rome receiving citizenship. The emotional tone is raised by the exclamatory wish expressed by the use of *utinam* and the subjunctive *possent*. The idea is expressed by a pleasing antithesis: those who fight on behalf of our state ought to be rewarded with citizenship, while those who fight against it ought to be deprived of Roman citizenship. The sentence is periodic, but not lengthy. The use of the cognates *propugnatores* and *oppugnatores* imparts more force to the antithesis. The use of the demonstrative article *huius* and *hanc* is emphatic; it is employed only in the first clause and not in the second. The two clauses are almost parallel: *propugnatores/oppugnatores huius imperii / rei publicae possent in hanc civitatem / de civitate venire / exterminari*. The finite verb stands in the middle of the first clause, which slightly imbalances the symmetry, as does the use of the demonstrative only in the first clause. Cicero could easily have achieved complete balance between the two clauses had he wanted to by placing *possent* between the two clauses, and either omitting the demonstrative or employing it in both clauses. In the latter instance he places the demonstratives where he wants to have an emphasis. The asymmetry seems at first less "artistic," but it is not.[52] The words denoting the republic are interlocked with verbs whose subject is the men who ought to be enfranchised.

The following sentence increases the emotional tone in a crescendo by the mention of Ennius (not by name; he is referred to as *summus poeta noster*) and Hannibal.[53] Cicero introduces the quote in a clever fashion by declaring that Ennius believed that it was the general view of commanders that foreigners ought to be enfranchised for assisting Rome in battle (*communem imperatoriam voluit esse*). Ennius' quotation does not say this; Cicero is interpreting it to mean so, and thus, in a sense Ennius becomes a prestigious witness on Balbus' behalf. Ennius' authority is emphasized by the words *ille summus poeta noster*, the quotation itself carries authority because of its antiquity. The parallel between Ennius' view and Pompey's is stated in the last clause of this sentence, thereby drawing together the poet, Pompey, and the long line of generals between them: "id habent hodie leve et semper habuerunt." The repetition of the verb in different tenses together with the use of the adverbial *semper*, stresses the great extent of time from the present to the distant past.[54] *Semper habuerunt* is in the emphatic final position, emphasizing the lengthy precedence which Pompey was following. The two words have the same rhythm (— u u u — —) as *esse videatur*, Cicero's favorite ending for a period sentence.

The main verbs of the following sentence are in the third person plural, referring to this long line of generals. By using this plural, Cicero widens the argument so that he appears to be defending all the generals from Ennius' time who have enfranchised foreigners. The sentence expresses a clever antithesis and employs artistically crafted word arrangement to do so. The idea contains a couple of contrasts. The first is that a man may be of humble birth (*ignobilium*) and yet be capable of fulfilling the ideal of personal achievements in the service of the state (*virtutem*);[55] the second that a high-born man (*nobilitatis*) might be lacking in energy (*inertiae*). The words are arranged in A B A B form (noun, adjective; noun, adjective), and the two contrasting men are separated by the word *persaepe*, a word which qualifies the statement. It is interesting that in his contrast between noble and humble man, Cicero does not use opposite qualities. *Ignavia* is the opposite of *virtus*,[56] while *fortis* and *stenuus* are often contrasted with *iners*.[57] After the courage of the humble man is noted, one would expect cowardice to be the quality mentioned in respect to the noble. For obvious reasons Cicero shies away from stating this. The orator also reworks the antithesis Ennius presents. As Ennius sets it up, the contrast is between known and unknown. As Cicero sees it, it is between low-born and high-born. If a peasant could be rewarded, there is all the more reason to reward Balbus, who is a high-born Gaditan. Balbus can only be considered *ignobilis* by Romans because he is a Spaniard and not a true born Roman, and more specifically, has no consular ancestors.

The following is the final passage from the *argumentatio* to be examined (54). The appeal to the emotions manifest in the previous passage continues.

Here at the end of the *argumentatio* Cicero moves into a high style appropriate to the pathos he expresses:

> An lingua et ingenio patefieri aditus ad civitatem potuit, manu et virtute non potuit? Anne de nobis trahere spolia foederatis licebat, de hostibus non licebat? An, quod adipisci poterant dicendo, id eis pugnando adsequi non licebat? An accusatori maiores nostri maiora praemia quam bellatori esse voluerunt?

> Could the right of admittance to the state lie open by means of oratory and talent but not by means of military service and courage? Was it permitted for nations bound to us by treaties to haul away spoils from us, but not permitted to do so from our enemies? Were they able to acquire by oratory that which they were not permitted to attain by fighting? Did our ancestors want there to be greater rewards for a prosecutor than a warrior?

The style of this passage assists in the arousal of pathos. The passage develops a variation on the ancient, antithetical theme of the contrast between the pen and the sword: here the antithesis is between oratory and military prowess. The anaphora of *an/anne* at the beginning of each of the four rhetorical questions adds vehemence to the antithesis, as does the shortness of the sentences. The shortness of the questions is also geared to rouse the emotions of the listeners.[58] The *anne* in the second sentence jars the parallelism. One would expect either *an* in this sentence, or *anne* in the fourth question to produce a balance.

Each of the rhetorical questions contains two clauses, the one contrasting the other. The first sentence is beautifully balanced. Cicero employs *elaboratio* and metonymy to dress up his theme. Two concrete parts of the body and the abstract qualities of character associated with them are contrasted: *lingua et ingenio* with *manu et virtute*. The word order in the second clause parallels that in the first, with the unnecessary words (*patefieri aditus ad civitatem*) ellipsed. *Potuit* in the first clause is paralleled and contrasted by *non potuit* in the second.

The second sentence elaborates upon the *manu et virtute* theme, with a contrast between the ability the *foederati* have to take spoils from Rome, but not from Rome's enemies. Here the two clauses are also balanced, with parallel word order: *de nobis* is contrasted by *de hostibus*; and *licebat* is paralleled and contrasted by *non licebat*.

In the third sentence Cicero returns to the contrast between oratory and warfare. He breaks the parallelism somewhat by using *poterant* in the first clause and *non licebat* in the second. The two gerunds, *dicendo* and *pugnando* are contrasted, but the word order is not parallel; in fact each word changes position in the second clause. In the first clause the word order runs: infinitive, finite verb, gerund (*adipisci poterant dicendo*) and in the second it is: gerund, infinitive, finite verb (*pugnando adsequi non licebat*). After two parallel clauses in the first two sentences, the audience might be expecting a third parallel clause. By upsetting the audience's expectations, Cicero creates a more interesting passage.

The fourth sentence repeats the antithesis between the orator and the warrior (*accusatori/bellatori*), this time by introducing the potent authority of the *maiores*. The anaphora between *maiores* and *maiora* helps to drive home Cicero's point.

Finally, I shall examine a passage from the *peroratio* (64). I chose this passage because it contains the requisite appeal for pity, a rather difficult emotion to rouse in regard to Balbus, given his unpopularity. Here style assists Cicero in accomplishing a formidable goal:

Miseremini eius qui non de suo peccato sed de huius summi et clarissimi viri facto, non de aliquo crimine sed periculo suo de publico iure disceptat. Quod ius si Cn. Pompeius ignoravit, si M. Crassus, si Q. Metellus, si Cn. Pompeius pater, si L. Sulla, si P. Crassus, si C. Marius, si senatus, si populus Romanus, si, qui de re simili iudicarunt, si foederati populi, si socii, si illi antiqui Latini, videte ne utilius vobis et honestius sit illis ducibus errare quam hoc magistro erudiri.

Pity this man [Balbus] who is involved in a dispute not about some wrongdoing of his own, but about an action of this illustrious and most distinguished man, not about some charge touching him personally, but about an issue of public law. But if Gnaeus Pompeius was unaware of this law, if Marcus Crassus, if Quintus Metellus, if Gnaeus Pompeius his father, if Lucius Sulla, if Publius Crassus, if Gaius Marius, if the senate, if the Roman people, if those who have made judgment about a similar case, if people bound to us by treaty, if our allies, if the ancient Latins [were unaware of this point of law] consider whether it will be more useful and more honorable for you, to err with them as guides rather than to be schooled with this man [the prosecutor] as a teacher.

The passage begins with an imperative, bidding the jury to have pity on his client. The first sentence is complex, containing a combination of antithesis and balance. It consists of two parallel relative clauses, the first introduced by *qui*, each containing a contrasting smaller phrase, signaled by *non*, and introduced by *sed*. The first relative clause picks up a theme introduced at the beginning of the speech: that Balbus was not on trial for any wrongdoing of his own (*peccato suo*) but for an action of Pompey's. The *huius* probably indicates that Cicero pointed to Pompey. Names are not necessary at this point of the speech; referring to Pompey as *huius summi et clarissimi* enables Cicero to remind the audience one more time of Pompey's merit, *auctoritas*, and his presence at the scene. There is some parallelism in these two contrasting clauses: both *peccato* and *facto* are placed last, and the contrast between the two is stressed by the use of anaphora. The two phrases which follow are in a sense parallel, in that the first begins with *non de* and the second with *sed*, but even here Cicero manages to create variety: in the first relative clause of the sentence (*non de suo peccato*) Cicero began by describing what the case was not about, in terms of Balbus (*suo*), in this second relative clause (with a suppressed *qui*), one would expect another *suo* to complete the parallelism, but Cicero upsets these expectations with <u>*aliquo*</u> *crimine*. *Periculo suo* in the final clause of the sentence creates a kind of chiastic order: *suo . . . huius . . . aliquo . . . suo*. *Periculum* is a word that carries a great deal of resonance in this speech. Cicero employed it earlier to describe the risks brave allies incurred in aiding Rome. By this point the word carries all the connotations that Cicero associated with it previously. But the contrast between the *non de aliquo crimine* and the *sed periculo suo de publico iure* clauses does not end here. Grammatically, the contrast is between *non de aliquo crimine* and *sed . . . de publico iure*; but Cicero, very cleverly also manages to tie in *periculo suo* by creating a contrast between *aliquo* and *suo*. In the following sentence, Cicero sums up the precedents he had cited earlier in the *argumentatio*. After the first *si* clause, which contains the verb *ignoravit*, the verb is ellipsed in the remaining *si* clauses. These thirteen clauses spill out like an endless cascade of precedents, moving from prestigious individuals to groups of people. The ellipsis of the verb in these *si* clauses assists the argument from precedents by concentrating the main points of each clause, and thus giving them more impact.

The use of style in this speech is closely linked to the "ethical," "pathetic," and rational argumentation. With careful use of diction and the placement and repetition of individual words, the orator can arouse emotions in the audience, as for example with the repetition of the word *pericula* (22–23), and also create vivid portrayals of character, as seen in the *peroratio* by the reference to Pompey by his characteristics rather than by his name (*huius summi et clarissimi*). The use of ellipsis and word order can assist "ethical" and "pathetic" argumentation, but also rational arguments, as seen in the passage above from the *peroratio*. The style in this speech shows great variety, from the elegant, careful, and almost poetic structuring of the sentences of the *exordium* to the clear, lucid diction and simple sentence structure of some passages from the *argumentatio*, to the more stirring style of the *peroratio*. There is no one style characteristic of the *argumentatio*, although the style of the *exordium* and *peroratio* appear fairly uniform. The *argumentatio* varies from the straightforward style mentioned above to an instructional style employing questions and exclamations, as when Cicero creates a dialogue between the prosecutor and himself, to a more vivid, dramatic style when Cicero attempts to rouse emotions (as in 22–23). In addition to the style aiding the argumentation of the speech, the creation and then foiling of expectations when Cicero at times avoids balance in clauses, creates a pleasing variety. At other times his intricate, balanced phrases, as in the *exordium*, create a pleasing rhythm which make his arguments even more attractive.

Conclusions

IN THE *PRO BALBO*, CICERO DEMONSTRATES HIS MASTERY OF THE USE AND arrangement of arguments, and of stylistic usage. In "ethical" argumentation we found that Cicero gives his defense the shape he wants by substituting Pompey as defendant, and emphasizing the *auctoritas*, experience, and ability of the general. The portrayal of Pompey is designed to present him as a thoroughly credible and prestigious character who could not possibly have made a legal mistake in enfranchising Balbus. This characterization is achieved through the repetition of Pompey's qualities, and through the use of *exempla* such as Quintus Numidicus Metellus and the unnamed, venerable Greek. The prosecutor is depicted as the antithesis of Pompey. In the face of Pompey's glory, the prosecutor's insignificance is stressed by the fact that he is never referred to by name. While Pompey is *peritissimus*, the prosecutor is *imperitissimus*. Whereas Pompey had rewarded a brave Spaniard by enfranchising him, the prosecutor wishes to strip the same Spaniard of his Roman citizenship. Cicero's major technique in portraying the prosecutor is the use of biting sarcasm and irony, particularly in addressing him as if he were a great font of legal wisdom. The prosecutor is also presented as the antithesis of Balbus. For example the prosecutor, according to Cicero, desires to harm Gaditan interests, while Balbus has done his best to help his fellow citizens.

In portraying Balbus, Cicero's goal is to diminish the *invidia* directed at his client, and arouse compassion for him. Cicero accomplishes this by emphasizing Balbus's self-sacrifice, hard work, and compassion for Cicero's family during the exile. Balbus is also strongly associated with Pompey, as mentioned above, but also with Cicero, Caesar, and brave foreigners in general. By talking about brave foreigners as a whole, Cicero is able to elaborate on the kind of risks Balbus took on Rome's behalf without mentioning Balbus by name, and thereby arousing jealousy. This tactic also universalizes the case, and thus raises its importance. Cicero depicts himself as a wise senior statesman who is able to cast aside personal enmities in the interests of the state. Cicero thus associates himself with the good of the state, and since he had earlier associated himself with Balbus, he therefore indirectly links Balbus to the good of the republic. The jurors, on the other hand, are portrayed in such a way as to suggest characteristics and behaviors Cicero would like them to show.

Pathos is described as evoking intense emotions in the audience. It is not, however, always pitched at one high level, but rises and falls in a series of crescendos and diminuendos. Pathos is used extensively in this speech, and emotion is often aroused by a portrayal of character, as with Balbus, Pompey, and Marius. In these cases pathos is distinguished from ethos by its intensity, and also often by the linking of strong admiration (in the case of Pompey and Marius) with the emotive concepts of patriotism and empire. Pathos may also be differentiated from ethos by the style of a particular passage, pathos being characterized by force and vigour (*vis*). Pathos is also generally characterized by the "high" style, especially when Cicero's subject is important, as with Pompey and Marius. Here figurative language, diction and the repetition of certain words, sentence phrasing, invocations, and questions all increase emotion. In the *digressio* on Marius the use of vivid depiction is another technique employed to stir strong feelings. Cicero also uses the technique of association, a tactic he also employs in "ethical" argumentation, and in "pathetic" argumentation. Pompey and Caesar are linked with the good of Rome and therefore with the good of the jurors. By bringing the interests of the jurors into the case, Cicero makes it easier to intensify their feelings of indignation against the prosecutor. Not all pathos in the speech is linked to ethos. For example, Cicero works on the fears of Romans that they will not be able to find allies in desperate times.

Cicero's main arguments in logos are that the *lex Cornelia Gellia* legally permitted Pompey to enfranchise Balbus, that the Gaditans were not entitled to give consent to the enfranchisement, and in any event, their behavior in appointing Balbus guest friend demonstrated that they had given consent. The *in utramque partem* argument is the main type used: Cicero argues that Gades had no legal right to give consent; and that even if the Gaditans had been given this right, the *lex Cornelia Gellia* would have overridden the right; and finally, if the *lex* had not overridden the treaty, that the Gaditans had behaved as though they had given consent. In addition to the *in utramque partem*, Cicero also employs *a fortiori* arguments, as for example, when he argues at 60 that if he were able to set aside personal enmities for the sake of the republic, then the jurors ought to be able to do the same. *A minore* arguments are also present, as when Cicero argues at 24 that if *stipendarii*, enemies, and slaves may become Roman citizens, then *foederati* ought to be permitted to do so. And finally *exempla* and precedents, which often have little similarity with Balbus' case (as for example the enfranchisement of the Greek priestess at 55) are liberally sprinkled throughout the speech. One of Cicero's most interesting tactics is the interweaving of "pathetic" arguments with weaker rational arguments.

In my fourth chapter, we have seen that Cicero employs *dispositio* to prepare his audience psychologically and make them as receptive as possible to his arguments. Central to his use of arrangement is the strategic blending and arranging of different *genera* of arguments and the manner in which he develops individual arguments. The overall structure of the speech is bipartite: the first part deals with the ethos of Pompey and the second with the issue of Gaditan consent. The most interesting feature of the speech is the use of the two *ethicae digressiones*. The first *ethica digessio*, on Pompey, functions as a *praemunitio*, and is designed to win over the audience and to make them more receptive to Cicero's attempts to diminish the *invidia*. Cicero's remarks on *invidia*, which follow the *digressio* on Pompey, precede his legal arguments so that any sympathy obtained might influence the jurors' impressions of the legal issues. The second *digressio* is positioned in such a way as to prepare for the argument that all of Rome sided with Pompey's interpretation of the law. Some of the most important tactics in the arrangement of Cicero's arguments are the interweaving of "pathetic" and rational arguments, particularly when the latter are weak, the interweaving of "ethical" and "pathetic" arguments, particularly in the two *digressiones*, and the sprinkling of sarcastic insults directed at the prosecution throughout the speech and usually placed next to a rebuttal by Cicero of one of the opposition's arguments. The sprinkling of insults builds up through resonance throughout the speech and helps Cicero destroy the credibility of the prosecutor.

In my fifth chapter, on *elocutio*, I studied the style of the speech, with special emphasis on the effect of style upon rhetoric. It was shown that the speech is not written in one style, but in several. The *exordium* is written in the middle style, and the *peroratio*, for the most part, in the grand style. The *argumentatio*, however, varies from the grand style, seen in the *digressiones* on Pompey and Marius, to the plain style, as seen in the passage selected from section 35. It became apparent that the use of stylistic techniques in the *Pro Balbo* assists in maneuvering arguments. The use and repetition of words, for example can stir emotions, as can the placement of phrases. Word order and other stylistic features, such as ellipsis and purposefully unbalanced clauses, can assist rational and "ethical" arguments by concentrating and focusing the sentences so that they emphasize the point being made.

The *Pro Balbo* is a fine example of Cicero's abilities as an orator. From circumstances which were at best difficult, given the hostility towards Balbus and Cicero's own position *vis-à-vis* Pompey and Caesar, Cicero fashions a powerful and credible defense. He deftly defuses these two problems, lays out the legal issues, but at the same time, bolsters these issues with national pride, security fears, ridicule of the prosecutor, and intense admiration for figures such as Pompey and Marius. Despite the fact that the law was probably on Balbus' side, Cicero is not content to rest with legal arguments. He knows his audience well enough to realize this would not be sufficient. With tremendous thoroughness he seeks out every possible argument, character-based and emotion-based in addition to legally grounded ones, and arrays them with the brilliance of a master chess player. He then blends them together to make each individual argument stronger by association. His use of diction, ellipsis, word order, and unbalanced clauses all demonstrate the attention he pays to detail. But also close attention is paid to the larger elements of the speech. *Inventio*, *dispositio*, and *elocutio* do not function entirely independently of one another, but are integrated in a way that is geared to make the most persuasive speech possible.

Notes

INTRODUCTION

[1] See below, p. 9

[2] Dio Cassius 48.32. For a biography of Balbus see Alföldi (1976), Reid (1890), Münzer (1901) 1259–1267, and Syme (1939).

[3] von Albrecht (1972) 1305–1308.

[4] Badian (1954, 1959), Levick (1967).

[5] For example Parker (1938).

[6] Kennedy (1968, 1972), May (1979, 1981, 1988).

[7] May (1988).

[8] Neumeister (1964), Stroh (1975), Classen (1981) 149–192, (1985), Gotoff (1986, 1993).

[9] It should be noted that both May and Craig also agree that persuasion is the goal of forensic oratory. Classen (1985) 5 admits a forensic speech may also have a political purpose.

[10] Neumeister cites Quint. *Inst. Or.* 2.13.6 and *De Or.* 1.145. See also *De Or.* 1.146.

[11] Neumeister derives these principles from the ancient rhetorical divisions of *inventio*, *dispositio*, and *elocutio*.

[12] Neumeister (1964) 32–34, 56–59. He studies *Div. in Caec.*; *In Verr.* 1; and *Pro Lig.* in light of this principle. Among others, Neumeister cites Quint. *Inst. Or.* 4.1.44; 8.3.11; and *De Or.* 2.291.

[13] Neumeister (1964) 71–82, 99–100. This principle is applied to the *Pro Milone*. He cites Quint. *Inst. Or.* 4.2.83; Isocrates 8.132; 15.140; and *De Or.* 2.307, among other ancient sources.

[14] Neumeister (1964) 110–127. The *Pro Milone* is examined in respect to this concept. He cites Quint. *Inst. Or.* 7.1.24; 10.1.20; etc.

[15] Neumeister (1964) 130–148. He investigates this concept in the rhetorical theory of Cicero and Quintilian and its use in the history of Greek and Roman rhetoric.

[16] Neumeister (1964) 156–192. He cites Quintilian extensively.

[17] Nisbet (1992) 1.

[18] *De Or.* 1.53; 2.215; *Brut.* 89; 276; *Or.* 69; Quint. *Inst. Or.* 4.5.6; 6.2.2.

[19] At *Pro Balbo* 9–16 and 46–49 respectively.

[20] Ward (1970) 121, Plutarch *Cic.* 8.3, Cic. *Har. Resp.* 49, Suet. *Tib.* 15.1, Vell. Pat. 2.77.1, and Dio 48.38.2.

[21] Ward (1970a) 121.

[22] Ward (1970a) 123–126.

[23] Ward (1970a) 60–67.

[24] Ward (1970b) 67.

[25] Johannemann (1935) 8–14.

[26] Johannemann (1935) 14–16.

[27] Johannemann (1935) 35 *et seq.*

[28] Johannemann (1935) 35.

[29] Johannemann (1935) 35.

[30] Johannemann (1935) 46–47.

[31] Johannemann (1935) 56.

[32] Johannemann (1935) 59–60.

[33] Johannemann (1935) 60–63.

[34] Reid (1890) 7, Cousin (1962) 231.

[35] Cousin (1962) 232.

[36] *Pro Balbo* 19. See also Brunt (1982) 136–147 for a detailed analysis of the legal issues in the *Pro Balbo*.

[37] See Brunt (1982) 136.

[38] *Pro Balbo* 8, 14, and 32.

[39] *Pro Balbo* 19.

[40] *Pro Balbo* 34 and 35.

[41] *Pro Balbo* 32 and 47.

[42] *Pro Balbo* 35.

[43] *Pro Balbo* 29.

[44] *Pro Balbo* 21.

[45] *Pro Balbo* 27–29, and 43.

[46] Quint. *Inst. Or.* 10.5.20; Alexander (2002) 3–5, 30.

[47] Alexander (2002) 3. See Alexander (2002) 29–30 for a list of guidelines for evaluating evidence in forensic speeches.

CHAPTER ONE: *INVENTIO*: **ETHOS**

[1] *Rhetoric* 1.2.1356a13.

[2] Ibid. 1.2.1356a1–13; 3.7.1408a25–36; 3.16.1417a16–36; 2.12.1388b32–2.17.1391b8. See also Cope (1867) 108–113, May (1988) 2–3, and Kennedy (1994) 59–60 for a discussion of ethos in Aristotle's *Rhetoric*.

[3] *Rhetoric* 2.1.1378a6–20; Fortenbaugh (1992). Aristotle states that the speaker must appear to possess these qualities, thus implying simulation is possible.

[4] Fantham (1973) 271.

[5] Wisse (1989) 222–249, especially 234. See also Wisse (2002) 386 for a comparison of the use of ethos in Aristotle and Cicero.

[6] For a discussion about the relation between Cicero's *conciliare* and Aristotle's ethos, see Fantham (1973), Wisse (1989) 222–249, and Gill (1984). See also A. Dihle (1955) 303 *et seq.*

[7] Fortenbaugh (1988) 261; (1992) 225–228; Kennedy (1972) 42.

[8] Wisse (1989) 234.

[9] The significance of ethos in traditional Roman rhetoric can be seen in Cato's *De Sumptu Suo* (*ORF* Vol.1.41 fr.171), in P. Cornelius Scipio Africanus maior's speech against M. Naevius (Gell. 4.183), in Antonius' speech against Norbanus (*De Or.* 2.200), among others. See Kennedy (1972) 42, 57; McClintock (1975) 37,41; and May (1988) 6–9 for a discussion of character in both rhetoric and society.

[10] See Heinze *Hermes* 60 (1925) 348–366, Hellegouarc'h (1963) 295–314 and 330–335, and Galinsky (1996) 10–41 for *auctoritas*.

[11] May (1988) 47.

[12] I am using the terms *patron* and *client* in the rhetorical sense as *trial advocate* and *defendant*, rather than in the ancient historical sense. See Badian (1960) 275–276. For a different view: Douglas (1960) 133–134.

[13] Kennedy (1968) and May (1981).

[14] *De Or.* 2.182: "Conciliantur autem animi dignitate hominis, rebus gestis, existimatione vitae." ("Moreover, minds may be won over by the worth of a man, by his actions, by his good name in life"). The close temporal proximity of the *Pro Balbo* (late summer of 56 B.C.) and the *De Oratore* (finished in the winter of 55 B.C.) should be noted. See also Loutsch (1994) 357 ff., especially 362–365 for a discussion of Cicero's characterization of Pompey and Crassus in the exordium.

[15] See Heinze (1925) 348; and 365, as follows:

> Was liegt ihr (*auctoritas*) zugrunde? Ich denke, das Gefühl, daß nicht jeder alles, und besonders nicht alles allein versteht; der Respekt vor einer Verantwortungsgefühl verkörpert sind, verbunden mit dem Wunsche, immer möglichst sicher zu gehen; das Misstrauen gegen jede "Eingebung"; letzten Endes der nüchterne und klare, illusionsfreie Sinn des Römers für Zweckmässigkeit des Handelns.

Heinze's article on *auctoritas* is reprinted in Vom Geist des Römertums, ed. E. Burck, 3rd edn., Darmstadt, 1960. See also Hellegouarc'h (1963) 297: "Le sentiment d'auctoritas était profondément ancré au coeur de tous les Romains et il commendait leur action dans de nombreuses circonstances de la vie; car c'était un principe constant dans leur vie publique ou privée de ne jamais prendre de décision importante sans recourir a l'avis d'une personne compétente"; and Galinsky (1996) 10–41. See also Loutsch (1994) 357 ff.

[16] Frier (195) 140. See also Heinze (1925) and *De Or.* 3.133–135.

[17] In general this was so, however it was not invariable. Scipio Aemilianus' *auctoritas* was used against him when he prosecuted L. Aurelius Cotta in 138 B.C.

[18] Hellegouarc'h (1963) 230.

[19] Hellegouarc'h (1963) translates this word as "[un] attachement passioné." See also Loutsch (1994) 362 ff.

[20] *Topica* 73: "Naturae auctoritas in virtute inest maxima; in tempore autem multa sunt quae adferant auctoritatem: ingenium opes aetas fortuna ars usus necessitas, concursio etiam non numquam rerum fortuitarum. Nam et ingeniosos et opulentos et

aetatis spatio probatos dignos quibus credatur putant" ("The authority derived from one's character depends especially upon moral worth; at the appropriate time, there are many things which convey authority: natural ability, wealth, age, good fortune, skill, experience, exigency, and sometimes even a concourse of fortuitous events.").

[21] *De Or.* 2.216–290, *Brutus* 109, Hellegouarc'h (1963) 281. This is not to say, however, that an orator can never be *levis*, as Cicero demonstrated in the *Pro Murena* and the *Pro Caelio*.

[22] Alexander (1990) lists Pompey as an advocate in only two trials, one of which is this trial of Cornelius Balbus. It is possible that the second trial in which he acted as advocate, on behalf of T. Ampius Balbus, was subsequent to that of Cornelius Balbus. Alexander also lists Pompey as a witness in three trials: that of M. Fonteius in 69(?) B.C., that of T. Annius Milo in 56 B.C. and that of M. Aemilius Scaurus in 54 B.C.

[23] Hellegouarc'h (1963) 279; Loutsch (1994) 365.

[24] Ernesti (1962) 97–98.

[25] Gotoff (1986) 122–132 notes that we cannot trust Cicero's account of other speeches. It should be noted that in this instance it is unlikely that Cicero is misleading the audience.

[26] *De Or.* 2.185–186.

[27] McClintock (1975) 171.

[28] *Pro Balbo* 18, 19, 56-58.

[29] *De Inv.* 1.24: "Si causae turpitudo contrahit offensionem, aut pro eo homine, in quo offenditur, alium hominem, qui diligitur, interponi oportet; aut pro re, in qua offenditur, aliam rem, quae probatur . . . ut ab eo, quod odit, ad id, quod diligit, auditoris animus traducatur . . ." ("If the baseness of the case occasions offense, it is necessary to substitute another man who is esteemed in place of that man who causes the offense; or other subject matter, which is approved, in place of that which causes offense . . . in order that the mind of the listener may be drawn from that which he hates to that which he esteems . . ."). (The text edited by Stroebel (1915) is used for all citations of the *De Inv.*) In this case it is the jealousy of Balbus which occasions the offense.

[30] May (1981, 1988) 89, 90. Cicero also uses this tactic in the *Pro Balbo* (1 and 58). (See pages 4–6, 14–15, 17, 18 and 22 for discussion of the use of association in 1 and 58.)

[31] In the *Pro Roscio Amerino*, an early speech given at a time when Cicero did not have a great amount of *auctoritas*, the orator also, although to a lesser extent, substitutes more powerful patrons for himself (2–4, 15, 27, 149).

[32] It was possible for experienced generals to make illegal enfranchisements, as for example Marius did during the war against the Cimbri and Teutons. Even Marius himself admitted that the enfranchisement was not legitimate in his famous statement that the clash of arms prevented him from hearing the sound of the law. See Plutarch *Marius* 28.

[33] There is a textual problem at 3. The manuscripts read *recte tractare*. Madvig suggests *recte se dare*, and Reid *recte cadere*. I have followed Reid's reading.

[34] See *Paradoxa Stoicorum* 4: "Quae quia sunt admirabilia contraque opinionem omnium (ab ipsis [Stoics] etiam παραδόξα appellantur)" ("These doctrines are astonishing, and contrary to universal opinion—they are called *paradoxa* by the Stoics them-

selves"), 17–19, Stobaeus 2.66, 14–67.4 (SVF 3.560) apud Long, A.A., Sedley, D.N. (1987) 379, Reid (1890) 48, and Cousin (1962) 241. The quoting of the paradox adds authority to Cicero's statement. See also *Pro Murena* 60–61, where Cicero satirizes the Stoic paradoxes to criticize Cato's behavior in prosecuting Murena. For Cicero's view of the appropriate use of Greek learning in Roman oratory see *De Or.* 2.152 and following.

[35] The Stoic definition of "well" does not mean that Pompeius will win, although this is the implication here.

[36] Cicero no doubt chose L. Crassus as a man to compare Pompey with because Cicero believed L. Crassus to be the best Roman orator. L. Crassus is one of the characters Cicero chose to espouse his theories on rhetoric in the *De Oratore*, on which he was at work around the time of this speech. See also *Brutus* 143–165 for an assessment of Crassus' abilities as an orator.

[37] All quotations of the *Pro Balbo* are from the Oxford Classical Text, edited by Peterson (1911), unless otherwise noted. I have also consulted the texts edited by Cousin (1962), Klotz (1919), and Bellardi (1975). In translating into English I made use of Reid's suggestions in his commentary (1890).

[38] The status of the case is its fundamental issues. See Kennedy (1972) 110, 620–625, *De Inv.* 1.10–1.19, *Ad Her.* 1.18–1.25.

[39] *De Inv.* 1.14–15, Kaden (1912) 39, Rohde (1903) 154.

[40] Although enemies of Pompey may have been using the accusations against Balbus as a way of indirectly attacking Pompey (Gelzer (1984) 133, Reid (1890) 10–11, (1879) 11, Seager (2002) 120–121), the actual charge before the court involved Balbus.

[41] This is common in Ciceronian speeches, although there may be different reasons for arguing from ethos in each speech; cf. in the *Pro Roscio Amerino, Pro Murena*. See also May (1988) 23, 60. It should be noted that an argument based on ethos does not have to be illogical, it is simply characterized by its focus on character.

[42] Heinze (1925) 357, Galinsky (1996) 14.

[43] It is possible that it was the prosecutor who made the connection between Balbus and Pompey, but I think it more likely that Cicero did so, since the tactic was more to his advantage, and since he has Sulpicius describe a similar tactic employed by the defense in his comments about Norbanus' trial (*De Or.* 2.203). "Ecce autem, cum te nihil aliud profecisse arbitrarer, nisi ut homines tibi civem improbum defendenti ignoscendum propter necessitudinem arbitrarentur, serpere occulte coepisti, nihil dum aliis suspicantibus, me vero iam pertimuiscente, ut illam non Norbani seditionem, sed populi Romani iracundiam neque eam iniustam, sed meritam ac debitam fuisse defenderes." ("See then, when I was thinking that you had accomplished nothing other than that men might think you should be forgiven since you were defending a base citizen because of your relationship to him, you began to worm your way in, while the others suspected nothing, but I indeed was already fearful that you were not defending that mutiny of Norbanus but the anger of the Roman people, and [implying] not that it was unjust, but deserved and justified.")

[44] *De Inv.* 1.23. Generally Cicero increases the significance of a case by broadening it from the specific to the universal (*Or.* 45, *De Or.* 3.120, Kennedy (1968) 431, and May (1988) 27, 39, 66, 80), as he does later in this speech (23, 24). Here he uses a different approach to augment importance.

[45] Cicero's praise of Pompey in this speech is similar to his praise in *Pro Leg. Man.* 10 and 27–50.

[46] See Alexander (1990) 51. The trial likely took place in either 110 or 106 B.C. Q. Caecilius Metellus Numidicus was charged under the *lex Acilia de repetundis* for malfeasance possibly in the year after his praetorship in 112 B.C., when he may have been governor, or as proconsul in 108–106 B.C. He was acquitted after the jurors, who were *equites*, refused to examine his records.

[47] For a detailed analysis of Cicero's portrayal of non-Romans in his speeches, see Vasaly (1993) 191–244.

[48] Cicero also praises Metellus in the *Pro Sestio* 101; *Post Red. in Sen.* 38; and *In Pisonem* 20. In the latter speech he draws a parallel between himself and Metellus.

[49] *Ad Her.* 1.9: ". . . aut aliquorum iudicium de simili causa aut de eadem aut de minore aut de maiore proferemus, deinde ad nostram causam pedetemptim accedemus et similitudinem conferemus." ("Or shall we offer the judgment of others regarding a similar case, whether that case be of the same, or less or more importance, then step by step approach our case and turn to the similitude.") I use the Teubner edition, edited by Marx (1894) for all passages from the *Ad. Her.* There was no formal charge by the presiding magistrate to the jury, whereby the jury would receive instructions on the law or on the issues. See Riggsby (1999) 15. Due to this lack of a formal charge, the paradigms which the advocate provided to the jurors as models for their decision-making were very influential. See Riggsby (1999) 19.

[50] In the *Pro Flacco*, Cicero makes a similar argument from *exempla* that the jurors should acquit his client. In that case, Cicero binds an acquittal of Flaccus to the safety of the Roman republic: "Cum tabella vobis dabitur, iudices, non de Flacco dabitur solum, dabitur de ducibus auctoribusque conservandae civitatis, dabitur de omnibus bonis civibus, dabitur de vobismet ipsis, dabitur de liberis vestris, de vita, de patria, de salute communi" (99) ("When the voting tablet is given to you, jurors, you will be giving judgment not about Flaccus alone, but also about the leaders and promoters of the preservation of the state, about all good citizens, about you yourselves, your children, your lives, your fatherland, and about our common safety").

[51] See my chapter on logos, and Rohde (1903) 105, 109.

[52] Neumeister examines the use of this technique in the *Pro Milone* (1964) 110–112.

[53] Neumeister (1964) 73, 83–99, Quint. *Inst.* 4.2.54. See also my chapter on *dispositio*.

[54] By contrast Cicero does name the prosecutor in the *Pro Archia* (8), who is unknown apart from the reference in that speech. See Reid (1879) 13, 42.

[55] *De Inv.* 1.22; *De Or.* 2.208.

[56] Cicero also uses this technique in the portrayal of the prosecutor C. Erucius in *Pro Sexto Roscio*. See *Pro Sexto Roscio* 45–46, 50, 54–55, 59, 61, and 82 in particular.

[57] *De Or.* 2.229–230.

[58] Hellegouarc'h (1963) 227 et seq.; Livy 8.7.2; Sallust *Cat.*3.1.

[59] (1963) 321.

[60] Heinze (1925) 349; Hellegouarc'h (1963) 295 *et seq.*

[61] See *De Divinatione* 2. 61 "ille divinationis auctor" of Chrysippus and OLD at *auctor* 4–5.

[62] Tacitus, who did not like Pompey ("occultior non melior") ("more secretly is not better") (*Hist.* 2.38) nonetheless states (*Ann.* 3.28) "Pompeius, tertium consul corrigendis moribus delectus" ("Pompeius, as consul for the third time was chosen to reform public morals"). Tacitus' remark demonstrates that Pompey was associated with public morals.

[63] The terms "*imperitus*" and "*imperite*" occur over a hundred times in Cicero, and are generally the harshest expressions he employs to criticize an opponent.

[64] Gelzer (1968) 70 *et seq.*

[65] Lintott (1992) 88–109, especially 90, and Gelzer (1968) 70.

[66] *Iudicio publico* is a reference to the prosecutor's loss of Roman citizenship through a trial such as Balbus'. See Reid (1890) 11 and (1879) 35.

[67] The Latin technical term for guest-friend, *hospes*, corresponds to the Greek term πρόχενος. For a detailed discussion of the Latin term, see Mommsen (1952–1953) 3. 65 and 3. 602.

[68] An important quality in winning goodwill (*De Or.* 2.207, 210). In actuality, however, if Balbus benefits other Gaditans, they owe him, and hence Balbus' self-interests are looked after.

[69] Brunt (1982) 137 is no doubt correct in stating that "even if Balbus had a cast-iron defense . . . the jury might have convicted him out of prejudice unless Cicero had countered it by dwelling on matters extraneous to the legal issue, and unless Pompey and Crassus had exerted their influence on his behalf."

[70] For more on *invidia* see Pöschl (1983) 11, a study of *invidia* in the *Pro Cluentio* and *In Verr. Actio Primo*, and also the interesting article (1983) 7–37 in which K. Dunbabin and M. Dickie document the representation of *invidia* in literature and mosaics.

[71] Although Balbus was a non-Italian, Cicero Romanizes him right from the beginning of the speech as "L. Cornelius." Balbus undertook the delicate negotiations with Cicero in 59 B.C. when the "First Triumvirate" wished to have Cicero join them: *Ad Att.* 2.3.3, Münzer (1901) 4 1261, Reid (1890) 7. He also kept Caesar advised of events in Rome when the general was in Gaul (*Ad Quint. Frat.* 3.1.12, Münzer (1901) 4 1262, Reid (1890) 7, 8). The *invidia* did not die out. In 44 B.C. Balbus was quite disturbed by it (*Ad Att.* 14.21, 15.2).

[72] *Pro Sulla* (22–23); *In Ver.* 2.180–182; May (1988) 41–42, 69. An excellent example is Cicero's relationship with Hortensius, which Dyck (1996) discusses at 589–590. See also Sallust *Iug.* 85 for Marius' speech on suffering from the *invidia* of the nobles.

[73] (*Ad Att.* 7.7.6). Cicero's feelings towards Balbus appear to be contradictory and dependent upon their relative political positions at each given instance. At times he begrudges Balbus, but at other times he wishes to relieve the Spaniard of the hostility felt towards him (*Ad Att.* 15.2).

[74] May (1988) 22.

[75] *De Or.* 2.210.

[76] Hellegouarc'h (1963) 276, Liegle (1967) 229–273, Traina (1988) 93–101, Galinsky (1996) 86–88.

[77] Hellegouarc'h (1963) 244 *et seq.*, 476–483, Earl (1967) 20, Weinstock (1971) 230–233, Ramage (1987) 76–86, Galinsky (1996) 84.

[78] *In Verr.* 2.4.81; *Pro Sestio* 136; *Pro Murena* 17; Earl (1967) 47.

[79] Balbus became a *novus homo* later. See Burckhardt (1990) 77–99 for a discussion of *novus homo* and *nobilitas*.

[80] Neither Pompey nor Caesar would favor an incompetent subordinate (in theory at least); hence the mere fact that Balbus served under these excellent generals suggests (again in theory) that he shared some of their qualities.

[81] Earl (1967) 68–69, 76–77, Galinsky (1996) 80–90.

[82] The reference to "nullius laboris" is important in quenching jealousy (*De Or.* 2.210).

[83] *De Or.* 2.182, 207. Balbus, however, did not relinquish all political interests in Gades, since the Gaditans made him their guest-host in Rome.

[84] Hellegouarc'h (1963) 420–421.

[85] And was directed toward any who were *novi homines.* As Wiseman notes, "At every stage the new man's career was likely to be obstructed" (1971) 166; 165–166 for a discussion.

[86] Wiseman (1971) 1.

[87] Wiseman (1971) 6 and Scullard (1968) 84.

[88] Wiseman (1971) 69.

[89] Wiseman (1971) 69.

[90] *De Or.* 2.211: "Iam misericordia movetur, si is, qui audit, adduci potest ut illa, quae de altero deplorentur, ad suas res revocet, quas aut tulerit acerbas aut timeat, ut intuens alium crebro ad se ipsum revertatur." ("Now pity is aroused, if he who listens can be prompted to apply his own troubles, whose harshness he either bears or fears, to those which are being lamented regarding another man, so that while observing another, he frequently turns back to himself.")

[91] *De Or.* 2.182.

[92] Wiseman (1971) 109, Cicero *Topica* 73.

[93] Earl (1967) 20–21 and Moore (1989) 5–13.

[94] *De Or.* 2.208.

[95] See footnote 44.

[96] See *Post Red. in Sen.* 6, 7, 11, 12, 16, 20; *Post Red. ad Quir.* 14; *De Harus. Res.* 3, 4, 15; *De Domo Sua* 26, 56, and especially 73: ". . . decrevit ut omnes qui rem publicam salvam esse vellent ad me unum defendendum venirent, ostenditque nec stare potuisse rem publicam si ego non fuissem, nec futuram esse ullam si non redissem." ("[the senate] decreed that all who desired the republic to be free should come to defend me alone, and it showed that the republic could not stand if I had not existed, nor would it exist if I should not return"). See also Fuhrmann (1992) 95.

[97] *Pro Sestio,* for example. See May (1988) 93–94. The author of *Ad Her.* (1.8) suggests the winning of goodwill through mention of the speaker's former services on behalf of the Republic. Cicero's innovation is to identify the Republic so closely with himself that Balbus can help the Republic by helping him. See also *Pro Plancio* 1, 2, 3, 18, 26, 68, 77; *Pro Milone* 34–39; and *Pro Rab. Post.* 47, 48.

[98] May (1988) 30.

[99] Cicero's point here appears to be that Balbus is not getting above himself, although he may also be implying that the house is modest.

[100] See also my discussions at 73–75, 94–97, and 104.

[101] It is possible that Crassus was not actually present at Luca, and that Caesar represented his interests there. For a more detailed analysis, see Seager (2001) 117–118. In any case, it was agreed at Luca that Pompey and Crassus would run for consul in 55 B.C., that Caesar's command in Gaul would be renewed for another five years, and that Pompey would restrain Cicero from any more attacks on Caesar's legislation.

[102] May (1988) 126–127.

[103] Habicht (1990) 52–56, Fuhrmann (1992) 102–103. Mitchell (1991) 185–186 has a somewhat different interpretation.

[104] *De Or.* 2.182.

[105] *Pro Archia* begins in a similar fashion.

[106] *De Inv.* 1.22. In another case in which there was great hostility towards the defendant, that of Gaius Norbanus, Antonius wins the goodwill of the audience by stressing he was defending Norbanus from a sense of duty. *De Or.* 2.198: ". . . vix ut mihi tenuis quaedam venia daretur excusationis, quod tamen eum defenderem, qui mihi quaestor fuisset." (". . . so scarcely was a slender indulgence granted to me for the excuse that at any rate the man I was defending had been my quaestor.") Also: *De Or.* 2.202: "Ut tu illud initio, quod tibi unum ad ignoscendum homines dabant, tenuisti, te pro homine pernecessario, quaestore tuo, dicere!" ("How you held on at the beginning to that one thing which men excused you for, that you spoke on behalf of a man you were very closely connected to, your quaestor!") See also Thompson (1962) 346 *et seq.*

[107] *Ad Att.* 2.1.6; 2.18.3; 2.19.4; see also Brunt (1965) 10, Gelzer (1969) 148–149 and (1984) 125.

[108] See this chapter 18 and May (1988) 93–94.

[109] See *Pro Plancio* 1–4 and Hellegouarc'h (1963) 46, 53.

[110] Cicero demonstrates a great aptitude throughout his career for turning disadvantageous positions into advantageous ones. See May (1988) 20, 45, 64.

[111] See Fantham (1972) 117–119. See May (1980) 259–264 for the metaphor of the ship of state in the *Pro Sestio.*

[112] See also section 23.

[113] Cicero talks as if Pompey was Balbus' major patron, but in reality, by this point the Gaditan was much closer to Caesar, although Pompey does have a special connection to Balbus on the issue of citizenship. See Münzer (1901) 4 1261 *et seq.* Pompey, in his speech, also acted as if he were the major patron (and real target) of the opponents: "quos quidem hesterno die Cn. Pompeius copiosa oratione et gravi secum, si vellent, contendere iubebat, ab hoc impari certamine atque iniusta contentione avocabat." (59) ("whom indeed yesterday in an eloquent and weighty speech Gnaeus Pompeius called off from this unequal and unjust dispute, and told them if they wished to fight, to do so with himself.")

[114] This ties in with earlier mention of Balbus' military valor and contributions.

[115] This is one of the oldest rhetorical tactics. See *Rhet. ad Alex.* 29.9 and 36.6. Here, Cicero is flattering the jury by suggesting they have a sense of justice, but also by emphasizing that quality he no doubt desires that the jurors put aside any feelings of jealousy and hatred against his client. It should be noted that the statement about the jury's *aequitas* immediately precedes a plea for the jury not to hold Balbus' qualities against

him.

[116] Cf. 19.

[117] Hellegouarc'h (1963) 268.

[118] See Riggsby (1993) 264–265.

[119] See my previous discussion of this *exemplum* at 8–9.

[120] See also 21–25.

[121] See also Sullust *Cat.* 6.2 and Livy 1.11, where early Rome is seen as morally superior to the Rome of their own times.

[122] Earl (1967) 30, 39. Earl (1967) 30 also suggests political reasons for the upper classes holding antiquity and custom in such reverence. For a different perspective see Döpp (1989) 73–101, see also Meier (1980) 190–200 (especially 192) for context.

[123] Hellegouarc'h (1963) 303.

CHAPTER TWO: *INVENTIO*: PATHOS

[1] Aristotle *Rhet.* 1356a 14–17; Solmsen (1941) 38–39, Neumeister (1964) 30 n.59, Kirby (1990) 52.

[2] See also Wisse (1989) 234, who states Cicero discusses ethos from three standpoints: from that of speaker/client, from the speech, and from the audience.

[3] Quint. *Inst. Or.* 6.2.8 *et seq.*

[4] Neumeister (1964) 30 n.59 pinpoints the origin of this confusion as being caused by the translation of the rhetorical terminology from Greek into Latin.

[5] Lussky (1928)11.

[6] Lussky (1928) 8, 10, 11.

[7] Kennedy (1972) 220–223, May (1979) 245–246 and (1988) 5, Vasaly (1993) 20, 24, 36, Kirby (1990) 53 (Kirby suggests some modifications). See also Fantham (1973) 262.

[8] Wisse (1989) 233 *et seq.*

[9] *De Or.* 2.188; 2.197; 2.200; 2.212; 2.213; 2.214.

[10] This will be discussed later in this chapter. See also my chapter on *dispositio*.

[11] Although in this work Cicero does not use the term pathos, it is nonetheless his most complete treatment of the rousing of emotions.

[12] *De Or.* 2.178; *Brutus* 276, 279, 322; *Or.* 69; *De Opt. Gen.* 3. See also Leon (1935) 34.

[13] *De Or.* 2.185.

[14] *De Or.* 2.201.

[15] As Fantham (1973) 152–153 also notes.

[16] Fantham (1973) 262 notes the convergence of content and style in Cicero's use of *conciliare*. The same applied to his use of pathos, or *movere*; *vis, atrox, vehemens* all refer to both the manner in which the orator arouses pathos, and to what he says.

[17] Norbanus, a tribune of the plebs in 103 B.C., was charged under the *lex Apuleia de maiestate* as a sympathizer of Saturninus and for his conduct during his year in office. See Alexander (1990) 86 and Lengle (1931) 306 *et seq.*

[18] As proconsul in 106 B.C. at the battle of Arausio in Gaul, Q. Servilius Caepio did not co-operate with his superior, the consul, Cn. Mallius Maximus. The result was the

worst defeat the Romans had suffered since Cannae. Caepio was blamed. Caepio had previously been responsible for legislation which removed some of the control of the *quaestiones* from the Equites. Lengle (1931) 302–316.

[19] *In Verr.* 1.1; see also May (1988) 39.

[20] *Pro Sexto Roscio* 153–154.

[21] A term used to characterize a type of vivid description in which the author or orator describes someone or something in great detail in order to bring the image of that person or thing into the person's mind and thereby work on his emotions. See Vasaly (1993) 19–20.

[22] These fears do not have to be irrational to qualify for discussion in this chapter, the mere fact that Cicero is attempting to rouse intense feelings, whether rational or irrational, demonstrates a use of pathos.

[23] Nisbet (1992) 1–17.

[24] Lussky (1928) 84–85.

[25] Lussky (1928) 84. It should also be pointed out that pathos is not necessarily expected in a citizenship case, as demonstated by the *Pro Archia*.

[26] Brunt (1982) 137.

[27] An example of blending pathos and ethos (*De Or.* 2.200; 2.212).

[28] 5–6.

[29] Lussky (1928) 84.

[30] *De Inv.* 1.22, Leon (1935) 35.

[31] Lussky (1928) 85.

[32] It is possible to dispute whether this is truly an *ethica digressio*, which normally appear between the proof and the *peroratio*. Kaden (1912) 58 labels this passage a digression and I follow him, since strictly speaking the case is about Balbus and not Pompey. It is a testament to Cicero's skill that the digression is integrated so well into the speech that it appears to be a vital element of proof.

[33] See my chapter on Ethos for further discussion of this tactic, which Cicero puts to clever use in this speech. Here ethos and pathos are complementary; the description of Pompey's character provides the foundation for building up emotion.

[34] See Vasaly (1993) 134 for comment on the cultural mythology of ethos and locus.

[35] Quintilian (*Inst. Or.* 11.3.169 and12.10.27–33) considered this sound cacophanous. See also Wilkinson (1963) 11.

[36] This is an example of what Cicero has Antonius describe in *De Or.* 2.212 as a blending of the two genera, the mild (*lene*) and the emotional (*vehmens*). An example may be found in Antonius' description of his defense of Gaius Norbanus, where Antonius states he varied the emotional intensity of his pleadings (*De Or.* 2.200). Thus arguments based on both ethos and pathos form an indivisible strategy. See my earlier discussion at 28.

[37] The *exempla* were discussed in greater detail in chapter 1 8–9.

[38] See Vasaly (1983) 66 and (1993) 25, 223–224 for comment on the *Imp. Pomp.* passage. Reid (1890) 58 cites the *Imp. Pomp.* passage without discussion.

[39] See Plutarch *Pompey* 24–26, de Souza (1999) 149–178, and Pohl (1993) 266–278.

[40] Vasaly (1983) 198 states: "It has been shown that the orator uses both his audience's direct experience of places (those actually seen) and their indirect experience (those

described or named) in order to manipulate their feelings for his own ends. It is not surprising that the most striking uses of place in the speeches involve this kind of appeal, since Cicero himself testified to the power of emotional response of an audience in persuasion." Also ibid. 206: "In many cases, then, the use of place as part of the description of action involves an attempt by the orator to draw on the feelings and thoughts raised in his audience's minds by the places he mentions. His purpose in doing this is to manipulate their reaction to the actions described."

[41] See Classen (1981) 154 *et seq.*

[42] Cf. the *Pro Caelio* 33–35, where Cicero draws on similar emotions with his *prosopopoeia* of Appius Claudius the Blind. But whereas in that speech, Cicero pretended to bring an ancient character into contemporary Rome, in the *Pro Balbo* he imagines Pompey placed in the past, more associatively. See also the *Pro Sexto Roscio* 50, where Cicero employs the reverse strategy. In that speech the orator presents an unfavorable comparison of Erucius by placing him in the past. See also Roloff (1938) 57–71 and 96–130.

[43] Nisbet (1992) 5.

[44] See Craig (1979).

[45] See Iser (1974) 30–31, 37–39.

[46] Scullard (1963) 53–61.

[47] Scullard (1963) 113.

[48] Cf. the Italian allies and the Social War, which is a somewhat different case, since the reason for the war was the allies' demands for citizenship. See Brunt (1988) 93 *et seq.* See Griffith (1935) 234–235 for mercenaries and Rome.

[49] Gades was a Phoenican, but not a Carthaginian colony. See Reid (1890) 81, the Oxford Classical Dictionary (1996) 618, and Richardson (1986) 50–53.

[50] See Beard *et. al.* (1998) 173–174, Bayet (1926) 127–154 and (1957) 123, Coarelli (1988) 61–67, Fantham (1992), Steinby (1993) 15–17, Winter (1910), and Wissowa (1912) 273–275.

[51] (1972) 127.

[52] Anderson (1928) 37–39 and Ritter (1995) 64–65.

[53] Winter (1910) 256, Bayet (1957) 123.

[54] Galinsky (1972) 142 *et seq.* Vergil gives a description of the battle in *Aeneid* 8.205 *et seq.*

[55] Ritter (1995) 18–21, 64–65, 149–159.

[56] Since the main function of this passage is to stir the emotions of the audience, and since it contains some of the most powerful appeals to pathos in the speech, it is best to include it in this chapter even though it is a *digressio.*

[57] For example: *In Verr.* 1: 2.2.110, 2.2.113; *In Verr.*2: 3.209, 5.14, 5.25, 5.181; *Pro Rosc. Amer.* 33; *De Leg. Man.* 47, 60; *Pro Caec.* 87; *Pro Cluent.* 87; *Pro Rab. Perd.* 20, 27, 29–30, 35; *In Cat.* 1.4, 1.24, 3.15, 3.24; *Pro Mur.* 17; *Pro Sulla* 23; *Pro Arch.* 9, 19–20; *Pro Planc.* 20, 26, 51, 61, 78, 88; *Ad Quir.* 7, 11, 19; *De Har. Resp.* 24, 25; *Pro Sest.* 37, 50, 116; *De Prov. Cons.* 19, 26, 30. The only possible exception is in *Ad Quir.* 7–10; 20 where Cicero compares himself more favorably. See Carney (1960) 83–122.

[58] *Pro Rab. Per.* 27; *In Cat.* 3.24; *Ad Quir.* 7; *Pro Sest.* 37, 116; *De Leg. Man.* 47, 60.

[59] *Pro Sulla* 23; *Ad Quir.* 7, 19; *De Har. Resp.* 24.

[60] The end of the war enabled the *Equites* to trade safely in Africa once again. See Scullard (1968) 52–53. See also Brunt (1988) 184.

[61] Scullard (1968) 59.

[62] Scullard (1968) 60.

[63] Scullard (1968) 62.

[64] See Lintott (1974) 62–78, and especially 63, for a detailed analysis of the fighting between Clodius and Milo, and Cicero's relationship with Milo.

[65] Although Pompey was a protégé of Sulla, the latter could not be used as an example because he was detested. See Diehl (1988).

[66] See Quint. *Inst. Or.* 8.3.61–71 and 9.2.40–41 for more on this technique. See also Vasaly (1993) 19, 20, 90–104, 111.

[67] For example, that of Appius Claudius the Blind in the *Pro Caelio*: "Exsistat igitur ex hac ipsa familia aliquis ac potissimum Caecus ille . . ." (33–34) ("Therefore let someone from this family itself come forth, especially that Caecus. . ."). See also *Pro Milone*: "Fingite igitur cogitatione imaginem huius condicionis meae, si possimus efficere Milonem ut absolvatis, sed ita si P. Clodius revixerit . . ." (79) ("Shape in your mind, therefore, a mental picture of this stipulation of mine, if we could cause you to acquit Milo, but only if P. Clodius shall have come back to life . . ."). It is also similar to that of the pupils of Plato summoned up in the *De Fin*: "Quid si reviviscant Platonis illi et deinceps qui eorum auditores fuerunt et tecum ita loquantur?" (4.61) ("What if those students of Plato were to come back to life again and thereafter their audience, and were to speak with you in such a way?").

[68] See Quint. *Inst. Or.* 6.2.32 "Insequitur ἐνάργεια, quae a Cicerone inlustratio et evidentia nominatur, quae non tam dicere videtur quam ostendere, et adfectus non aliter, quam si rebus ipsis intersimus, sequentur." ("The result will be *enargeia*, what Cicero calls *illustratio* and *evidentia*, a quality which makes us seem not so much to be talking about something as exhibiting it. Emotions will ensue just as if we were present at the event itself.") I use Russell (2001) for all passages from Quintilian.

[69] Both in Greco-Roman art and in the literary tradition, envy is often depicted as a bird or wild animal biting or tearing at its victims. See Dunbabin and Dickie (1983) 7–37.

[70] See Lussky (1928) 85.

[71] Vasaly (1993) 134 refers to this passage while discussing the political perception of Rome as world empire.

[72] Lussky (1928) 85.

[73] I disagree with Lussky (1928) 86 who states "[t]he emotional appeal is not diffused through the entire *oratio*." As I argue throughout this chapter, appeals to emotion can be seen throughout the speech.

[74] (1964) 76.

CHAPTER THREE: *INVENTIO*: LOGOS

[1] See *De Inv.* 1.51–77; *Top.* 53–57; *Ad Her.* 28–30. For an account of rhetorical deductive argumentation from Aristotle to Cicero see Craig (1979) 7–11.

[2] Cousin (1962) 214.

[3] I follow Reid's (1890) 16–20 division of arguments in the *argumentatio*, except for the last section (56–65). I divide this (as does Kaden [1912] 58) into two: 56–59, which contains arguments, and 60–65 which consists of the *peroratio*.

[4] Cicero himself admits this: "Donatum esse L. Cornelium praesens Pompeius dicit . . . accusator fatetur" (19) ("That Roman citizenship was conferred upon Lucius Cornelius, Pompeius states in this court . . . the prosecutor acknowledges").

[5] Cf. Riggsby (1995) 245 *et seq.*

[6] Cf. Nisbet (1992) 7, Neumeister (1964) 172.

[7] *Pro Balbo* 1–2.

[8] For a discussion of the term *fundos fieri* see Kaden (1912) 41–43, *Thesaurus Linguae Latinae* (1924) 1580.50 *et seq.*, Mommsen (1952–1953) 3 693 n. 4, 3 796 n. 3, and Cousin (1962) 218–226.

[9] See Brunt (1982) 142, 143–144.

[10] Reid (1890) 64, 65.

[11] Kaden (1912) 42–43.

[12] Although Cicero will talk about the most dangerous or refutable point of the other side's case and not necessarily the most prominent, in this particular instance it is likely the *fundus fieri* issue formed an influential part of the prosecutor's argument. If there were other arguments by the prosecutor Cicero would at least have had to pay lip service to them in *Pro Balbo*.

[13] Further evidence that the major portion of the prosecutor's speech did not consist of an outright attack on Pompey is Cicero's assertion at 59 that Pompey in his speech the previous day had told the prosecutor to attack him, but to leave Balbus alone. If the prosecutor had spent most of his speech attacking Pompey, Pompey's request would not make sense.

[14] For more detail on these laws see Berger (1953) 552, 561, Reid (1890) 65–66, Gaius *Instit.* 2.225–2.226, Justinian *Instit.* 2.22; 2.14n; *De Fin.*2.17; *In Verr.* 1.43. There is no reason to suppose, from the information available about these laws, that either law had a *fundus fieri* clause or any reference to non-Romans. Cicero's point here is to contrast Roman laws which other states could adopt and which would apply to all their citizens, with a Roman law which enfranchised individuals.

[15] Reid (1879) 8, Cousin (1962) 252, Berger (1953) 553.

[16] Brunt (1982) 143–144; see also Reid (1890) 16: "When the status of a whole community was to be changed, its assent was necessary, but to suppose that no single individual from the community could change his status to that of a Roman citizen without its assent, was absurd." For a different view see Braunert (1966) 51–73 and Galsterer (1976) 132–133, 162–164. For a rebuttal: Brunt (1982) 136–147.

[17] Sherwin-White (1973) 188 n.3: "The longer discussion in 19–22 shows that Cicero merely means that this was a purely internal law that concerned non-Romans as individuals only, not as states."

[18] It should be noted that the *lex Aquilia* shows that Rome could make unilateral, viritim grants of citizenship.

[19] Brunt (1982) 143.

[20] See pages 49–50 of this chapter.

[21] Rohde (1903) 118.

[22] See chapter one, page 18–19.

[23] Clerc (1971) 1.178 et seq., 2.1 et seq., Reid (1890) 67, and Wackernagel (1930) RE 14.2 2132.34 et seq.

[24] Richardson (1986) 20–29, 39–40, 54–55, 63–64, 73–74; Reid (1890) 67.

[25] See chapter one, page 4–6, 14–15, 17, 18, and 22.

[26] See sections 20 and 22, and page 00 (93) of this book.

[27] Rohde (1903) 78 refers to it as an argument de rebus negotio *adiunctis ex collatione*.

[28] Cicero also discusses change of Roman citizenship in *Pro Caec*. 96–105 and *De Domo* 77. See Reid (1890) 70 and Kaden (1912) 51–53 for comment.

[29] *Top*. 36, 37; Reid (1890) 71; Kaden (1912) 53–54; Watson (1967) 237–255.

[30] Cf. page 49 of this chapter and Nisbet (1992) 7.

[31] That is not to say that the statement that Rome can enfranchise anybody is incorrect; but merely that this conclusion is not supported by the proofs.

[32] "Iure enim nostro neque mutare civitatem quisquam invitus potest" (27) ("by our law a man cannot change his citizenship against his will"); "ne quis invitus civitate mutetur neve in civitate maneat invitus!" (31) ("that no one should be removed from or remain on the citizen roll against his will").

[33] Brunt (1982) 143.

[34] Reid (1890) 76

[35] Brunt (1982) 141.

[36] Scullard (1975) 601 n. 3.

[37] I.e. (a) that there was no saving clause in the Gaditan treaty, but (b) that even if there were such a clause, the *lex Cornelia Gallia* would invalidate it. I use *in utramque partem* in the same sense as Craig (1979) ii, 234; that is: if X, then Y; if not X, then still Y.

[38] Hardy (1917) 133.

[39] Rohde (1903) 68.

[40] Such a clause is called a *sanctio* and governs the relationship between the *lex* and earlier legislation, and sometimes the *lex* and any possible future legislation designed to abrogate it. Schiller (1978) 245.

[41] An *obtestio* is a prayer to the gods to punish transgressors, while a *consecratio* stipulates human punishment. A *lex sacrosancta* generally contained both. See Reid (1890) 76–77.

[42] Reid (1890) 18 "He [Cicero] even contends that any such treaty stipulation would be overridden by the *lex Gellia Cornelia*. Here he treads on rather dangerous ground, for his argument really involves the assumption that the resolutions of the *comitia* ought to override all treaty obligations." Brunt (1982) 141 hesitantly puts forth the same view, with a caution about textual problems in Section 33: "the general rule of the Twelve Tables 'ut quodcumque postremeum populus iussisset, id ius ratumque esset' would hardly have applied to the extent of justifying the abrogation of 'anything sacrosanct,' even though no saving clause had been inserted in the later statute." For comment on the text in 33 see Reid (1890) 106.

[43] Polybius 6.14; Sallust *Bell. Jug*. 39; Livy 7.17.12. See also Brunt (1982) 138–140. For a different view, see Braunert (1966) 62–65. Brunt (1982) 139 refutes him.

[44] Braunert (1966) 65–66 again disagrees, and is refuted by Brunt (1982) 140.

[45] See Reid's (1890) 77 note on this term.

[46] For the purposes of his speech, Cicero says this was the only clause in the treaty: "Nihil est enim aliud in foedere, nisi ut 'pia et . . .'" (35) ("For there is nothing else in the treaty save that 'There shall be a holy and . . .'"). Livy (32.2.5) mentions another clause regarding a *praefectus*.

[47] Reid (1890) 79, Cousin (1962) 263, Brunt (1982) 142, Kunkel (1973) 38.

[48] See Heuer (1941) 25 *et seq.* for a refutation of the suggestion that *comiter* means the same thing as *communiter*.

[49] Rohde (1903) 67.

[50] Rohde (1903) 43. This is an argument *de locis extrinsecus assumptis de testimoniis*.

[51] Kaden (1912) 55; Sherwin-White (1973) 301; see also Brunt (1982) 143.

[52] See chapter one, pages 7–10 and 12–13.

[53] Rohde (1903) 43.

[54] Brunt (1982) 137.

[55] Plutarch, *Mar.* 28: "δοκοῦντος εἶναι τούτου παρανόμου καί τινων ἐγκαλούντων, εἰπεῖν, ὅτι τοῦ νόμου διὰ τὸν τῶν ὅπλων ψόφον οὐ κατακούσειεν." ("And when some complained that this seemed to be against the law, he said that he did not hear the law because of the noise of arms.") See Kaden (1912) 48, Reid (1890) 13, Sherwin-White (1973) 295, Badian (1958) 206, 259.

[56] Reid (1890) 13 states that there is no record of even an *ex post facto* enabling act. Kaden (1912) 48–49 argues that Marius must have had an enabling act because Cicero presents Marius' case as an analogy to Balbus'. He states that Marius enfranchised these men under a enabling act, which Marius did not yet know about when he made the bestowal (hence the word δοκοῦντος). Kaden's argument is weak because Cicero presents several analogies quite dissimiliar to Balbus' as if they are the same throughout the speech (especially in 51 and 53–55).

[57] Brunt (1982) 145.

[58] See Reid (1890) 86, Cousin (1962) 269.

[59] Pages 39–42.

[60] Cf. sections 22, 23, 24, 25, 31, 37. Resonance will be discussed in my chapter on *dispositio*. See Craig (1979) 3–4, 38–39, 52–53.

[61] See Reid (1890) 88, 13.

[62] See Cousin (1962) 272 on Cicero's calling Utica a *civitas foederata*.

[63] See Cousin (1962) 273. Probably from a speech Hannibal gave before the battle of Tessin.

[64] Sherwin-White (1973) 301.

[65] Sherwin-White (1973) 301. See also Greenidge (1901) 426, n 2; the term *repetitio* is used also in Livy 7.32.1, and in *Pro Domo* 144: see Reid (1890) 89, 80.

[66] First stated at the end of section 52: "nemo umquam est de civitate accusatus, quod aut populus fundus factus non esset, aut quod foedere civitatis mutandae ius impediretur" ("no one of them has ever been prosecuted for his assumption of citizenship, either because his own people had not "given its consent," or because his right to change his citizenship was debarred by a treaty.")

[67] Brunt (1982) 144.

[68] It is irrelevant because all this argument proves is that no case where consent was

an issue had ever come before the court; it does not mean that because no case had come before the court, it was impossible for a state to give consent (as Cicero suggests).

[69] Reid (1890) 13–14.

[70] See Reid (1890) 89 and Cousin (1962) 274 for discussion about the date of the treaty.

[71] Rohde (1903) 109.

[72] Sherwin-White (1973) 97.

[73] Levick (1967) 256–8. See also Gruen (1969) 8–11, Sherwin-White (1973) 96–97. Badian (1954) 101–102 holds a different view.

[74] Dionysius (6.17) puts the commencement of these rites at Rome in 476 B.C. See Cousin (1962) 275, Scheid (1995) 15–31, esp. 20–21.

[75] See Münzer (1919) *RE* 10.2 1655.

[76] In *De Oratore* (1.172–173) Cicero has Crassus criticize other orators who do not have a good knowledge of the law.

[77] See *De Legibus* 3.30, where Lucullus makes a similar point about houses and *dignitas*.

[78] This tactic is similar to the one (appropriation and reversal) analyzed in several speeches by Riggsby (1995) 245–256.

[79] This seems the best interpretation; the actual facts regarding the inheritance are unclear. See Reid (1890) 94, Kaden (1912) 37.

[80] Rohde (1903) 51.

[81] Rohde (1903) 57.

[82] Rhode (1903) 134.

[83] Cicero considered *in utramque partem* arguments very important and the mark of an excellent orator (*De Or.* 3.80). See also Leeman (1981) 67.

CHAPTER FOUR: *DISPOSITIO*

[1] Quintilian also compares rhetors and sculptors at 5.12.20–21.

[2] Neumeister (1964) 11, Stroh (1975) 8, Classen (1985) 7. I agree with Classen (1985) 5–6 that a forensic speech may also have a political purpose. Classen gives the example of Cicero's speeches from his consular year.

[3] *De Or.* 1.142: "deinde inventa non solum ordine, sed etiam momento quodam atque iudicio dispensare atque componere" ("Then, not only must he find the order [for the arguments], but he must also distribute and arrange them with discernment as to their influence"), and *De Or.* 2.313 where Cicero is critical of orators who place their weakest points first: "Atque etiam in illo reprehendo eos, qui, quae minime firma sunt, ea prima conlocant" ("And moreover I reproach those who place those argument which are weakest first"). See also *Ad Her.* 3.18; Stroh (1975) 16; and Classen (1981) 172.

[4] Stroh (1975) 19–20, 71, 178, 255.

[5] Riggsby (1995) 245–256.

[6] In *Pro Cluentio* (1), Cicero states his speech is divided into two parts. See Stroh (1975) 226–227; 268; Kirby (1990) 121.

[7] Cf Cousin (1962) 214; see also my chapter on logos, 47–48.

[8] According to ancient rhetorical theory, speeches were generally composed of four

parts: an *exordium, narratio, argumentatio* (consisting of *refutatio* and *confirmatio*) and *peroratio*. Different rhetoricians make various minor changes to this arrangement *Ad Her.* 1.4; Quint. *Inst. Or.* 4. Pr.6; *De Or.* 1.143.

[9] The difficulty the *dispositio* of the *Pro Balbo* poses for modern commentators is demonstrated by the differing breakdowns given for the speech. Reid [(1890) 15–20] considers 1–16 the *exordium*; 17–19 a separate section which he does not label; 19–56 the *argumentatio*; and 56–65 the *peroratio*. Kaden [(1912) 58] divides the speech as follows: *exordium* 1–4; *narratio, partitio, propositio* 5–19 (*digressio* 9–16); *confirmatio, refutatio* 20–59; *peroratio* 60–65. Cousin [(1962) 236] has a rather confusing arrangement: *exordium* 1–4; *narratio* 5–19; *propositio* 5–6; *divisio* 6; *refutatio* 7–59; *peroratio* 59–65. Hoche [(1882) 10–16] divides the speech as follows: *exordium* 1–4; *propositio* and *narratio* 5–7; *confirmatio* 7–56; *peroratio* 56–65.

[10] On the contrary, both Cicero and Quintilian state that it is important for the orator to hide his "art," that is, his rhetorical technique from the judges (*De Or.* 2.177 and *Inst. Or.* 4.5.6). See also Neumeister (1964) 133. Although here the two orators are talking about blurring the transitions between arguments, Cicero in this speech applies the technique to his entire speech. The result is a speech which seems extemporaneous and thus more from the heart—from both Cicero's own heart, and that of the case. Both Cicero and Quintilian consider such an appearance of extemporization desirable. Quintilian (4.1.54–55) even suggests that the orator should give an impromptu *exordium* so that the entire speech would appear *ex tempore*, even though in truth the remaining speech would have been carefully worked out. Cicero, on the other hand, disapproves of *exordia* which are truly extempore, as is clear from the criticism of Philippus in *De Or.* 2.316. Doubtless such an appearance of spontaneity gave an impression of truthfulness.

[11] Neumeister (1964) 201, Stroh (1975) 12.

[12] As Quint. (*Inst Or.* 7.10.10) states: "Quare plurima petamus a nobis et cum causis deliberemus, cogitemusque homines ante invenisse artem quam docuisse." ("Let us therefore look for most of what we need from our own resources, take counsel with the Cause we are to plead, and realize that men discovered our art before they taught it.")

[13] Quint. *Inst. Or.* 7.10.11: "Illa enim est potentissima, quaeque vere dicitur oeconomica totius causae dispositio, quae nullo modo constitui nisi velut in re praesente potest" ("For the most powerful, and properly called the orderly arrangement of the entire case is that which it is in no way possible to establish unless the matter is at hand.")

[14] Unfortunately we know nothing of either Pompey's or Crassus' speeches. Reid (1890) 14, quoting *De Leg.* 2.5, states that Pompey's speech contained praise of Cicero. The *De Leg.* passage, however, discusses Ampius Balbus' trial, and not Cornelius'.

[15] Classen (1981) 171–172. Cf. *Pro Mur.*; *Pro Sulla*; *Pro Flacco*; *Pro Caelio*; *Pro Scauro*; *Pro Plancio*. This is not quite accurate, since there is a very brief *narratio* in the *Pro Balbo*.

[16] *Brutus* 190.

[17] As Classen states (1981) 151 in regard to other speeches [*Pro Roscio* 83; *Pro Caec.* 10; *Pro Tull.* 37; *Pro Q. Roscio* 15; *In Verr.*2.3.144; 2.4.105; *Pro Cluent.* 11; 17; 20; 30; 66; 149; *Pro Sestio* 31; 96]: "wo er [Cicero] solche Abschnitte ankündigt, sucht er den Eindruck zu erwecken, dass ein weites Ausholen zum rechten Verständnis der Sache oder aus anderen Gründen unerlässlich sei. Bisweilen zieht es der Redner auch vor, durch eine

sorgfältige Disposition Aspekte, die nicht zur Sache gehören, gleichberechtigt neben den eigentlichen Redegegenstand zu stellen und damit deren gegenseitiges Verhältnis zu verdunkeln."

[18] Chapter one (ethos) 6–7.

[19] Kirby (1990) 122 and Craig (1979) 156.

[20] *Ad Her.* 2.28; 3.16; *De Inv.* 1.97; *De Or.* 3.312. See also May (1988) 28, who states that the *ethica digressio* placed between *argumentatio* and *peroratio* became a regular feature in Cicero's forensic speeches. Cf. *Pro Sexto Amer.*; *Div. in Caec.*; *Pro Sulla*; *Pro Flacco*; *Pro Sestio*; *Pro Milone*. In *De Or.* Cicero is more flexible about the positioning of digressions. The digression on Sassia in *Pro Cluentio* is also placed in an unusual place—at the beginning of the *narratio/argumentatio*. See Stroh (1975) 226 who sees the year *Pro Cluentio* was delivered (66 B.C.) as a beginning of a new epoch in rhetoric as Cicero breaks away from the restraints of the rhetorical tradition.

[21] I argue that Cicero's arrangement produces a crescendo because he moves from individuals to important groups of people to the entire Roman world.

[22] See also *De Or.* 2.325.

[23] McClintock (1975) argues convincingly that Cicero's narrative technique produced fundamental changes in the *narratio*. See 34: "It will be Cicero's triumph to combine all three [ethos, *narratio*, logos] into his narrative technique in such a subtle way that persuasion will begin unnoticed in the narration, without having to be suspended until the argument." McClintock examines both the tradition of judicial narration up until Cicero's time, and Cicero's own increasingly innovative use of *narratio* throughout his career. See also McClintock (1975) 73–74, 191. In the *Pro Balbo* Cicero introduces "ethical" proofs in the *exordium* and the *digressio*, the latter of which takes the place of a *narratio*.

[24] This is because traditionally the *narratio* was a simple account of events. See McClintock (1975) 11–58.

[25] In *De Or.* (2.319), Cicero states that points raised in the *exordium* must come from the essential parts of the defense. Cicero also shifts arguments forward into the *exordium* in *In Q. Caecilium* (Stroh (1975) 186). See also Stroh (1975) 226, who discusses such a technique in terms of *Pro Cluentio* and Neumeister (1964) 134–135.

[26] This is not to denigrate the intelligence of the jurors, but to emphasize the clever rhetorical ability of Cicero.

[27] This "seed-planting" is one of the *insidiae* mentioned by Quintilian (10.1.21): "Saepe enim praeparat, dissimulat, insidiatur orator, eaque in prima parte actionis dicit, quae sunt in summa profutura" ("For often the orator prepares the listeners, dissembles, lays ambushes for them, and speaks about things in the first part of the action which will be profitable at the end").

[28] Neumeister (1964) 110 *et seq.*, especially 111, cites a similar tactic in *Pro Milone* where Cicero brings up the example of Orestes, who killed his mother and afterwards was acquitted.

[29] For the role of *dispositio* and *invidia* in *Pro Cluentio* see Kirby (1990) 121, Stroh (1975) 199–227, and Classen (1965) 104–142.

[30] *Pro Cluentio* (1). See also Stroh (1975) 199 and Kirby (1990) 55.

[31] I do not mean to imply that these extant speeches *had* to take the form they actu-

ally did, but to demonstrate that the *dispositio* was not haphazard, and that Cicero had good reasons for the arrangement of his arguments.

[32] In *De Or.* 2.208–209 Cicero explains that if something wrongful is done against good men in general, or anybody in general, then a disgust (*offensio*) is created not unlike *invidia* or hatred (*odium*). But people are especially jealous (*invident maxime*) when those who are their equals or their social inferiors rise above them. Cicero's analysis would suggest that feelings would run more strongly against Balbus than against Cluentius.

[33] See, for example, *Pro Fonteio*, *Pro Scauro*, and *Pro Flacco*. See also Vasaly (1993) 136, 152, and especially 191–243, Balsdon (1979) 30–76, and Thompson (1989).

[34] See also my discussions at 14–20, 94–96, and 104.

[35] Chapter three (logos) 48.

[36] De Or. 2.313. As Stroh (1975) 74 points out, the jury expect to hear convincing arguments from the start, and it is important to satisfy that expectation as soon as possible. A point which Cicero can depict as conceded by the opposition fulfills this requirement.

[37] The ridicule of the prosecutor is an important psychological tool. It helps to ruin the jury's trust in the opposition. As Stroh (1975) 75 states, the principle of psychological *praeparatio* calls for the first arguments to prepare for and support what follows either by the establishment of the listeners' goodwill towards the speaker or the destruction of the opponent's credibility. Cicero employs both techniques.

[38] Sherwin-White (1973) 160.

[39] Although based on the emotion of fear, this argument is not irrational.

[40] Chapter three (logos) 54.

[41] Inst. Or. 7.1.17. See also De Or. 2.313–314, quoted in my previous discussion at 72–73. Cicero believes one must begin with a strong argument, and save the most resounding argument until the end of the speech.

[42] The crescendo only appears within the larger framework of arguments: the *lex Cornelia Gallia* (19), the issue of when consent could be given (20), the consequences of Rome's inability to enfranchise foreigners (22–26), Roman citizenship laws including the appeal to patriotism (27–31), the invalidity of the Gaditan treaty (33). Each of these arguments is more potent than the preceding one. The one argument which could be considered weaker than the preceding one, that is, the argument about Roman citizenship laws, is strengthened by being bound to an emotional appeal to patriotism. The importance of *dispositio* within this framework can be seen when one attempts to reposition one of the arguments. For example, if one placed the last argument (that about the invalidity of the Gaditan treaty) first, it would make all the other arguments appear redundant. Within each group of arguments, however, as seen above, there is not necessarily such a crescendo. In fact, weak arguments are often buried between stronger ones.

[43] See Reid (1890) 76 and my chapter three (logos) 56.

[44] See Reid (1890) 18, Brunt (1982) 141, and my chapter on logos 56–57.

[45] In De Oratore 2.310 Cicero advocates the interweaving of arguments based on ethos, pathos, and logos throughout speeches: "Et quoniam, quod saepe iam dixi, tribus rebus homines ad nostram sententiam perducimus, aut docendo aut conciliando aut permovendo, una ex tribus his rebus res prae nobis est ferenda, ut nihil aliud nisi docere velle videamur, reliquae duae, sicuti sanguis in corporibus, sic illae in perpetuis ora-

tionibus fusae esse debebunt" ("And since, as I have often said already, we lead men to our opinion by three methods, either by instructing them, or by winning them over, or by rousing their emotions, we must employ one of these three methods openly, so that we appear to want to do nothing other than instruct. The other two, just like blood in our bodies, must be spread throughout the entire speech.").

[46] In *De Or.* 2.332 Cicero advocates the following: "Omnia autem concludenda sunt plerumque rebus augendis vel inflammando iudice vel mitigando" ("Moreover for the most part they all must be concluded by embellishment or by inflaming or assuaging the jurors").

[47] This argument demonstrates Cicero's ability to employ foreigners' and provincials' ethos for his own purpose. Cf. *In Verr.*; *Pro Fonteio*; *Pro Flacco*.

[48] The theme gains force with each repetition. See Neumeister (1964) 75, and 112, 118 *et seq.* for a description of these techniques as used in *Pro Milone*. See also Craig (1979) 3, 38–39, 52–53.

[49] See above, note 42.

[50] *De Or.* 2.314; 2.332.

[51] See chapter two (pathos) 39–40.

[52] Plutarch *Pomp.* 13.4–13.5 also gives a second version of the origins of Pompey's title "Magnus," namely that Pompey's men gave him the title, which was afterwards confirmed by Sulla.

[53] Resonance occurs when an argument made earlier in a speech is repeated conjointly with another argument. If the second argument is weaker, it gains strength through its association with the repeated stronger argument. In addition an argument can gain strength through sheer repetition. For a more detailed explanation of resonance see Craig (1979) 3, 38–39, 52–53.

[54] The appeal to the jury (in 18) to lay aside their *invidia* comes after the emotional digression on Pompey, see page 74 *et seq.* of this chapter.

[55] See pages 73–74 of this chapter.

CHAPTER FIVE: *ELOCUTIO*

[1] See also *De Or.* 3.37; 3.91.

[2] Laurand (1965) 307: ". . . le *Pro Balbo*, et plus encore le *Pro Tullio* ressemblent au *Pro Caecina*: ce sont des plaidoyers civils. Le *Pro Tullio*, qui a pour sujet une question d'indemnité, est naturellement plus simple; le *Pro Balbo*, traitant du droit de cité, l'est un peu moins."

[3] For a discussion of Cicero's style, see von Albrecht (1973, 1989), Gotoff (1979), Johnson (1971), Laurand (1965), Lebreton (1901) and Leeman (1963).

[4] Cicero works hard, both through his use of types of arguments and style, to demonstrate to the jurors that in fact the case was of the highest importance to Rome and that their verdict could affect the security of the republic.

[5] Of course Cicero argues from the other end in the *Pro Balbo*: that what is really at stake is Pompey's enfranchisement. This is an attempt on his part, among other things, to elevate the importance of the case.

[6] In *De Or.* 3.211 Cicero states that criminal cases require one style and civil suits and

unimportant cases another style.

[7] Interestingly enough, the *Pro Archia*, which also concerned a citizenship case, is written in a more elevated style, but for different reasons. Archias was a poet, and Cicero employs the style of the speech to demonstrate the stylistic debt he declares he owes to Archias (1). Cicero feels it is necessary, however, to apologize for employing an elevated style in the *Pro Archia* (3).

[8] There is some controversy about whether there were actually three different styles or not. Laurand (1965) 231–233 argues that there were, while Johnson (1971) 3 disputes this. See also Hendrickson (1905) 249–290 for a thorough analysis of the three styles.

[9] Laurand (1965) 321, 323, 327–331.

[10] Laurand (1965) 321.

[11] Although he cites this sentence, Laurand does not comment on it.

[12] Because of the careful artistry of the sentences in the *exordium*, I have made line divisions in order to draw attention to the construction of these sentences.

[13] The *Pro Caecina, Pro Archia, Post Reditum in Senatu, Pro Sestio, In Vatinium, Pro Caelio, De Prov. Cons.*, for example.

[14] See Gotoff (1979) 68–69 for a discussion of periodicity.

[15] Gotoff (1979) 137, 138, 231

[16] See Gotoff (1979) 96 *et seq.* for a stylistic analysis of the opening to the *Pro Archia*.

[17] Classen (1981) 175 *et seq.*, with reference to *Pro Quinctio* and *Pro Caecina*, points out that the repetition of single words influences and prepares the audience for the orator's argumentation.

[18] As Reid (1890) 47 notes.

[19] Robinson (1994) 475 *et seq.* notes that Cicero never refers to his banishment as exile but instead employs euphemisms.

[20] See *Ad Her.* 4.44 and 4.18 for hyperbaton. See also Gotoff (1979) 252.

[21] There are textual problems at this point; the italics are Peterson's. *Procedere* is Peterson's emendation.

[22] Cicero often employs repetition of the word *nihil*. See *De Nat. Deor.* 1. 51, 1. 75, 1. 92, 2.18, 2. 39, 2. 47, 2. 104, 3. 23, 3.30; *Off.* 1. 151; and *Tusc.* 4. 61. See also Pease (1955) 1.75.

[23] A technique remarked on by Quintilian *Inst. Or.* 9.4.29–30. See also Neumeister (1964) 157, 159.

[24] An important element in style: cf. *De Or.* 3.173 *et seq.*

[25] Such a technique is not lost upon modern television advertisers, who also seek to persuade.

[26] Classen (1981) 172–173. See also Quintilian *Inst. Or.* 2.17.21.

[27] McClintock (1975) 34, 73–74, Neumeister (1962) 8, 110–112, and my chapter 4 on *dispositio* 73.

[28] Here I would like to emphasize that I do not mean to underestimate the intelligence of the jurors, but to comment on the skill of the orator. Cf. *De Or.* 2.202–203, and also Cicero's comments that he had thrown sand in the jurors' eyes in his *Pro Cluentio*.

[29] My italics throughout.

[30] Lebreton (1901) 78 cites this passage as one of two examples in Cicero's entire cor-

pus in which the name of a people is used in the singular in a collective sense. (The other example is found in *Ad Att.* 5.16.4.) In my view Cicero's reason for employing the singular here is rhetorical. The case is about an individual enfranchisement and Cicero wants the audience to think in terms of brave foreign individuals.

[31] This movement from individuals to the whole Roman people foreshadows the movement of the *peroratio* at section 64. See page 107 of this chapter.

[32] See Classen (1981) 180 for Cicero's use of individual words that have a strong emotional effect. In the *Pro Balbo* Cicero focuses on and repeats these emotive words throughout the speech.

[33] Both are legal terms in foreign relations. See *In Caec.* 66, *lex Acilia* l.1, Lintott (1993) 32–33, Mommsen (1952–1953) 3. 659 and 3. 1026, and Wegner (1969) 72–94.

[34] Neumeister (1962) 110.

[35] See Classen (1981) 168 for general comment about this technique.

[36] See *De Or.* 3.202 for the importance of visual presentation of events in creating an impression on the audience.

[37] As von Albrecht (1989) 41 points out, it is Cicero's ability to break events down into small, sequential units that largely creates vividness.

[38] In *De Or.* 3.104–105 Cicero remarks on the effectiveness of using the stylistic device of amplification in rousing emotion.

[39] In *De Or.* 2.177 Cicero states that sometimes it is better for the orator not to state expressly a proposition. Here, by phrasing the proposition as a question, he makes it explicit, but allows the audience to come to the conclusion themselves by answering the question.

[40] See also my discussions at 14–20, 73–75, and 104.

[41] A common technique, cf. *Pro Roscio Amer.* 40 *et seq.*; *Pro Cluentio* 113 *et seq.*; *Pro Rab. Perduell.* 29; *Pro Plancio* 31 *et seq.*; *Pro Caelio* 62 *et seq.* In *Pro Archia* 15 Cicero imagines an objector raising a point.

[42] *De Or.* 2.177.

[43] See Classen (1981) 181–182 for a discussion of Cicero's strategic reasons for employing questions. Classen believes that Cicero often employs questions to get himself out of difficult situations. It is quite possible Cicero is employing questions for this reason in this passage from the *Pro Balbo*, but I also believe that Cicero is doing so to shape the argument, and for the other reasons I give above.

[44] See Reid (1890) 106 for a discussion of textual problems in this passage.

[45] Livy 7.17; Reid (1890) 77. See also Crawford (1996) 2. 721, who believes that the clause is not truly from the Twelve Tables, but instead is a first century B.C. invention.

[46] Reid (1890) 77 suggests that either the terms of the clause were not uniform (which is unlikely) or Cicero has misquoted it, since he does not use the same words each time he mentions the clause. Cf. *Pro Caec.* 95–96 and *De Dom.* 106.

[47] This characterization through imagined quotation is common in Cicero's speeches and it is an effective tactic. See May (1988) 17–18, 26, 33–34, 133–134, 137–138, 145, 166.

[48] Reid (1890) 79. Although neither Reid (1890), Peterson (1911), Cousin (1962), Klotz (1919), nor Bellardi (1975) have suggested emending *nusquam*, some of the manuscripts offer different readings (*enim se nusquam, senus enim quam, enim senus quam,*

enim se nunquam): see Cousin (1962) 262. In any case, since nusquam is the *lectio dif-ficilior*, it is most likely the correct reading.

[49] The use of two words such as *commendatione* and *iudicio*, and *voluntate* and *sen-tentiis* to express the same or a similar thought is characteristic of Cicero's style. See Laughton (1961) 46.

[50] *De Or.* 2.177.

[51] As always: Menge (1995) 343.

[52] In *De Or.* 2.177 Cicero stresses the importance of variety so that the listener does not perceive the orator's art (this is especially important in the *argumentatio*) or become bored by too much monotony.

[53] Classen (1981) 182.

[54] The repetition of a verb in different tenses together with an adverb is also common in Roman poetry. See Horace *Epist.* 1. 2. 42–43, Ovid *Her.* 4. 109, Ovid *Met.* 7. 690–691, 14. 379, and Wills (1996) 302.

[55] Hellegouarc'h (1963) 244 *et seq.*, 476–483, Earl (1967) 20, Weinstock (1971) 230–233, Ramage (1987) 76–86, Moore (1989) 5 *et seq.*, Galinsky (1996) 84. See also my previous discussion at 14–20, 73–75, and 94–96.

[56] Moore (1989) 12.

[57] Moore (1989) 16, Hellegouarc'h (1963) 250.

[58] See Neumeister (1964) 177 for a discussion of Cicero's use in the *Pro Milone*.

Bibliography

Alexander, Michael C. 1990. *Trials in the Late Roman Republic, 149 B.C. to 50 B.C.* Toronto: University of Toronto Press.

———. 2002. *The Case for the Prosecution in the Ciceronian Era.* Ann Arbor: The University of Michigan Press.

Alföldi, Andreas. 1976. *Oktavians Aufstieg zur Macht.* Bonn: Rudolf Habelt Verlag GmbH.

Anderson, Andrew Runni. 1928. "Hercules and His Successors." *Harv. Stud. in Class. Phil.* 39, 7–58.

Austin, R. G., ed. 1952. *M. Tulli Ciceronis Pro M. Caelio Oratio.* Oxford: Clarendon Press.

Axer, Jerzy. 1989. "Tribunal-Stage-Arena: Modeling of the Communication Situation in M. Tullius Cicero's Judicial Speeches." *Rhetorica* 7, 299–311.

Ayers, Donald M. 1954. "Cato's Speech Against Murena." *CJ* 49, 245–254.

Badian, E. 1954. "*Lex Servilia.*" *CR* 4, 101–102.

———. 1958. *Foreign Clientelae.* Oxford: Clarendon Press.

———. 1960. "Neuhauser, W., *Patronus und Orator.*" *JRS* 50, 275–276.

Balsdon, J. P. V. D. 1960. "*Auctoritas, Dignitas, Otium.*" *CQ* 10, 43–50.

———. 1979. *Romans and Aliens.* London: Duckworth.

Bailey, D. R. Shackleton. 1971. *Cicero.* London: Gerald Duckworth & Co.

Bayet, Jean. 1926. "Les origines de l'Hercule romain." *BEFAR* 132, 127–154.

———. 1957. *Histoire politique et psychologique de la religion romaine.* Paris: Payot.

Beard, Mary, John North, & Simon Price. (1998) *Religions of Rome.* Cambridge, UK: Cambridge University Press.

Bellardi, Giovanni. 1975. *Le Orazioni di M. Tullio Cicerone.* Vol. 3. Torino: Unione Tipografico.

Berger, Adolf. 1953. "Encyclopedic Dictionary of Roman Law." *Transactions of the American Philosophical Society* 43/2. Philadelphia: American Philosophical Association.

Bitzer, Lloyd F. 1968. "The Rhetorical Situation." *Philosophy and Rhetoric* 1, 1–14.

Braunert, Horst. 1966. "Verfassungsnorm und Verfassungswirklichkeit im Spätrepublikanischen Rom: Eine Interpretation zu Ciceros Rede für Balbus." *Der altsprachliche Unterricht* 9, 51–73.

Brunt, P. A. 1965. "'Amicitia' in the Late Roman Republic." *Proceedings of the Cambridge Philological Society* 191, 1–20.

————. 1982. "The Legal Issue in Cicero, *Pro Balbo*." *CQ* 32, 136–147.

————. 1988. *The Fall of the Roman Republic*. Oxford: Clarendon Press.

Buchheit, Vinzenz. 1975. "Chrysogonus als Tyrann in Ciceros Rede für Roscius aus Ameria." *Chiron* 5 193–211.

Büchner, Wilhelm. 1866. *Annotationum criticarum ad M. Tulli Ciceronis orationem pro L. Cornelio Balbo habitam particula I [—II]*. 18–29. Schwerin: F. W. Bärensprung.

Burke, Kenneth. 1975. "The Nature of Form." *Contemporary Rhetoric*. New York. 183–199.

Burckhardt, L. A. 1990. "The Political Elite of the Roman Republic: Comments on Recent Discussion of the Concepts *Nobilitas* and *Homo Novus*." *Historia*. 39, 77–99.

Canter, H. 1936. "Irony in the Orations of Cicero." *American Journal of Philology* 57, 457–464.

Caplan, Harry, tr. 1954. *(Cicero) ad C. Herennium de Ratione Dicendi*. London: William Heinemann.

Carney, Thomas Francis. 1960. "Cicero's Picture of Marius." *WS* 73, 83–122.

————. 1970. *A Biography of C. Marius*. Chicago: Argonaut.

Cary, Earnest, tr. 1953. *The Roman Antiquities of Dionysius of Halicarnassus*. Vol. 3–4. London: William Heinemann.

————, tr. 1969. *Dio's Roman History*. Vol. 3, 6. London: William Heinemann.

Clark, Albert Curtis, ed. 1901. *M. Tulli Ciceronis Orationes*. Vol. 2. Oxford: Clarendon Press.

————, ed. 1905. *M. Tulli Ciceronis Orationes*. Vol. 1. Oxford: Clarendon Press.

————, ed. 1909. *M. Tulli Ciceronis Orationes*. Vol. 4. Oxford: Clarendon Press.

Clark, Donald Leman. 1957. *Rhetoric in Greco-Roman Education*. New York, NY: Columbia.

Clark, Mark Edward & James S. Ruebel. 1985. "Philosophy and Rhetoric in Cicero's *Pro Milone*." *Rheinisches Museum für Philologie* 128, 57–72.

Clarke, M. L. 1945. "Ciceronian Oratory." *Greece & Rome* 14, 72–81.

————. 1963. *Rhetoric at Rome: A Historical Survey*. New York: Barnes & Noble.

Classen, Carl Joachim. 1973. "Ciceros Rede für Caelius." *Aufstieg und Niedergang der Römischen Welt* 1.3, 60–94.

————. 1981. "Éloquence et rhétorique chez Cicéron." *Entretiens sur l'antiquité classique* 28. Geneva: Fondation Hardt.

————. 1985. *Recht-Rhetorik-Politik: Untersuchungen zu Ciceros rhetorischer Strategie*. Darmstadt: Wissenschaftliche Buchgesellschaft.

————. 1988. "Ars Rhetorica: L'essence, possibilities, Gefahren." *Rhetorica* 6, 7–19.

Clerc, Michel. 1971. *Massilia. Histoire de Marseille dans l'antiquité à la fin de l'empire romain*. 1, 2. Marseille: Laffitte Reprints.

Coarelli, F. 1988. *Il Foro Boario*. Rome: Quasar.

Cope, E. M. 1867. *An Introduction to Aristotle's Rhetoric*. London: MacMillan.

Cousin, Jean. 1962. *Cicéron: Discours Tome XV: Pour Caelius, Sur les Provinces Consulaires, Pour Balbus*. Paris: Budé.

Craig, Christopher. 1979. *The Role of Rational Argumentation in Selected Judicial Speeches of Cicero*. (Dissertation.) Chapel Hill: University of North Carolina.

———. 1981. "The *Accusator* as *Amicus*: An Original Roman Tactic of Ethical Argumentation." *TAPA* 111, 31–37.

———. 1985. "The Structural Pedigree of Cicero's Speeches *Pro Archia*, *Pro Milone*, and *Pro Quinctio*." *CP* 80, 136–137.

———. 1989. "Reason, Resonance, and Dilemma in Cicero's Speech for Caelius." *Rhetorica* 7, 313–328.

———. 1993. *Form as Argument in Cicero's Speeches: A Study of Dilemma*. Atlanta, Georgia: Scholar's Press.

Crawford, M. H., ed. 1996. *Roman Statutes*. London: Institute of Classical Studies, School of Advanced Study, University of London.

Crook, J. A. 1967. *Law and Life of Rome*. London: Thames and Hudson.

Davies, J. C. 1969. "A Slip by Cicero?" *CQ* 19, 345–346.

Diehl, Hermann. 1988. *Sulla und seine Zeit im Urteil Ciceros*. Olms: Hildesheim.

Döpp, Siegmar. 1989. "Nec omnia apud priores meliora. Autoren des frühen Principats über die eigene Zeit." *RhM* 132, 73–101.

Dorey, T. A., ed. 1965. *Cicero*. New York: Basic Books.

Donnelly, F. 1935. *Cicero's Milo: A Rhetorical Commentary*. New York: Bruce.

Douglas, Alan Edward. 1960. "Neuhauser: *Patronus and Orator*." *CR* 10, 133–134.

———. 1973. "The Intellectual Background of Cicero's Rhetorica: A Study in Method." *Aufstieg und Niedergang der Römischen Welt* 1.3, 95–138.

Dunbabin, Katherine M. D. & M. W. Dickie. 1983. "*Invidia Rumpantur Pectora*." *Jahrbuch für Antike und Christentum* 26, 7–37.

Dunkle, J. Roger. 1967. "The Greek Tyrant and Roman Political Invective in the Late Republic." *TAPA* 98, 151–171.

Dyck, Andrew. 1996. *A Commentary on Cicero, de Officiis*. Ann Arbor: University of Michigan Press.

Earl, Donald. 1961. *The Political Thought of Sallust*. Cambridge: Cambridge University Press.

———. 1967. *The Moral and Political Tradition of Rome*. Ithaca: Cornell University Press.

Enos, Richard Leo. 1975. "The Epistemological Foundation for Cicero's Litigation Strategies." *Central States Journal* 26, 207–214.

Ernesti, Johann Christian Gottlieb. 1962. *Lexicon technologiae latinorum rhetoricae*. Hildesheim: Olms.

Fantham, Elaine. 1972. *Comparative Studies in Republican Latin Imagery*. Toronto: University of Toronto Press.

———. 1973. "Ciceronian *Conciliare* and Aristotelian Ethos." *Phoenix* 27, 261–275.

———. 1992. "The role of Evander in Ovid's *Fasti*." *Arethusa*. 25, 155–171.

Fisher, C. D., ed. 1906. *Cornelii Taciti Annalium*. Oxford: Clarendon Press.

Fortenbaugh, William W. 1988. "*Benevolentiam conciliare* and *animos permovere:* Some remarks on Cicero's De oratore 2.178–216." *Rhetorica* 6, 259–273.

———. 1992. "Aristotle on Persuasion through Character." *Rhetorica* 10, 203–244.

Foster, B. O., tr. 1988. *Livy.* Vol. 1. London: William Heinemann.

Freese, John Henry. 1967. *Cicero VI: Pro Publio Quinctio, Pro Sexto Roscio Amerino, Pro Quinto Roscio Comoedo, de Lege Agraria 1, 2, 3.* London: William Heinemann.

Frier, Bruce. 1985. *The Rise of the Roman Jurists: Studies in the Pro Caecina.* Princeton: Princeton University Press.

Fuhrmann, Manfred. 1984. *Die Antike Rhetorik.* München: Artemis Verlag.

———. tr. W. E. Yuill. 1992. *Cicero and the Roman Republic.* Oxford: Blackwell.

Galinsky, Karl. 1972. *The Herakles Theme.* Oxford: Blackwell.

———. 1996. *Augustan Culture.* Princeton: Princeton University Press.

Galsterer, Hartmut. 1976. *Herrschaft und Verwaltung im Republikanischen Italien.* München: C. H. Beck'sche Verlagbuchhandlung.

Gardner, R. tr. 1966. *Cicero XII: Pro Sestio and In Vatinum.* London: William Heinemann.

———. 1970. *Cicero XIII: Pro Caelio, De Provinciis Consularibus, Pro Balbo.* London: William Heinemann.

Gasquy, Armand. 1886. *De M. Tulli Ciceronis Pro L. Cornelio Balbo Oratione.* (Dissertation.) Paris: Thorin.

Geffcken, Katherine. 1973. *Comedy in the* Pro Caelio. Leiden: E. J. Brill.

Gelzer, Matthias. tr. P. Needham. 1968. *Caesar: Politician and Statesman.* Cambridge, MA: Harvard University Press.

———. 1969. *Cicero; ein biographischer Versuch.* Wiesbaden: F. Steiner.

———. tr. Robin Seager. 1969. *The Roman Nobility.* New York: Barnes & Noble.

———. ed. Herrmann-Otto, E. 1984. *Pompeius.* Wiesbaden: F. Steiner.

Gill, Christopher. 1984. "The Ethos/Pathos Distinction in Rhetorical and Literary Criticism." *CQ* 34, 149–166.

Goodfellow, Charlotte E. 1935. *Roman Citizenship.* (Dissertation.) Bryn Mawr, PA: Bryn Mawr College.

Gotoff, Harold C. 1979. *Cicero's Elegant Style: An Analysis of the* Pro Archia. Urbana: University of Illinois Press.

———. 1986. "Cicero's Analysis of the Prosecution Speeches in the *Pro Caelio:* An Exercise in Practical Criticism." *CP* 81, 122–132.

———. 1993. *Cicero's Caesarian Speeches.* Chapel Hill: The University of North Carolina Press.

Grant, Michael. 1946. *From Imperium to* Auctoritas. Cambridge: Cambridge University Press.

Greenidge, A. H. J. 1901: *The Legal Procedure of Cicero's Time.* London: Clarendon Press.

Greenwood, L. H. G., tr. 1989. *Cicero VII & VIII: The Verrine Orations.* Vol. 1–2. Cambridge, MA: Harvard University Press.

Griffith, G. T. 1935. *The Mercenaries of the Hellenistic World.* Cambridge: Cambridge University Press.

Grube, G. M. A. 1962. "Educational, Rhetorical, and Literary Theory in Cicero." *Phoenix* 16 234–257.

Gruen, Erich S. 1969. "Cicero: *Pro Balbo* 54." *CR* 19 8–11.

———. 1974. *The Last Generation of the Roman Republic.* Berkeley: University of California Press.

Habicht, Christian. 1990. *Cicero the Politician.* Baltimore: The Johns Hopkins University Press.

Hall, Jonathan Charles Redvers. 1992. *Style and Design in Cicero's* De Oratore. (Dissertation.) Austin: University of Texas.

Hardy, E. G. 1914. "The Table of Heraclea and the *Lex Iulia Municipalis.*" *JRS* 4, 65–110.

———. 1916. "The Transpadane Question and the Alien Act of 65 or 64 B.C." *JRS* 6, 63–82.

———. 1917. "Cicero's Argument in *Pro Balbo*, VIII. 19–22." *CR* 21, 132–134.

Heinze, R. 1925. "*Auctoritas.*" *Hermes* 60 348–366; Reprint: Burck, E., ed. 1960. *Vom Geist des Römertums.* Stuttgart: Teubner.

Hellegouarc'h, J. 1963. *Le Vocabulaire Latin des Relations et des Partis Politiques sous la République.* Paris: Société D'Édition "Belles Lettres."

Hendrickson, G. L. 1905. "The Origin and Meaning of the Ancient Characters of Style." *AJPh* 26, 249–290.

———, tr. 1971. *Cicero: Brutus.* London: William Heinemann.

Hett, W. S., H. Rackham, tr. 1983. *Aristotle. Problems, Books 22–38. Rhetorica ad Alexandrum.* 1983. Cambridge, MA: Harvard University Press.

Heuer, K. H. 1941. *Comitas—facilitas—liberalitas: Studien zur gesellschaftlichen Kultur der ciceronischen Zeit.* Lengerich: Lengericher Handelsdruckerei.

Hildebrandt, Paulus, ed. 1907. *Scholia Ciceronis Orationes Bobiensia.* Lipsiae: Teubner.

Hoche, Johannes. 1882. *de L. Cornelio Balbo.* Rossleben: Halle a. S.

van Hook, LaRue. 1915. "The Influence of Isocrates on Cicero, Dionysius, and Aristides." *CW* 9, 79.

Hodge, H. Grose, tr. 1927. *Cicero, the Speeches:* Pro Lege Manilia, Pro Caecina, Pro Cluentio, Pro Rabirio Perduellionis. London: William Heinemann.

Hornblower, Simon and Anthony Spawforth, ed. 1996. *Oxford Classical Dictionary.* Oxford: Oxford University Press.

Hubbell, H. M., tr. 1949. *Cicero: de Inventione, de Optimo Genere Oratorum, Topica.* London: William Heinemann.

———, tr. 1971. *Cicero: Orator.* London: William Heinemann.

Hübner. 1912. "Gades." *Paulys Realencyclopädie der classischen Altertumswissenschafft* 7, 439–461.

Innes, Doreen. 1988. "Cicero on Tropes." *Rhetorica* 6, 307–325.

Iser, Wolfgang. 1974. *The Implied Reader.* Baltimore: The Johns Hopkins University Press.

Johannemann, R. 1935. *Cicero und Pompeius in ihren wechselseitigen Beziehungen bis zum Jahre 51 vor Christi Geburt.* Emsdetten: Dissertations-Druckerei Heinr. & J. Lechte.

Johnson, W. R. 1971. *Luxuriance and Economy: Cicero and the Alien Style.* Berkeley: University of California Press.

Jullien, Aemilius. 1886. *De L. Cornelio Balbo Maiore.* (Dissertation.) Paris: Leroux.

Kaden, Hans. 1912. *Quaestionum ad Ciceronis Balbianam Spectantium Capita Tria.* (Dissertation.) Berlin: Denter & Nicolas.

Kennedy, George Alexander. 1963. *The Art of Persuasion in Greece.* Princeton: Princeton University Press.

————. 1968. "The Rhetoric of Advocacy in Greece and Rome." *American Journal of Philology* 89, 419–436.

————. 1972. *The Art of Rhetoric in the Roman World.* Princeton: Princeton University Press.

————. 1994. *A New History of Classical Rhetoric.* Princeton: Princeton University Press.

King, J. E., tr. 1950. *Cicero: Tusculan Disputations.* London: William Heinemann.

Kinsey, T. E., ed. 1971. *M. Tulli Ciceronis Pro Quinctio Oratio.* Sydney, Australia: Sydney University Press.

Kirby, J. T. 1990. *The Rhetoric of Cicero's* Pro Cluentio. Amsterdam: Gieben.

Klotz, A. 1919. *M. Tulli Ciceronis Scripta Quae Manserunt Omnia.* 7 Lipsiae: Teubner.

Konstan, David. 2001. *Pity Transformed.* London: Duckworth.

Kornemann, Ernst. 1935. "*Municipium.*" *Paulys Realencyclopädie der classischen Altertumswissenschaft* Series 1. Vol. 16, 570–634.

Kroll, W. 1950. "Rhetorik." *Paulys Realencyclopädie der classischen Altertumswissenschaft* Supplementband 7, 1039–1138.

Kunkel, Wolfgang. Tr. J. M. Kelly. 1973. *An Introduction to Roman Legal and Constitutional History.* Oxford: Clarendon Press.

Kurke, Alexander David. 1989. *Theme and Adversarial Presentation in Cicero's Pro Flacco.* (Dissertation.) Michigan.

Laqueur, R. 1934. "Theophanes." *Paulys Realencyclopädie der classischen Altertumswissenshaft* Series 2. Vol. 5, 2090–2127.

Larson, Richard L. 1970. "Lloyd Bitzer's 'Rhetorical Situation' and the Classification of Discourse: Problems and Implications." *Philosophy and Rhetoric* 3, 165–168.

Laurand, L. 1965. *Études sur le Style: Discours de Cicéron.* Amsterdam: Hakkert.

Lebreton, Jules. 1901. *Études sur la Langue et la Grammaire de Cicéron.* Paris: Hachette.

Leeman, A. D. 1963. *Orationis Ratio.* Vol. 1, 2. Amsterdam: Hakkert.

————. 1981. *Marcus Tullius Cicero De Oratore Libri III Kommentar.* Vol. 1. Heidelberg: Carl Winter Universitätsverlag.

Leeman, A. D., Harm Pinkster, and Hein L. W. Nelson. 1985. *Marcus Tullius Cicero De Oratore Libri III Kommentar.* Vol. 2. Heidelberg: Carl Winter Universitätsverlag.

————. 1989. *Marcus Tullius Cicero De Oratore Libri III Kommentar.* Vol. 3. Heidelberg: Universitätsverlag.

Lengle, J. 1931. "Die Verurteilung der römischen Feldherrn von Arausio." *Hermes* 66, 302–316.

Leon, Harry L. 1935. "The Technique of Emotional Appeal in Cicero's Judicial Speeches." *Classical Weekly* 39, 33–37.

Lepore, Ettore. 1954. *Il Princeps Ciceroniano.* Napoli: nella sede dell'istituto.

Levick, Barbara. 1967. "*Acerbissima lex Servilia.*" *CR* 17, 256–258.

Lintott, Andrew. 1974. "Cicero and Milo." *JRS* 64, 62–78.

————. 1992. *Judical Reform and Land Reform in the Roman Republic.* Cambridge: Cambridge University Press.

———. 1993. *Imperium Romanum: Politics and Administration.* London: Routledge.

Loutsch, C. 1994. *L'exorde dans les discours de Cicéron.* Brussels: Latomus.

Ludwig, W., ed. 1981. *Éloquence et rhétorique chez Cicéron. Entretiens sur l'Antiquité Classique.* Vol. 28. Geneva: Fondation Hardt.

Lussky, Ernest Alfred. 1928. *The appeal to the emotions in the judicial speeches of Cicero as compared with the theories set forth on the subject in the De Oratore.* (Dissertation.) Minneapolis: University of Minnesota.

MacDonald, C., tr. 1977. *Cicero X: In Catilinam I-IV, Pro Murena, Pro Sulla, Pro Flacco.* London: William Heinemann.

Malcovati, H. 1930. *Oratorum Romanorum Fragmenta.* Vol. 1. Torino: Paraviae et Soc.

Marouzeau, J. 1921. "Pour Mieux Comprendre les Textes Latins." *Révue de Philologie* 45, 149–193.

Marx, Fridericus, ed. 1894. *Ad C. Herennium Libri 4.* Lipsiae: Teubner.

May, James M. 1979. "The Ethica Digressio and Cicero's *Pro Milone:* A Progression of Intensity from Logos to Ethos to Pathos." *CJ* 74, 240–246.

———. 1981. The Rhetoric of Advocacy and Patron-Client Identification: Variation on a Theme." *American Journal of Philology* 102, 308–315.

———. 1988. *Trials of Character: The Eloquence of Ciceronian Ethos.* Chapel Hill: North Carolina Press.

———, ed. 2003. *Brill's Companion to Cicero.* Leiden: Brill.

McCall, Marsh H., Jr. 1969. *Ancient Rhetorical Theories of Simile and Comparison.* Cambridge, MA: Harvard University Press.

McClintock, Richard Clare. 1975. *Cicero's Narrative Technique in the Judicial Speeches.* (Dissertation.) Chapel Hill: University of North Carolina.

Meier, Christian. 1980. *Res Publica Amissa.* Wiesbaden: Suhrkamp Verlag.

Menge, Hermann. 1995. *Repetitorium der lateinischen Syntax und Stilistik.* Darmstadt: Wissenschaftliche Buchgesellschaft.

Meyer, Dieter. 1957. *Cicero und das Reich.* Köln: Photostelle der Universität zu Köln.

Miller, Arthur B. 1972. "Rhetorical Exigence." *Philosophy and Rhetoric* 5, 111–118.

Miller, Walter, tr. 1961. *Cicero* De Officiis. London: William Heinemann.

Mitchell, Thomas N. 1991. *Cicero the Senior Statesman.* New Haven: Yale University Press.

Mommsen, Theodor. 1952–1953. *Römisches Staatsrecht.* Graz: Akademische Druck—u. Verlagsanstalt.

Moore, Timothy J. 1989. *Artistry and Ideology: Livy's Vocabulary of Virtue.* Frankfurt: Athenäum.

Münzer, Friedrich. 1901. "L. Cornelius Balbus." *Paulys Realencyclopädie der classischen Altertumswissenschaft* Series 1. Vol. 4, 1260–1268.

———. 1919. "Kalliphana." *Paulys Realencyclopädie der classischen Altertumswissenschaft* Vol. 10.2, 1655.

Neumeister, Christoff. 1964. *Grundsätze der Forensischen Rhetorik.* München: Max Hueber Verlag.

Nisbet, R. G. M. 1992. "The Orator and the Reader: Manipulation and Response in Cicero's *Fifth Verrine*." *Author and Audience in Latin Literature.* Cambridge, UK: Cambridge University Press.

Oliver, James H. 1981. "Civic Status in Roman Athens: Cicero, *Pro Balbo* 12.30." *GRBS* 22, 83–88.

Paton, W. R., tr. 1979. *Polybius: the Histories.* Vol. 3. London: William Heinemann.

Pease, Arthur Stanley, ed. 1955. *M. Tulli Ciceronis. De Natura Deorum.* Cambridge, MA: Harvard University Press.

Peterson, W., ed. 1907. *M. Tulli Ciceronis Orationes.* Vol. 3. Oxford: Clarendon Press.

———, ed. 1911. *M. Tulli Ciceronis Orationes.* Vol. 5. Oxford: Clarendon Press.

———, tr. 1970. *Tacitus Dialogus.* Cambridge, MA: Harvard University Press.

Pinkster, Harm. tr. Hotze Mulder. 1990. *Latin Syntax and Semantics.* London: Routledge.

Pohl, Hartel. 1993. *Die römische Politik und die Piraterie im östlichen Mittlemeer vom 3. bis zum 1. Jh. v. Chr.* Berlin: Walter de Gruyter.

Pöschl, Victor. 1983. "'Invidia' in den Reden Ciceros." *Literatur und geschichtliche Wirklichkeit* 11–16. Heidelberg: Carl Winter Universitätsverlag.

Prill, Paul. 1986. "Cicero in Theory and Practice: The Securing of Good Will in the *Exordia* of Five Forensic Speeches." *Rhetorica* 4.2, 93–109.

Rackham, H., tr. 1914. *Cicero De Finibus Bonorum et Malorum.* London: William Heinemann.

———, tr. 1942. *Cicero De Oratore Bk. III De Fato, Paradoxa Stoicorum, De Partitione Oratoria.* Cambridge, MA: Harvard University Press.

———, tr. 1950. *Pliny Natural History.* Vol. 5. London: William Heinemann.

———, tr. 1967. *Cicero De Oratore Books I, 2.* Cambridge, Mass: Harvard University Press.

Rahn, Helmut. 1966. "Zur Struktur des ciceronischen Rede-Prooemiums." Der *Altsprachliche Unterricht* 11, 5–24.

Rawson, Elizabeth. 1975. *Cicero: A Portrait.* Ithaca: Cornell University Press.

Reid, J. S. 1879. *M. T. Ciceronis Pro A. Licinio Archia Poeta Oratio.* Cambridge: Cambridge University Press.

———. 1890. *M. T. Ciceronis Pro L. Cornelio Balbo Oratio Ad Iudices.* Cambridge: Cambridge University Press.

———. 1915. "Problems of the Second Punic War." *JRS* 5, 87–124.

———. 1915. "The So-Called 'Lex Iulia Municipalis.'" *JRS* 5, 207–248.

Reynolds, L.D., ed. 1998. *Cicero, Marcus Tullius. De finibus bonorum et malorum.* Oxford: Clarendon Press.

Richardson, J. S. 1986. *Hispania. Spain and the Development of Roman Imperialism, 218–82 B.C.* Cambridge, UK: Cambridge University Press.

Riggsby, Andrew. 1991. "Elision and Hiatus in Latin Prose." *C.A.* 10, 326–343.

———. 1993. *Criminal Defense and the Conceptualization of Crime in Cicero's Orations.* (Dissertation.) Berkeley: University of California.

———. 1995. "Appropriation and Reversal as a Basis for Oratorical Proof." *CP* 90, 245–256.

———. 1999. *Crime and Community in Ciceronian Rome.* Austin: University of Texas Press.

Ritter, Stefan. 1995. *Archäologie und Geschichte, Band 5: Hercules in der Römischen Kunst.* Heidelberg: Verlag Archäologie und Geschichte.

Roberts, W. Rhys, tr. 1984. *Aristotle: Rhetoric.* New York: Modern Library.

Robinson, Arthur. 1994. "Cicero's References to his Banishment." *CW* 87, 475–480.

Rohde, Franciscus. 1903. *Cicero, quae de inventione praecepit, quatenus secutus sit in orationibus generis iudicalis.* (dissertation) Königsberg: Huntungiana.

Rolfe, John C., tr. 1929. *Cornelius Nepos.* London: William Heinemann.

———, tr. 1985. *Sallust.* Cambridge, MA: Harvard University Press.

Roloff, Heinrich. 1938. *Maiores bei Cicero.* Leipzig: Göttingen.

Rubio, Lisardo.1949. "Los Balbos y el Imperio Romano." *Anales de Historia Antigua y Medieval* 67–119.

Russell, Donald, tr. 2001. *Quintilian. Institutiones Oratoriae.* Cambridge, MA: Harvard University Press.

Sanders, Henry A. 1910. *Roman History and Mythology.* London: MacMillan.

Scheid, John. 1995. "Graeco Ritu." *HSPh* 97, 15–31.

Schiller, A. Arthur. 1978. *Roman Law.* The Hague: Mouton.

Schlesinger, Alfred C., tr. 1959. *Livy.* Vol. 14. London: William Heinemann.

Schulz, Fritz. tr. Marguerite Wolff. 1936. *Principles of Roman Law.* Oxford: Clarendon Press.

Scullard, H. H. 1976. *From the Gracchi to Nero: A History of Rome From 133 B.C. to A.D. 68.* London: Methuen.

Seager, R. 2002. *Pompey the Great: A Political Biography.* Oxford: Blackwell.

Sherwin-White, A. N. 1973. *The Roman Citizenship.* Oxford: Clarendon Press.

Sintenis, Carolus, ed. 1891. *Vitae Parallelae.* Vol. 2. Lipsiae: Teubner.

Smith, R. E. 1966. *Cicero the Statesman.* Cambridge: Cambridge University Press.

Solmsen, Friedrich. 1936. "Aristotle and Cicero on the Orator's Playing upon the Feelings." *CP* 33, 390–404.

———. 1938. "Cicero's First Speeches: A Rhetorical Analysis." *TAPA* 69, 542–546.

———. 1941. "The Aristotelian Tradition in Ancient Rhetoric." *American Journal of Philology* 62, 35–50.

de Souza, Philip. 1999. *Piracy in the Graeco-Roman World.* Cambridge, UK: Cambridge University Press.

Steinby, E. M. 1993. *Lexikon Topographicum Urbis Romae.* Rome: Quasar.

Stevenson, G. H. 1919. "Cn. Pompeius Strabo and the Franchise Question." *JRS* 9, 95–101.

Strasburger, Hermann. 1966. *Caesars Eintritt in die Geschichte.* Darmstadt: Wissenschaftliche Buchgesellschaft.

Stroh, Wilfried. 1975. *Taxis und Taktik: Ciceros Gerichtsreden.* Stuttgart: Teubner.

Sutton, E. W., tr. 1988. *Cicero* De Oratore. London: William Heinemann.

Syme, Ronald. 1939. *The Roman Revolution.* Oxford: Oxford University Press.

Taylor, Lily Ross. 1971. *Party Politics in the Age of Caesar.* Berkeley: University of California Press.

Thesaurus Linguae Latinae. 1924. Leipzig: Teubner.

Thompson, Lloyd A. 1962. "The Relationship between Provincial Quaestors and Their Commanders-in-Chief." *Historia* 11, 339–355.

———. 1989. *Romans and Blacks.* London: Routledge.

Tyrell, R. Y. and L. C. Purser. 1918. *The Correspondence of Cicero.* Vol. 4. Dublin: Dublin University Press Series.

Usher, S. 1965. "*Occultatio* in Cicero's Speeches." *AJPh* 86, 175–192.

Vasaly, Ann. 1983. *The Spirit of Place: The Rhetorical Use of 'Locus' in Cicero's Speeches.* (Dissertation.) Bloomington: Indiana University.

————. 1985. "The Masks of Rhetoric: Cicero's *Pro Roscio Amerino.*" *Rhetorica* 3, 1–20.

————. 1993. *Representations: Images of the World in Ciceronian Oratory.* Berkeley: University of California Press.

Vatz, Richard E. 1973. "The Myth of the Rhetorical Situation." *Philosophy and Rhetoric* 6, 154–161.

von Albrecht, M. 1973. "M.T. Cicero, Stil und Sprache." *Paulys Realencyclopädie der classischen Altertumswissenschaft* Supplementband 13, 1237–1347.

————. tr. Adkin, N. 1989. *Masters of Latin Prose from Cato to Apuleius.* Leeds: Cairns Publications.

Wackernagel, H. G. 1930. *Paulys Realencyclopädie der classischen Altertumswissenschaft* Vol. 14.2, 2132–34.

Ward, A. M. 1970a. "Cicero and Pompey in 75 and 70 B.C." *Latomus* 29, 58–71.

————. 1970b. "The Early Relationship between Cicero and Pompey until 80 B.C." *Phoenix* 24, 119–129.

Warmington, E. H., tr. 1940. *Remains of Old Latin.* Vol. 4. London: William Heinemann.

Watson, Alan. 1967. *The Law of Persons in the Later Roman Republic.* Oxford: Clarendon Press.

————. 1970. *The Law of the Ancient Romans.* Dallas: Southern Methodist University Press.

Watts, N.H., tr. 1979. *Cicero XI: Pro Archia Poeta, Post Reditum in Senatu, Post Reditum ad Quirites, de Domo Suo, de Haruspicum Responsis, Pro Plancio.* London: William Heinemann.

Wegner, Michael. 1969. "Untersuchungen zu den lateinischen Begriffen *socius* und *societas.*" *Hypomnemata* 21 Gottingen: Vandenhoeck.

Weische, Alfons. 1966. *Studien zur politischen Sprache der römischen Republik.* Münster, Westf.: Aschendorffsche Verlagsbuchhandlung.

White, Horace, tr. 1912. *Appian's Roman History.* Vol. 1. London: William Heinemann.

White, Peter. 1993. *Promised Verse.* Cambridge, MA: Harvard University Press.

Wilkins, A. S., ed. 1902. *M. Tulli Ciceronis Rhetorica.* Vol. 1. Oxford: Clarendon Press.

————, ed. 1903. *M. Tulli Ciceronis Rhetorica.* Vol. 2. Oxford: Clarendon Press.

Wilkinson, L. P. 1963. *Golden Latin Artistry.* Cambridge: Cambridge University Press.

Williams, W. Glynn, tr. 1927. *Cicero: The Letters to His Friends.* Vol. 1–3. London: William Heinemann.

Wills, Jeffrey. 1996. *Repetition in Latin Poetry.* Oxford: Clarendon Press.

Winstedt, E. O., tr. 1928. *Cicero's Letters to Atticus.* Vol. 1–3. London: William Heinemann.

Winter, J.G. 1910. "The Myth of Hercules at Rome." *Roman History and Mythology.* New York: Macmillan.

Wiseman, T.P. 1971. *New Men in the Roman Senate 139 B.C. - A.D.14*. Oxford: Oxford University Press.

Wisse, Jakob. 1989. *Ethos and Pathos from Aristotle to Cicero*. Amsterdam: Hakkert Amsterdam.

Wissowa, G. 1971. *Religion und Kultus der Römer (Handbuch der Altertumswissenschaft)*. Munich: C.H. Beck.

Wood, Neal. 1988. *Cicero's Social and Political Thought*. Berkeley: University of California Press.

Woodman, Tony & Powell, Jonathan, ed. 1992. *Author and Audience in Latin Literature*. Cambridge: Cambridge University Press.

General Index

Index of Ancient Authors

For Product Safety Concerns and Information please contact our EU
representative GPSR@taylorandfrancis.com
Taylor & Francis Verlag GmbH, Kaufingerstraße 24, 80331 München, Germany